Launched in 1999, Greenline Publications introduced a list of unique books: *Extraordinary Guides for Extraordinary Travelers*. The *25 Best Civil War Sites* continues the **Greenline Historic Travel Series**, which also includes The *25 Best World War II Sites: Pacific Theater* and The *25 Best World War II Sites: European Theater*. Greenline's willingness to explore new approaches to guidebooks, combined with meticulous research, provides readers with unique and significant travel experiences.

Never settling for the ordinary, Greenline's **Fun Seeker's** travel series covers the world's most fun events and destinations. The flagship books in the series, *The Fun Seeker's North America* and *The Fun Seeker's International*, take readers to the world's most fun places—from the Opera Ball in Vienna to the Calgary Stampede to the world's greatest food fight, the Tomatina in Buñol, Spain. The series also includes Fun Seeker's destination guides devoted to the world's greatest cities.

To reach us or for updated information on all Greenline books, visit the Greenline Publications website at www.greenlinepub.com.

The 25 Best Civil War Sites is an independent guide. We welcome your views on our selections. The information contained in this book was checked as rigorously as possible before going to press. The publisher accepts no responsibility for any changes that may have occurred since or for any other variance of fact from that recorded here in good faith.

ISBN: 0-9759022-4-5
Library of Congress Control Number: 2005926513
Distributed in the United States by National Book Network (NBN)
Printed in the United States
First Edition 2005
Published by Greenline Publications
Copyright © 2005 by Clint Johnson
All rights reserved

Executive Editor	Alan S. Davis
Series Editor	Christina Henry de Tessan
Copy Editor	Gail Nelson-Bonebrake
Cover Designer	Samia Afra
Production Editor	Jo Farrell
Cartographer	Chris Gillis
Photographer	Clint Johnson (unless otherwise specified)
Photo Insert Designer	Amber Pirker
Indexer	Karen Bleske

The photo of Hampton Roads that appears on p.18 is courtesy of the Mariners' Museum. The photo of Petersburg that appears on p.38 is courtesy of Pamplin Historic Park. The photo that appears on p.28 in the Richmond chapter is courtesy of the Museum of the Confederacy.

GREENLINE PUBLICATIONS
Extraordinary Guides for Extraordinary Travelers
P.O. Box 590780
San Francisco, CA 94159-0780

GREENLINE HISTORIC TRAVEL SERIES

The Ultimate Traveler's Guide
to the Battlefields, Monuments
and Museums

THE 25 BEST
Civil War Sites

CLINT JOHNSON

GREENLINE PUBLICATIONS • SAN FRANCISCO, CALIFORNIA

ABOUT THE AUTHOR

Clint Johnson of Winston-Salem, North Carolina, has been studying the war for more than forty years and reenacting it for twenty-seven. He is a descendant of Confederate soldiers from Florida, Georgia, and Alabama. He is a member of the 26th Regiment of North Carolina Troops (www.26nc.org), which posts a sound file of a real rebel yell recorded in 1935 at a reunion of Confederate soldiers.

Johnson has written five other touring books covering the American Civil War, including: *Touring the Carolinas' Civil War Sites* (17 point-to-point driving tours in the two states), *Touring Civil War Sites in Virginia and West Virginia* (17 point-to-point driving tours), *In the Footsteps of Robert E. Lee, In the Footsteps of Stonewall Jackson,* and *In the Footsteps of J.E.B. Stuart.* He has also written *Civil War Blunders and Bulls-Eyes* and *Misfires: 50 People Whose Obscure Efforts Shaped the American Civil War.*
To order any personalized copies of those books, visit his website at www.clintjohnsonbooks.com.

OVERVIEW MAP

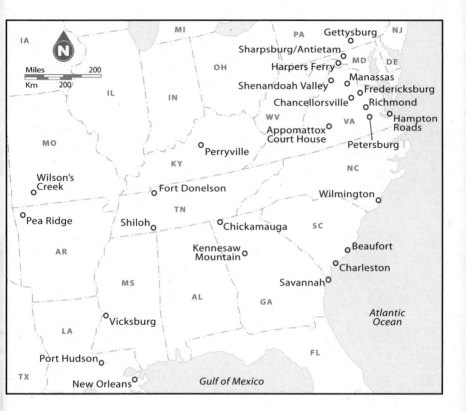

Statue of General G.K. Warrenat Little Round Top at Gettysburg.

TABLE OF CONTENTS

CHRONOLOGY OF THE CIVIL WAR

1859

October 17: John Brown raids Harpers Ferry, Virginia (now West Virginia).

1860

November 7: Lincoln is elected president.

December 20: South Carolina secedes from the Union. Six other states follow over the next several weeks to form the Confederate States of America.

1861

February 9: Jefferson Davis is named president of the seven-state Confederacy.

March 4: Lincoln is inaugurated as President of the U.S.

April 11: South Carolina discovers a supply ship nearing Fort Sumter.

April 12: South Carolina fires on Fort Sumter.

April 15: Lincoln asks remaining states for 75,000 troops to put down "rebellion."

April 17–May 20: Four more Southern states secede. Confederacy consists of eleven states.

June 10: Small Battle of Big Bethel, Virginia, takes place. It is a Southern victory.

July 11: Small Battle of Rich Mountain, Virginia, takes place. It is a Northern victory.

July 21: Large Battle of First Manassas takes place. It is a Southern victory.

July 27: George McClellan is appointed commander of the Army of the Potomac.

August 10: Large Battle of Wilson's Creek, Missouri, is a Confederate victory.

August 27–28: Union army captures Outer Banks of North Carolina.

November 1: Lincoln appoints McClellan commander of all Union armies.

November 7: Port Royal, South Carolina, is captured by U.S. Navy.

1862

February 6–14: Forts Henry and Donelson are captured by Union forces.

March 7–8: The Battle of Pea Ridge, Arkansas (Elkhorn Tavern), is a Union victory.

March 8: C.S.S. *Virginia* attacks wooden blockading ships at Norfolk, Virginia.

March 9: C.S.S. *Virginia* and U.S.S. *Monitor* battle in the first contest between ironclads. They fight to a draw.

March 15: McClellan begins his ponderous Peninsula Campaign up the Virginia Peninsula to try to capture Richmond.

April 5–May 4: Siege of Yorktown, Virginia, takes place.

April 6–7: The big Battle of Shiloh, Tennessee, shocks the nation with more than 24,000 casualties in two days.

April 24: New Orleans, Louisiana, falls without firing a shot in its own defense after Union fleet passes Forts Jackson and St. Phillip 70 miles south of the city.

May 31: At the Battle of Seven Pines, Virginia, General Joseph E. Johnston is wounded, leaving an opening for Robert E. Lee to be appointed general.

June 25–July 1: Lee directs the Seven Days Battles, which save Richmond from capture by McClellan's Army of the Potomac.

August 28–30: Lee wins the battles of Brawner Farm and Second Manassas, defeating Union General John Pope.

September 4: Lee's army invades the North to recruit Marylanders into the army and attract recognition from Europe.

September 17: Lee's 40,000-man army fights McClellan's 100,000-man army to a draw at Sharpsburg or Antietam.

September 22: Lincoln announces that he will issue an Emancipation Proclamation.

October 8: Battle of Perryville, Kentucky, is a Union victory. Confederates lose any hope of taking Kentucky out of the Union.

December 11–13: Battle of Fredericksburg, Virginia, is a Confederate victory.

1863

January 1: The Emancipation Proclamation, freeing only the slaves in the Confederacy, but keeping slaves in the Union states in bondage, is issued and read in public at Port Royal, South Carolina, which is in Union hands.

January 25: Joseph Hooker replaces Burnside as commander of the Army of the Potomac.

January 29: Grant is ordered to capture Vicksburg, Mississippi.

May 1–4: The Battle of Chancellorsville, Virginia, is a Confederate victory.

May 23: The Battle of Port Hudson, Louisiana, is a Union victory that sees the first extensive use of black troops in combat.

July 1–3: The Battle of Gettysburg, Pennsylvania, is a major Union victory.

July 4: The Confederates surrender Vicksburg, Mississippi, for a Union victory.

July 18: Fort Wagner, South Carolina, is attacked by the 54th Massachusetts, a regiment made up of free blacks. It is a Confederate victory.

September 19–20: The Battle of Chickamauga, Georgia, results in a major Confederate victory.

November 19: Lincoln delivers the Gettysburg Address.

November 23–25: Federals end the Confederate siege of Chattanooga with captures of Lookout Mountain and Missionary Ridge, a major Union victory.

1864

March 4: Lincoln appoints Grant to command all U.S. armies and orders him east to confront Lee.

May 5–6: Grant faces Lee for the first time at the Wilderness. The battle is a draw.

May 8–21: The battles for Spotsylvania Court House, Virginia, result in a draw.

June 3: Grant orders a disastrous charge at Cold Harbor, Virginia, resulting in 7,000 casualties. This is a Confederate victory.

June 15: Grant's forces arrive around Petersburg, Virginia, and start a siege that lasts ten months.

June 27: The Battle for Kennesaw Mountain results in a Confederate victory.

August 29: George McClellan becomes the Democratic candidate against Republican Lincoln for the 1864 presidential election.

September 2: Atlanta is captured by Union General William T. Sherman.

November 8: Lincoln is reelected president, carrying all but three states. The army unexpectedly votes for Lincoln rather than their old commander.

November 15: Sherman burns Atlanta and begins his "March to the Sea."

December 21: Sherman captures Savannah after capturing nearby Fort McAllister.

1865

January 15: The Battle of Fort Fisher, North Carolina, results in a Union victory. Wilmington soon surrenders.

February 18: Charleston surrenders to the Federals after a two-year siege.

March 4: Lincoln is inaugurated for second term with talk of peace.

April 2: Grant's army breaks through the Confederate trenches around Petersburg. Lee orders his army westward and orders the evacuation of Richmond.

April 6: At the Battle of Saylers Creek, one-third of Lee's army is captured.

April 9: Lee surrenders the Army of Northern Virginia at Appomattox Court House.

April 14: The U.S. flag is raised over Fort Sumter. President Lincoln is shot at Ford's Theater that night.

April 15: Lincoln dies at 7:22 a.m.

Ohio Monument at Vicksburg

INTRODUCTION

Years ago, while working in a corporate office in Florida, a Massachusetts-born executive asked me in an exasperated voice: "Why are you Southerners still fighting the Civil War?"

My answer was simple: "We are not still fighting the war. We just remember it."

We all have an obligation to remember a war that cost 620,000 American lives (two percent of the 1860 population of 31.5 million) in a conflict that pitted brother against brother, family against family, friend against friend. To really grasp how our nation came to be what it is today, we must understand why two parts of the country would fight each other fewer than ninety years after those same two parts had been united in ridding our fledgling nation of foreign domination. We must study how social differences between the two regions created an atmosphere so poisonous on both sides that battling to the death seemed the only way to settle those differences. And finally, we must appreciate the fact that a conflict that occurred so long ago can still bring forth expressions of pride and loyalty in the descendants of men and women who participated in it.

It is impossible to overstate the impact the war had on our nation, but its aftermath and legacies were recorded in varied, bitter, and sometimes poignant ways.

Until the last Confederate laid down his arms in 1865, most people thought of themselves as residents of their individual states first and residents of the nation second. Before the war, many people believed the nation was a collection of states formed into a union for the common good, but some believed that those states could leave the Union at any time. It was only after the war that it became clear to one and all that the Union was unbreakable. The matter of states' rights was settled for good: states' rights were secondary to the federal government.

After more than sixty years of debate about the continued existence of slavery, the war ended the practice forever. Politicians dating back to before the U.S. Constitution was written had questioned what to do about "the peculiar institution." Now armed conflict had settled the issue once and for all. But little thought had been given to the matter of what to do once that goal was accomplished. Remarkably little was done to integrate the 4 million suddenly freed slaves into the rest of society. The South's economy—which had employed the slaves on cotton and tobacco farms—had been destroyed by invading Union armies. Now, white planters and yeoman farmers and black freedmen all suddenly found themselves without work.

The eleven years of so-called Reconstruction imposed on the South from 1865 through 1876 involved very little construction, but left a great deal of residual anger toward the North and the freedmen who became the unintentional symbols of the South's loss of the war. The insults against white Southerners were sometimes small, such as forcing Confederates to cover their jacket's military buttons with black cloth, and occasionally big, such as not allowing former Confederates to hold political office in their own home states. Animosity toward Reconstruction also resulted in occasional racial violence against the freedmen and would mark the South as a dangerous place for minorities to live—an unfortunate, misleading, and untrue stereotype that still exists nearly 150 years later.

Why does this conflict that ended more than 140 years ago still pique the interest of so many? Why do Northerners who move to the South notice this interest as soon as they start talking to their native neighbors?

For one thing, the war took place here in the South. One cannot drive more than twenty minutes in any direction without running into some reminder of the war. It may be a battlefield park administered by the federal or state government, a skirmish or camp site known only to relic hunters, a soldiers' monument on a county courthouse lawn, a chimney marking the spot of a house burned down by Union soldiers, or maybe something as simple as an old cemetery with iron crosses marking Confederate veterans' graves.

No place in the South is far from the war. I grew up in Florida, now better known for its amusement parks and retirement communities than for its history. But within a half hour's drive of every place I ever lived or worked in the state was the site of a Civil War skirmish or battle. The Battle of Natural Bridge, the battle that captured my interest as a fourth grader, was just twenty-five miles south of Tallahassee. It was one of the first battles I ever reenacted. That weekend, I handled a six-pounder cannonball that one of my fellow reenactors had found. We knew the Federals had fired it from the area in which it was found. I was riveted by the fact that I was holding real history in my hand. I now live in Winston-Salem, North Carolina, near a community where raiding Yankees broke into residents' homes while they were in church *praying* that the Yankees would not break into their homes. The war is never far away—and therefore not easily forgotten.

Lastly, the war was not really that long ago. My grandmother told me stories of her grandfather, a veteran from Georgia who never uttered a word that she could remember. Later, I found his pension application, which pronounced him "addle-brained by the war." In modern terms, his Civil War combat service had left him with post-traumatic stress syndrome. When I look at a photograph of Captain Richard Newton Moore of Hilliard's Legion from Alabama, another great-great grandfather who fell mortally wounded at Chickamauga, I see my own facial structure.

The purpose of this book is to show busy history travelers how to find the twenty-five best Civil War sites in the nation. I have thrown in ten bonus sites that I thought were important as well. I define "best" using several criteria, which may explain why your favorite Civil War site is not on this list. A best site has to have had some significant impact on the war—which does not necessarily mean it had to be a major battle. For instance, Pea Ridge, Arkansas, is the site of a relatively small battle and is virtually unknown to the casual historian. But that battle ended the Confederacy's major attempts to take Missouri out of the Union. For Missouri, a slave state, to stay with the Union was vitally important to a Federal government insisting that preservation of the Union—not slavery—was the paramount reason it was fighting Southern secession.

In addition, a best site might be located in an area that has noteworthy or beautiful surroundings. The Shenandoah Valley in Virginia was not the scene of many huge battles, but it was of tremendous strategic importance as the breadbasket of the region. Its harvests fed countless soldiers during the war years. This rich land between the Blue Ridge and the Allegheny Mountains not only has sites that the history traveler can enjoy, but less historically inclined travelers along for the ride can gaze upon some of the most beautiful mountains in the nation.

The whole idea of this book is for readers to take the time to go see these sites for themselves. My opinion that General Lyon was in the wrong spot at the wrong time when he was killed at Wilson's Creek, Missouri, means nothing until visitors look back up the slope of Bloody Hill—and see for themselves that any good general should have been at the top rather than at the bottom of the hill. A history book simply can't adequately describe the firepower thrown against the U.S. Colored Troops (USCTs) as they walked up New Market Heights, Virginia. One has to see that long slope in person to understand what a killing ground that now-peaceful rural neighborhood must have been. One cannot understand the terrifying nature of the Pettigrew-Pickett-Trimble Assault (labeled incorrectly by Virginia newspaper editors as "Pickett's Charge") without going to Gettysburg in the summer, preferably in early July, and taking the same walk across that long mile of open field. One can read how hot, dusty, and dangerous it was that day, but until a person walks in the footsteps of those 12,000 Confederates and looks up at the Round Tops while thinking about being under artillery fire for more than a mile, one cannot begin to understand what these men suffered.

To grasp what it felt like to attack or be under siege at these battlefields, one really should set out on foot, preferably at or near the same time of the year as the battle. Those with plenty of energy can try climbing Kennesaw Mountain, Georgia, or Stitlington Hill, Virginia, and marvel that anyone carrying thirty pounds of gear could do the same walk while musket balls flew past his head. At Gettysburg, visitors can stand in the same swale in which the Confederates rested before pushing on into the hail of musket balls they knew awaited them once they left that little haven of safety. At Fort Moultrie, South Carolina, one can stand beside one of the cannons that fired on Fort Sumter to start the war and recognize how short a distance it really is across the channel.

By visiting these sites, history travelers will get a true sense of what the war was like for the soldier and civilian. Visitors can walk the same flat, sloping, or steep ground on which people walked 140 years ago; breathe the same air, mild, hot, or cold depending on the season; see the same blooming plants in the spring, the lush green forests in the summer, or the carpet of dead leaves in the fall and winter. With a little imagination, visitors can hear the Minie balls zing past their ears, feel the concussion as a twelve-pounder cannon is fired behind then, and see the blood on the ground as they near a wooden fence that offered little protection from that same musket and artillery fire. By visiting the many museums, big and small, visitors will be able to see the artifacts that the soldiers used while fighting for their country at these sites.

Each chapter lays out the historical importance of the site, suggests further reading, describes the primary points of interest and how visitors can reach the site, and finally lists a few places to stay near the site.

One word on accommodations. I list only lodgings that are in houses or buildings that either predate the war or look like they do (such as houses that were built in the Victorian era). In one case I do list a bed and breakfast where Lee really slept. I even show you where you can take a bath in the same place where Lee and Stonewall Jackson took baths. (I've done it, and it is the best $12 and one hour I've ever spent in my life.)

Those just getting interested in learning about the war will want to know which books best describe the conflict. Here are my picks for the best books for beginners drawn from my own extensive library of more books than I care to count:

The Historical Times Illustrated Encyclopedia of the Civil War, edited by Patricia Faust, Harper & Row, 1986, is the best single-volume encyclopedia I have ever seen. The many generals, battles, and other information are listed in alphabetical order with a concise description that provides a basic understanding of the subject.

The Encyclopedia of the American Civil War—A Political, Social, and Military History, edited by David S. Heidler and Jeanne T. Heidler, ABC-CLIO, 2000, comes in five volumes. There is a version of this that comes in one volume with the same information, but that book is so thick it is unwieldy. Go for the five volumes.

The Civil War—A Narrative, Shelby Foote, Random House, is the landmark three-volume history of the war. This wonderful work, written over nearly twenty years by Foote using a dip-in-ink pen, cannot be matched in terms of the visual images he creates in words. The only drawback—if you can call it that—is its length. It could take months to read all three books. The original three have been reprinted in paperback and converted into an illustrated version that covers several volumes.

The American Heritage History of the Civil War, Bruce Catton, Harper Collins, 1991, was originally published in 1960. This single volume was the first "adult" history of the war I ever owned. My parents gave it to me for Christmas in 1960 when I was seven years old. That same copy is still on my shelf. This version includes a CD-ROM, but is still the original text. If Foote, a Mississippian, brings a Southern slant to the war in his three-volume history, Catton, a Michiganer, brings a decidedly Northern bias to this one-volume history.

These books supply the reader with a firm grasp of the war, its major personalities, and all of the major battles. After reading these general histories, those who are interested can find countless more targeted histories of people, battles, and regiments on the market. But again, books can only tell half the story. It is only by standing on the grounds themselves that one can really understand what happened in 1861–1865 and how the nation rebuilt itself into a bigger and better United States. It is my great hope that this book supplies history travelers with all the tools they need to witness these sites first-hand and honor those who died there.

REENACTMENTS
As Close As You Can Come
To Living History

Civil War reenactments started around the time of the Civil War's Centennial commemorations in the 1960s. But even after the Centennial events were over in 1965, reenacting continued. Today, an estimated 50,000 men and women around the country put on uniforms or period civilian clothing to re-create specific events that occurred in 1861–1865. The hobby is not limited to the South, where most of the battles occurred. Virtually every state in the Union, some as far as 3,000 miles from the South, hosts a Civil War weekend event of some kind during the year. There are even American Civil War reenactments in Europe. Reenactors around the world save up their money so they can fly to the States to do big events. It is not uncommon to hear British, Australian, French, and German accents at these events.

Reenactments are generally open to spectators for an admission charge that allows people to tour the camps, shop on sutlers (merchants) row, and watch the action from a safe distance behind a rope barrier.

It is difficult to provide a list of the best reenactments because they tend to come and go depending on what groups are sponsoring them, the availability of local funding, even who is in command of the reenactors on both sides. Just as in the real war, some commanders are better and more popular than others. (Reenactors decide which events they support based on which general is directing the combat.)

Still, here are some guidelines that will help readers find some of the most worthwhile reenacting events:

Watch for major events held on the five-year anniversaries of the big battles. These generally attract the most reenactors from around the nation. For instance, in 2006, the 145th reenactment of First Manassas will probably be staged somewhere near the battlefield. In 2001, it was held near Leesburg, Virginia, about twenty-five miles from Manassas. In 2007, the 145th anniversaries of the battles of Shiloh, Tennessee, and Sharpsburg, Maryland, may be reenacted. In 2008, the 145th anniversary of Gettysburg, Pennsylvania, may be reenacted. In 2009, it will be time for the 145th anniversary of the Battle of Franklin, Tennessee. There is no guarantee that these future events will be held, but the past five-year anniversaries have been reenacted.

Remember that reenactments do not only take place in the South. Virtually every state has reenactors and reenactments.

Look for events where private foundations host battles to raise money to preserve the actual battlefield. For instance, the Battle of Cedar Creek, Virginia, is held each year, generally on the third weekend of October, on the actual battlefield south of the town of Middleton. The Battle of Fort Branch, North Carolina, holds an event on the first weekend of November each year at the actual dirt fort, which is east of Hamilton, North Carolina.

Contact state-maintained battlefields to see if they hold events. For instance, the Battle of Port Hudson, Louisiana, is held in the state park during the first weekend of each year. The Battle of Pickett's Mill, Georgia, is generally held the last weekend of May each year at the state park. The Battle of Perryville, Kentucky, is held the second weekend of October on the park site. But be advised that not all battlefield state parks hold reenactments, and some do not do events every year. For example, the Battle of Bentonville, North Carolina, is held every five years.

National battlefield parks do not hold reenactments (it is actually against federal law), but some of the battlefield parks host "living histories" where reenactors are invited to camp at specific spots on the battlefield and give demonstrations of drill and camp life to park visitors. This will usually include demonstrations of weapons firing. For instance, Gettysburg National Military Park allows Confederates to camp at Pitzers Woods on Seminary Ridge and Federals to camp around the Pennsylvania monument on Cemetery Ridge. Antietam National Military Park puts its reenactors across from Dunker Meeting House—some of the bloodiest and spookiest ground found in any national park. Call the national parks you plan to visit and ask them for a calendar of when living histories will be taking place.

Here are a few things to keep in mind as you research reenactments. First of all, check that the event is held where spectators can watch the action. One key to seeing the action is an elevated spectator area (often on a hillside). Secondly, be sure to look for events where spectator safety is assured, which may mean the spectators are a good distance from the mock fighting. The only difference between Civil War combat and reenactor combat is that reenactors are not firing lead. A musket shoots a flame about four feet in length and a cannon shoots one about twelve feet in length. Those flames are dangerous. Lastly, it is important to look for events that stress authenticity.

There are two sources where spectators can find details on events they may want to attend around the nation: *Civil War News* (www.civilwarnews.com, 800-777-1862) is a monthly newspaper that concentrates on news affecting sites associated with the war. Click on "Calendar" to use the website's interactive features to find out the upcoming events schedule. *Camp Chase Gazette* (www.campchase.com, 800-624-0281) is the only nationwide magazine dedicated exclusively to Civil War reenacting. Click on "Upcoming Campaigns" on its website to find events. Subscriptions to either or both of these publications will keep you informed of all events. Pay attention to the advertisements. If some reenactment sponsoring organization is well financed, it will place full-page ads in these publications, and the ads will generally list its web site.

What should you do if the reenacting bug bites and you want to participate in this hobby? Most groups are organized as regiments, which were the basic fighting unit in the Civil War. Smaller regiments are based around specific towns, but my own reenactment unit, the 26th Regiment of North Carolina Troops (www.26nc.org) welcomes members from our mountains to our coast (a distance of more than 400 miles), twelve other states, and Australia. Most reenactment units do both Union and Confederate impressions depending upon the needs of particular reenactments.

Other tips on joining a reenactment unit:
Find a reenactment unit that likes to drill. Drill was part of a Civil War soldier's life, so it is only natural that it be part of a reenactor's life. Regular drilling helps you build stamina and go into the event with a good understanding of what fighting in 1861–1865 would have been like.

Find a unit large enough (or affiliated with other units) to allow battalion drill to be practiced. These are the movements the real regiments used to put themselves into position so they could fight any enemy coming from any direction.

Find a unit that is strict on uniform and weapons authenticity. Plastic-frame glasses were not around in 1860. Neither were work boots. Polyester had not been invented. Most units carried three-banded muskets, not shotguns. If you are going to play at being a Civil War soldier, go all out and look like one too.

Look for a unit that has a field music component, which generally consists of fifes and drums. Field music is enormously entertaining to have in camp, and marching is much easier when you have such a group leading the way.

Most units also have an auxiliary organization for civilians such as the 26NCT's Soldiers Benevolent Society. This is made up mostly of women, but also men who have "retired" from the strain of the battlefield, or who just want to try a different impression. This is where children can participate if they do not play an instrument or are too young to carry a weapon (generally under age sixteen). Civilians often set up camps where they spin or dye cotton or wool to demonstrate what life was like before the war came along.

If you can't find a unit you like at a particular reenactment search on the web. Most reenactment units have a web site, and they are always recruiting. *Civil War News* and *Camp Chase Gazette* will have contact names for units that are recruiting. It will cost about $1,400 to outfit a soldier with uniform, musket and accoutrements, shoes, and hat. I still own the same musket, leather goods, and bayonets I bought in 1977.

What motivates reenactors to get out in the heat and the cold? (I've reenacted in 105-degree heat and minus–10-degree wind chill cold, and have fallen face first into a cold stream.) Why do we pick up a nine-pound musket; strap on thirty-five to fifty pounds of gear distributed in a backpack, haversack, and cartridge box; and then set out on a ten-mile march that we know will leave us with shin splints? We do it because it is the same emotional need that drives history travelers to spend their vacations touring Civil War battlefields. Reenactors love studying those who fought for what they believed.

That is the value of reenactments. These events bring us close to what real battles sounded, smelled, looked, and felt like. Spectators get a chance to see what lines of battle really looked like on the field. They see the flags fluttering in the breeze and realize why those bright colors attracted such fire that the life expectancy of a color bearer was short. On hot days, spectators can imagine what it must have been like for soldiers to be dressed in wool-blend uniforms, firing muskets until the hot barrels blistered their hands. They can watch as quartermaster sergeants drag wooden boxes of ammunition down a firing line as soldiers shout that their cartridge boxes are growing empty—but the enemy is still coming. When a line of cannons fire and the concussion sweeps over the crowd, followed by the acrid smell of burnt powder, they can imagine that smell lasting for hours as it would have in a real battle. Spectators can share in the thrill when reinforcements arrive to shore up a crumbling line. They can feel the terror soldiers felt when they saw that one end of a trench had been captured, which meant enfilading fire would soon be coming from that part of the lost line. Reenactments, for both those participating and those spectating, make history tangible and heighten the intensity and understanding of what took place in our country not so very long ago.

Hampton Roads

Virginia

The upside-down turret of the *U.S.S. Monitor* at the Mariners' Museum in Newport News, Virginia.

THE WAR YEARS

ampton Roads is the bay at the southern end of the peninsula formed by the James and York Rivers and the northern end of a knob of mainland encompassing several towns. This was the location of the most valuable piece of real estate lost to the Union in April 1861—Gosport Naval Yard, where tons of gun powder and thousands of cannons were stored. Today, naval and military museums in the area house and document the creation of ironclad warfare and preserve the cell where President Jefferson Davis was imprisoned.

Most nervous bureaucrats in Washington, D.C., in the winter of 1860–1861 were in the U.S. Naval Department. They were consumed by what would happen to the Gosport Naval Yard should Virginia secede. Gosport was the Navy's premier ship-repair and refitting facility. It boasted the nation's largest—perhaps the world's largest—dry dock, two large houses where ships could be repaired out of the weather, and dozens of support facilities. Perhaps most important was an arsenal where hundreds of tons of black powder and more than 3,000 heavy cannons were stored. Those cannons were designed to be loaded aboard ships or placed in forts to defend against ships. More than 300 of them were the latest-model smoothbore Dalhgrens designed to throw explosive shells.

The heart of the U.S. Navy's fleet was also undergoing repair at Gosport. Anchored or on blocks were several sloops, ships of the line, and a steam frigate named the *U.S.S. Merrimack,* which was undergoing repairs on its balky steam engines. The *Merrimack*'s engines had never worked the way their contractor had promised they would, but with forty eight- and ten-inch cannons, she was still one of the U.S.'s most formidable ships.

In early April, the Secretary of the Navy sent an engineer to Gosport to determine if the *Merrimack* could be moved before Virginia took a secession vote. The engineer repaired the ship's engines in days after the post commander told him that it would take weeks to ready the ship. When the engineer had the ship's boilers fired to make way, he was ordered to stay in port lest the departure of the ship anger the citizens of the towns around Gosport which had not left the Union as of yet.

On April 17, Virginia seceded in response to President Lincoln's call for 90,000 volunteers to put down the rebellion of the first seven states of the Confederacy. On April 20, a small combined force of the U.S. Navy and Army tried to burn both the ships and the naval yard in order to keep them out of Confederate hands. As the U.S. forces left, thinking the fire they had set and the gunpowder charges would consume the port and ships, Virginia civilians rushed in to extinguish the fires. They pulled fuses away from charges that had been set to blow up the dry dock and the powder magazine. The Federals were most successful in destroying the cannons, but the Confederates salvaged more than 1,000 heavy guns that would eventually be shipped as far west as Tennessee.

For the next year, Gosport Naval Yard gave the Confederacy great hope that it might defeat the superior and long-established shipbuilding tradition of the northern coastal states. All of those states had shipyards that were immediately pressed into service to build new fighting ships and convert civilian ships such as ferries into warships. The South had no shipbuilding tradition. It had always relied on Northern-owned ships to export goods such as cotton and import everything from English plows to slaves.

The Confederacy's leaders immediately recognized that they would never match the North's industrial might in building ships, so they chose the radical path of building a new kind of ship that would be technically superior to the wooden ships they expected to see off their ports. By the summer of 1861 plans were under way to build an ironclad ship at Gosport that would patrol the waters of Hampton Roads and rid the port of the growing presence of blockading ships. If that ironclad proved successful, copies of it would be manufactured and sent to other Southern port cities.

Soon the *C.S.S. Virginia,* built on the hulk of the *Merrimack* (which had burned only to the waterline) was under construction. It was to be a water-going battery of ten cannons, four of them rifled. The idea was that the armored ship would steam to within a few hundred yards of the wooden blockading ships, then blast them into oblivion while their return fire bounced off the iron plating. It was a simple idea that had been a theory for decades in Europe. Only the Confederates, desperate for some means of protecting their ports, had the audacity to put theory into practice.

Hearing that the *Virginia* was under construction, the North countered with its own crash ironclad-building program. The competition was won by an inventor who submitted a design for a ship that would be armed with only two cannons. He called it the *U.S.S. Monitor.*

The March 8, 1862, attack of the *Virginia* against the wooden blockading ships was matched in ferocity only by the March 9 battle between the two ironclads. The two ships fought each other to a fierce draw, each damaging the other, but not enough for a clear victor to be declared. In two days, the centuries-old history of naval warfare had changed forever. Every nation's navy would make ironclads the core of its fleet. The *Monitor* s rotating turret, which allowed it to bring its guns to bear more quickly than the broadside guns on the *Virginia,* would become a standard feature on every naval vessel.

Once the *Virginia* met its match the *Monitor* in Hampton Roads, the North gained the upper hand. More Union infantry arrived on ships to march up the Virginia Peninsula in an attempt to take Richmond. By late spring of 1862, Hampton Roads bay was under Union control, and the Federals recaptured Gosport Naval Yard. Sets of plans drawn by a Confederate ship designer were discovered. The plans were for small ironclad ships that could have been loaded onto railroad train cars and shipped to every coastal city in the South. Had the *Monitor* not arrived when it had, Gosport would have built scores of Confederate ironclads that might have broken the back of the Union blockade.

The Hampton Roads area remained under Union control. The Confederacy's dream of using the North's most important naval installation lasted only a year. When the shipyard was recaptured, the Confederacy's chance of breaking the Union blockade with superior ironclad technology all but disappeared. The Confederacy would be forced to build its ironclads at makeshift shipyards in cornfields beside shallow rivers. Moving supplies and equipment to those shipyards and transporting the completed ships to hot spots where they could fight the Federals would prove to be too difficult. That window of opportunity when the South had a chance of building a superior ironclad fleet had closed forever.

SITE
1

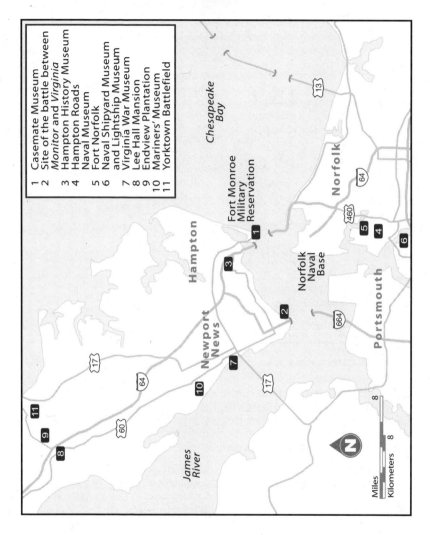

1 Casemate Museum
2 Site of the battle between
  Monitor and *Virginia*
3 Hampton History Museum
4 Hampton Roads
  Naval Museum
5 Fort Norfolk
6 Naval Shipyard Museum
  and Lightship Museum
7 Virginia War Museum
8 Lee Hall Mansion
9 Endview Plantation
10 Mariners' Museum
11 Yorktown Battlefield

Chesapeake Bay

Fort Monroe Military Reservation

Hampton

Newport News

James River

Norfolk Naval Base

Norfolk

Portsmouth

Miles
Kilometers

Hampton Roads Today

With 1.6 million people, the Hampton Roads metropolitan statistical area is Virginia's largest "city," outnumbering Richmond, the state capital, by more than a half million people. The MSA is made up of several municipalities, including Norfolk, Hampton, Portsmouth, Virginia Beach, and Chesapeake. The reason this region has grown so large can be traced back more than 140 years to Gosport Naval Yard. Today, Hampton Roads is home to scores of U.S. Navy warships, including five aircraft carriers. No other port is home to as many carriers. The original stone dry dock that was so important to both Union and Confederate navies is still on the same base.

That dry dock is off-limits to history travelers because of heightened security concerns, as are some other historically significant Civil War sites such as the graves of the sailors who went down with the frigate *U.S.S. Cumberland* after it tangled with the *C.S.S. Virginia* on March 8, 1862. Still, the region has done a fine job of retaining some of its Civil War atmosphere. For example, Fort Monroe, one of the oldest forts in the nation, which is on an active military base, is open to the public. You might have to look harder for them, but there are monuments and statues sharing space with modern-day buildings, an indication that the region has not forgotten its roots.

Points of Interest

1. Casemate Museum ★★★★★

Fort Monroe, Hampton
T: 757-788-3391
Daily, 10:30 a.m.–4:30 p.m.
Closed major holidays.
Free admission.

The Casemate Museum is located within Fort Monroe, an active military base, so be prepared to go through security before being allowed on the base. Everyone in the vehicle should have a photo identification. The guards will ask for a destination (the Casemate Museum) and may even ask to search the vehicle. Once past the guard house, follow the signs to the Casemate Museum, which is located in one of the walls of the fort. You will even drive over a moat to get inside the fort.

This point of land jutting out into Hampton Roads is the oldest continually guarded real estate in the nation. Captain John Smith, the military commander of the Jamestown colony, just up the James River, established a fort on the same site. It has been occupied ever since. After the British burned the Executive Mansion and Capitol in Washington in 1814, the U.S. government decided to build a system of forts to protect its inland cities from river attack. Fort Monroe was the first in what would be dozens of forts built in a ring stretching from the North Atlantic to the Pacific. It was started in 1819 and finished in 1834. Among its later engineers was Robert E. Lee, who also worked on a smaller fort in Hampton Roads called Fort Wool, which can be visited by tour boat.

Despite the fact that Norfolk and the other towns across Hampton Roads quickly fell into Confederate hands after Virginia seceded, Fort Monroe always remained under Federal control. It was used as a base from which Union troops marched out to fight one of the first true battles of the war, the Battle of Big Bethel, on June 10, 1861. The battle plan was supposed to be General Ben Butler's attempt to prove that politically appointed generals were just as good as professional soldiers. But Butler failed miserably. The two columns he sent to capture Confederate outposts at Big Bethel Church fired on each other by accident before they ever reached Confederate territory. When they finally did fight the Confederates, the vastly outnumbered Southerners won, leading to the oft-quoted expression that one Southern boy could whip ten from the North.

Monroe never came under Confederate attack, but slaves on neighboring plantations instinctively recognized it as a chance for freedom. They fled to the Union-held fort in such large numbers that Butler finally asked Washington what to do with the "contrabands," a term that referred to the humans as property. Butler let the word spread through the surrounding countryside that if other contrabands made it to the safety of the fort, they would not be returned to bondage. Since he was not quite declaring them to be forever free as other military commanders in former Southern territory had done, President Lincoln did not object.

The Casemate Museum tells two important stories, that of coastal fort artillery and that of the two years when Confederate President Jefferson Davis was imprisoned at the fort. Among the displays is a thirty-two–pounder cannon with its manikin loading crew. This type of smoothbore cannon was typical of the armament of most Confederate forts that Union forces would

attack. Once the Federals captured any forts, they would quickly replace such antiquated ordnance with rifled cannons of heavier and larger calibers than the Confederates could produce.

The cell or casemate in which Davis was kept for several months is faithfully reproduced. After his capture in Georgia in May 1865, Davis was immediately transferred to Fort Monroe on the assumption that he would be tried for treason. Initially, Davis was kept shackled, and a light burned in his cell twenty-four hours a day. He remained in the dark, dank cell until a fort doctor finally persuaded the fort's commander to move him to more healthful quarters in a nearby house.

Davis was imprisoned at the fort for nearly two years before he was finally released without any charges ever being brought against him. Some historians have speculated that the reason Davis was never tried may have been that the chief justice of the U.S. Supreme Court gave the government his secret opinion that secession was legal under the U.S. Constitution. Any public trial of Davis would have given him a very public chance to proclaim that the Confederacy had legitimately left the Union. General Robert E. Lee, who had also been threatened with trial, was also released without ever being tried. In fact, no high-ranking Confederate government official or military leader was ever tried for his role in leaving the Union.

2. Site of the Battle between *Monitor* and *Virginia* ★

South Hampton at the King-Lincoln Park before Monitor-Merrimack Bridge Tunnel

It is impossible, of course, to show a naval battlefield, but one can at least see the distances the two ships were operating in from the shore of Hampton looking south into Hampton Roads (a body of water, not an actual road) just before crossing the

Monitor-Merrimack Bridge Tunnel (I-664). The *Virginia* was hampered by the fact that she drew twenty-two feet of water under her keel, meaning that she had to stay a good distance from either bank lest she risk running aground—which she did once during the battle. The *Monitor*'s draft was less than eleven feet. The *Monitor*'s ability to operate in shallower water, her better maneuverability, and her rotating turrets helped make up for the *Virginia*'s heavier firepower. The *Virginia* was some-times referred to by its old U.S. Navy name, the *Merrimack,* even by some Confederates who were familiar with the five-year-old hull under the iron plating.

3. Hampton History Museum ★★

120 Old Hampton Lane, Hampton
T: 757-727-1610
Monday–Saturday, 10 a.m.–5 p.m.,
Sunday, 1–5 p.m.
Admission: $5

This museum covers more than 400 years of history of the area and includes gal-leries covering the antebellum period, the Civil War, and Reconstruction. This is the best place to learn about the first major land engagement of the war, the Battle of Big Bethel, which took place just north of Hampton. (The site is now under a water reservoir.) This was the first battle in which both Union and Confederate sol-diers lost their lives in direct combat with each other. Union General Ben Butler's offer to protect runaway slaves if they made it to Fort Monroe is also explained in some panels.

4. Hampton Roads Naval Museum ★★★★

Part of Nauticus in downtown Norfolk
T: 757-322-2987
Tuesday–Saturday, 10 a.m.–5 p.m.,
Sunday, noon–5 p.m.
Open Mondays during summer, limited hours between January and early March.
Free admission (if visiting the Naval

Museum only but there is a charge to visit Nauticus, the science museum).

This museum is on the waterfront in downtown Norfolk and reached by passing through the second floor of Nauticus, a scientific museum dedicated to describing the power of the sea. In addition to exhibits of artifacts from the *U.S.S. Cumberland,* a frigate sunk by the *Virginia,* there is some armor plating from the *Virginia* and a full-scale replica of the *Monitor*'s turret. Also boarded from this second floor is the *U.S.S. Wisconsin,* a World War II–era battleship.

5. Fort Norfolk ★

Corner of Front Street and Colley Avenue, Norfolk
Daylight hours, self-guided tours

This is the oldest and last-standing of nineteen harborfront forts ordered built by President George Washington in 1794. Though its thin walls and light guns were obsolete by 1861, the fort still had a full powder magazine when the Confederates captured it. The black powder and shells in the magazine were transferred to the *Virginia,* which used them to fight the Union wooden fleet one day and the *Monitor* the next. The fort is usually open for a self-guided tour. Follow the signs.

6. Naval Shipyard Museum and Lightship Museum ★★★

Two High St., Portsmouth
T: 757-393-8741
Monday–Saturday, 10 a.m.–5 p.m.;
Sunday, noon–5 p.m.
Winter hours: closed on Monday, open Sunday 1–5 p.m.
Admission: $3

Because the Navy shipyard where the stone dry dock that was so vital in the Civil War is off-limits to civilians, this little museum is the next best thing for learning about the region's centuries-old shipbuilding tradition. The museum explains why the Gosport Naval Yard's name was changed to Norfolk Shipyard, when the facility itself is actually in Portsmouth (there already was a shipyard by that name in New Hampshire). Artifacts, models, and uniforms are on display. Next door, and for the same admission price, is a lightship, a ship used as a lighthouse that was moored in the Atlantic.

7. Virginia War Museum ★★★

9285 Warwick Blvd., Newport News
T: 757-247-8523
Monday–Saturday, 9 a.m.–5 p.m.,
Sunday, 1–5 p.m.
Admission: $6

All of the wars in which Virginia has participated are covered in this museum, including the Civil War. This museum has some rare artifacts, including a French light tank from World War I and a light American tank from World War II.

8. Lee Hall Mansion ★★★★

163 Yorktown Rd., Newport News
T: 757-888-3371
Monday, Wednesday–Saturday, 10 a.m.–4 p.m.; Sunday, 1–5 p.m.
Closed Wednesdays January–March and major holidays.
Admission: $6

This is one of the few remaining prewar homes left in this part of Virginia, a testament to how much the region has been built up in recent years. Finished in 1859, in 1862 the house was the headquarters of two generals; John Magruder, a hard-drinking general who fooled Union General George McClellan into believing that 10,000 Confederates were really 100,000 at Yorktown; and Joseph E. Johnston, the overall commander of Confederate forces who was charged with defending Richmond from attack by Federals marching up the Peninsula. For three weeks, the meager Confederate forces in the region

commanded by these two generals slowed down McClellan's massive army, giving Richmond time to set up a defense. Once the defense was ready, Johnston pulled his troops back from this region to Williamsburg, where the Federals finally forced a major battle. The front yard of this house was the location of a small skirmish. The lower Peninsula remained in Union hands for the remainder of the war.

9. Endview Plantation ★★

362 Yorktown Rd., Newport News
T: 757-887-1862
Monday, Wednesday, Saturday,
10 a.m.–4 p.m.; Sunday, 1–5 p.m.
Closed Wednesdays January–March.
Admission: $6

This house dates back to before the American Revolution. General George Washington may have stopped here on his way to Yorktown. McClellan used it as a headquarters, and it was also a Union hospital during the Federal army's siege of Yorktown. A reenactment usually takes place here in March every year.

10. Mariners' Museum ★★★★★

100 Museum Dr., Newport News
T: 757-596-2222
www.mariner.org
Daily, 10 a.m.–5 p.m.
Closed major holidays.
Admission: $8

The Mariners' Museum houses and is restoring major artifacts from the *U.S.S. Monitor*, including the propellers, engine, and a turret that is deeply gouged in several places from rounds fired by the *C.S.S. Virginia*. Recovered over the last several years from the *Monitor*'s resting place off Cape Hatteras, North Carolina, these large pieces are undergoing preservation in large outdoor, water-filled tanks at the museum, and visitors can view them. Inside the museum are other displays of smaller artifacts recovered from the ironclad, including the red signal lamp that was the last thing seen above the waves before the ship sank in a storm in December 1862.

The rest of the *Monitor* will likely never be recovered. The thin armor plating of the hull has deteriorated so much that it is impossible to raise the hull without destroying it. The nine-foot-high, twenty-foot-wide turret was the most important and innovative aspect of the ironclad. It still contains the two eleven-inch Dahlgren smoothbore cannons. As the decades of accumulated sea growth is removed, historians are noting some dents in the turret. Some of the dents are quite deep, meaning some direct shots from the *Virginia* came close to penetrating the eight one-inch layers of iron plating. This was the only true battle the *Monitor* ever fought. She was unable to elevate her guns enough to reach Confederate land batteries. During the war, the U.S. Navy rushed through the construction of many other similar ships it called "monitors."

The rest of the museum includes other fine exhibits on ships and the sea, including a collection of wooden figureheads, a vast collection of wooden ship models showing naval technology from ancient times through today, and the personal history of a Norfolk ship designer who helped modernize the U.S. Navy.

11. Yorktown Battlefield ★★★★

Exit 250B from I-64
T: 757-898-2410
Visitor center 8:30 a.m.–5 p.m.
Grounds close at sunset.
Free admission

Though Yorktown is known and interpreted by the National Park Service as the battlefield where the British finally gave up trying to defeat the American Patriots during the American Revolution, the trenches on the south end of the battlefield are more likely left over from Confederate improvements in the spring of 1862 when the Confederates were defending the Virginia Peninsula from Union invasion. It was here that Confederate General John Magruder waged a successful psychological war against the Federals. Magruder would march regiments quietly to the rear and then noisily march them right back into the trenches. Officers would loudly shout out orders for nonexistent regiments, knowing that listening Federals would note the names of those regiments. McClellan interpreted the action as thousands of reinforcements coming in to face his 100,000-man army, so he slowed his advance and planned a lengthy siege. Magruder, a flamboyant man who enjoyed acting in his spare time, never had more than 10,000 men and an active imagination. His action at Yorktown allowed Richmond time to prepare a defense.

SOURCES & OTHER READING

Thunder at Hampton Roads, A.A. Hoehling, DeCapo Press, 1993.

Iron Afloat: The Story of the Confederate Ironclads, William Still, University of South Carolina Press, 1985.

Reign of Iron: The Story of the First Ironclads, the Monitor and the Merrimack, James L. Nelson, William Morrow, 2004.

Duel of the Ironclads U.S.S. Monitor and C.S.S. Virginia at Hampton Roads, 1862, Angus Konstam, Osprey Press, 2003.

Getting To and Around Hampton Roads

Norfolk International Airport has more than 200 departures and arrivals each day. Getting around the region will require a vehicle, a good local map, and detailed directions on how to reach sites from the major highways. There is one bridge tunnel leading to and from Norfolk on I-64 and one leading to and from Portsmouth on I-664, so traffic backups are common, particularly during weekday rush hours. Weekend touring of the Civil War sites is advisable, but even weekend travel is busy. The sites are too scattered to see by walking or biking. Public transit is not an option between cities, as the historic sites are not near bus routes. The best way to see all of the Civil War sites associated with Hampton Roads is by car. All of these sites are within twenty miles of each other, but those miles are urban, so be sure to give yourself plenty of time to get from one site to the next.

Accommodations

Patriot Inn Bed & Breakfast

201 North St., Portsmouth
T: 757-391-0157
www.bbonline.com/va/patriot
4 rooms
$100–$120

Located next to the Elizabeth River, this 1784 house witnessed General Cornwallis loading his troops up to take them to Yorktown to meet—and he assumed defeat—General Washington's rag-tag Colonials. The windows frame the same hand-blown glass that was installed when the house was built.

Glencoe Inn

222 North St., Portsmouth
T: 757-397-8128
www.glencoeinn.com
4 rooms
$95

Though the house was not built until 1890, it is located in a Civil War–era neighborhood called Old Towne. The current owners try to preserve the Scottish heritage of the original owners and builders of the house.

The Freemason Inn Bed and Breakfast

411 West York St., Norfolk
T: 757-963-7000
www.freemasoninn.com
4 rooms
$187–$277

Located in a turn-of-the-century inn, the rooms are decorated in an English style and have four-poster beds. Though it is a bed and breakfast, private dinners can be arranged in advance of visiting.

Page House Inn

323 Fairfax Ave., Norfolk
T: 757-625-5033
www.pagehouseinn.com
7 rooms and suites
$150–$175

Located in the Ghent historic district in downtown Norfolk, this bed and breakfast is within walking distance of Norfolk's attractions and is right next door to the Chrysler Museum of Art.

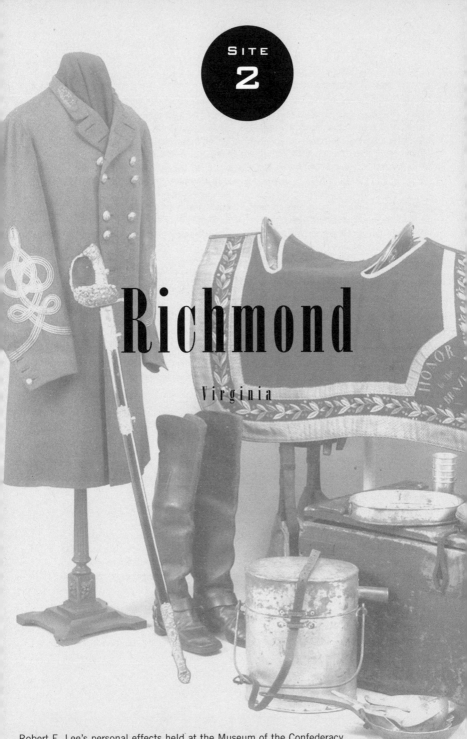

Richmond

Virginia

Robert E. Lee's personal effects held at the Museum of the Confederacy.

THE WAR YEARS

D uring the war Richmond was the primary objective of the Union Army of the Potomac for four years. Today, it is home to the Confederate White House, as well as the Museum of the Confederacy, which houses the largest collection of Confederate artifacts in the nation. Richmond, and the battlefields to its east, are among the nation's top Civil War destinations.

Historians today still wonder what was going on in the minds of Confederate congressmen when they voted on May 20, 1861, to move the Confederate capital from Montgomery, Alabama, to Richmond. Richmond was barely 100 miles, less than five days' march, from Washington, the capital of what would soon prove to be the most powerful nation on earth. Whether it was an attempt to be provocative and defiant in rebellion, or an attempt to show the Union that two separate countries could coexist close together is unknown. The practical effect was that Richmond was a target of capture for the duration of the war, and the Confederate government in Richmond reacted to that constant threat to the detriment of all others. While other cities (such as New Orleans) were strategically more important to the future of the Confederacy, attention and resources were always focused on saving the Confederate capital city from attack.

Richmond was a major metropolis in 1860. Although smaller than New Orleans and Charleston, it was more industrialized. Richmond was home to the Tredegar Iron Works, a large iron foundry that supplied almost all of the railroad rails in the south. Tredegar was even a major supplier of cannons for the U.S. government, which was a very good customer until Virginia seceded on April 17, 1861.

The city's prewar population of 38,000 was large by Southern standards. When the city was named Confederate capital, its population more than doubled within a few months as bureaucrats, war planners, suppliers, and profiteers all moved to Richmond to take over administration of the new national government and the war effort. Jefferson Davis and his family, Mississippians who had briefly lived in Montgomery before the capital was moved, moved into a hillside house that a wealthy businessman donated to the Confederate cause.

At first, war fever gripped the city, but as casualties began to arrive by rail, the fervor was replaced by the realization that war kills people. That was followed by fear that war would one day come to the city's doorsteps. Hospitals sprang up around the city in scattered houses. A huge hospital complex called Chimborazo was built, where hundreds of doctors and nurses took care of thousands of wounded men.

As the war dragged on, Richmond's confidence dwindled. Starting as early as the spring and summer of 1862, when Union General George McClellan's army came within sight of the city, a constant fear of capture and destruction plagued the populace. As early as the spring of 1863, the city began to experience food shortages. In April of that year, scores of lower-class women staged a "bread riot" and broke into stores to steal food. President Davis himself was forced to address the crowd, telling them that the only solution to food shortages was to defeat the Federals who were trying to strangle their city.

Starting with the Fredericksburg victory in December 1862, followed by the Chancellorsville victory in May 1863, Richmond's residents and the Confederate government returned to the belief that they could eventually win the war. Those high-flying emotions were dashed in July 1863 when word came simultaneously into the capital that Lee had retreated from Gettysburg on July 3 and that Vicksburg had surrendered the following day. Still, Richmond itself was relatively safe.

That sense of safety started to change in the spring of 1864 when Ulysses S. Grant took overall command of Union forces and began riding with the Army of the Potomac. Starting with the Battle of the Wilderness in May 1864, barely fifty miles northeast of Richmond, Grant changed the strategy of the war in the East. For the previous three years, under all previous commanders of the Army of the Potomac, the objective had been to capture Richmond. Grant's goal was the destruction of the Army of Northern Virginia. Once Lee's army was destroyed, then Grant would march on Richmond.

For the next eleven months, Grant doggedly pursued that strategy. When he lost at Wilderness, he moved further south to Spotsylvania Court House. When he lost there, he move further south to the North Anna River. When he lost there, he moved to the east of Richmond. When he lost at Cold Harbor, he crossed the James River and moved on Petersburg. When he couldn't capture Petersburg in its opening battles, he settled into a long siege of that vital rail city and Richmond. All the while, Lee's army was being whittled away, and Grant was inching closer to Richmond.

Finally on April 2, 1865, Grant made one giant push on the Petersburg trenches, and Lee's army, suffering from months of starvation and disease, finally yielded. The trench lines were broken, and Lee had to abandon both Petersburg and Richmond. He sent a telegram to Jefferson Davis urging him to abandon the city while he could still get a train out. As Davis and his cabinet were leaving, pent-up frustration and fear of the future got the better of the people still in Richmond. Looting began and a fire broke out that consumed most of the commercial district, including some 900 buildings in twenty city blocks. What the Federals had been threatening to do for four years—destroy Richmond—occurred while the Union army was still miles away. Richmond had been destroyed by the carelessness of its own citizens. Ironically, the total destruction of Richmond by fire was halted when the first Union troops to enter the city laid down their muskets and picked up fire-fighting equipment.

On April 4, President Lincoln, the man who had set the goal of capturing Richmond four years earlier, arrived for a surprise inspection of what was left. With just a small guard of sailors protecting him, Lincoln moved through the city to the Confederate White House. He sat in Jefferson Davis's chair before returning to the safety of the Union ship that had docked nearby.

Life would be hard in Richmond for the next ten years of Reconstruction, but not as hard as it might have been. When the fire started, the president of the Tredegar Iron Works armed his workers and told them to shoot anyone approaching company property who was carrying a torch. Word spread among the rioters, and Tredegar was never in danger. After the war, it returned to making rails and was one of the key economic engines to help restore economic stability to Richmond.

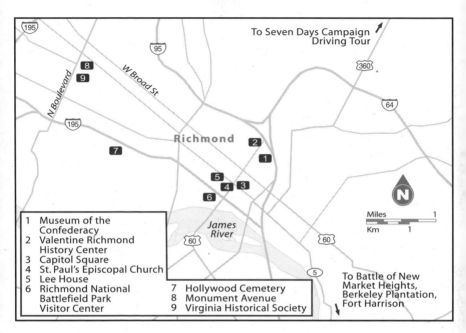

1 Museum of the Confederacy
2 Valentine Richmond History Center
3 Capitol Square
4 St. Paul's Episcopal Church
5 Lee House
6 Richmond National Battlefield Park Visitor Center
7 Hollywood Cemetery
8 Monument Avenue
9 Virginia Historical Society

To Seven Days Campaign Driving Tour

Richmond

James River

Miles 1
Km 1

To Battle of New Market Heights, Berkeley Plantation, Fort Harrison

SOURCES & OTHER READING

Ashes of Glory: Richmond at War, Ernest Ferguson, Vintage Press, 1997.

Richmond Burning: The Last Days of the Confederate Capital, Nelson Lankford, Penguin Press, 2003.

Chimborazo: The Confederacy's Largest Hospital, Carol C. Green, University of Tennessee Press, 2004.

To the Gates of Richmond: The Peninsula Campaign, Stephen Sears, Tickknor & Fields, 1992

City under Siege: Richmond During the Civil War, Mike Wright, Cooper Square Publishers, 2002.

Mary Chesnut's Civil War, edited by C. Vann Woodward, Yale University Press, 1983

The Confederate State of Richmond: A Biography of the Capital, Emory Thomas, Louisiana State University Press, 1998.

RICHMOND TODAY

Richmond, Virginia's capital and the former capital of the Confederacy, does not especially embrace that latter title. This city regularly saw Confederate heroes like Stonewall Jackson and Robert E. Lee walking its streets; more Confederate artifacts are housed in this city than anywhere else in the world; and several significant moments in American history took place here; but Richmond prefers to think of itself as a modern business city rather than a historic city centered on the events of 1861–1865. This means that history travelers will have to work a little harder to find sites associated with the Civil War.

POINTS OF INTEREST

1. Museum of the Confederacy ★★★★★

Exit 74C off I-95. Follow signs from exit. Take West Broad Street to 11th Street, then turn right. Drive two blocks to Clay. Turn right onto Clay and follow to Museum at 12th and Clay Streets.
Park in the hospital parking deck.
T: 804-649-1861
Monday–Saturday, 10 a.m.–5 p.m.; Sunday, noon–5 p.m.
Admission: $7 ($10 when combined with a tour of the Confederate White House).

This is, without a doubt, the best museum of Confederate artifacts and the best museum explaining the life and death of the Confederacy to be found in the nation. Any history tourist wondering what Southerners thought before, during, and after the war will find the answers in the permanent displays and the changing exhibits. The temporary exhibits are one of the museum's strengths, so it is worth visiting even if you have toured it previously. Not many history museums do this, but that has always been a hallmark of the Museum of the Confederacy. And the museum has never put any subject off-limits. Among its more popular exhibits have been those looking at slavery and the black experience in the South.

The permanent exhibit traces the war in chronological order on one floor using a mixture of general displays of weapons and uniforms and specific displays focusing on pivotal moments in the history of the Confederacy. Among the most poignant is a display of the sketchbook Stonewall Jackson's engineer was carrying the night Jackson was accidentally shot by a Confederate regiment. Lieutenant Keith Boswell, the engineer who shadowed Jackson in order to make sure roads and bridges were strong enough to carry his men, was shot through the heart in the same volley that wounded Jackson in the arm and hand. The sketch book is open to show the path two Minie balls took before killing Boswell. In the same case are the medical instruments used to amputate Jackson's arm. Other displays contain a cap that was worn by Jackson, a camp scene set up using Robert E. Lee's personal accoutrements and hat, and other uniforms worn by famous Confederates.

As noted, the museum has enough items (more than 500 battle flags, 200 uniforms,

6,000 original photographs) so that it can regularly host special exhibits that focus on a specific aspect of the war.

Next door to the museum is the White House of the Confederacy, the executive mansion of Jefferson Davis and his family. Built in 1818, the house was loaned to the Davis family as a residence when they moved to Richmond in 1861. During the war it functioned much like Lincoln's Executive Mansion in Washington. The first floor was devoted to official space where receptions were held in honor of visiting dignitaries. President Davis had an office on the second floor where he conducted meetings with politicians and generals on war strategy. Also on the second floor were his private quarters where he played with his children. At ease while in the family quarters with his wife and family, the stiff, mercurial Davis became like any other loving husband and father.

The Confederate White House did know tragedy. One day, Davis's small son, Joe, was playing, when he fell from a third-floor railing to the bricked pavement below. Within hours the child had died from a head injury. Davis was inconsolable. Among the letters of regret that arrived was one from President Lincoln. He was returning the favor of a sympathy note Davis had sent when one of Lincoln's sons had died of fever in the U.S. Executive Mansion.

As of 2005, the future of the museum and the Confederate White House is being debated by its board of directors. All of the land around the two structures is controlled by Virginia Commonwealth University Medical School. The traffic caused by the hospital's construction intrudes on the accessibility of the two historic structures. The board assures its members that the museum will always exist, but there is a possibility that it may

be moved in order to make it easier for history travelers to find it. The board also assures its members that the Confederate White House will not be separated from the Museum of the Confederacy.

2. Valentine Richmond History Center ★★★

1015 East Clay St.
T: 804-649-0711
Tuesday–Saturday, 10 a.m.–5 p.m.;
Sunday, noon–5 p.m.
Admission: $7

This museum opened in 1898, so it has had plenty of time to collect what it calls "Richmond's thises and thats." Among the items on display is a plaster death mask of Stonewall Jackson. The detail is so great that scratches can be seen in his face, made on the night of his wounding when his horse bolted and dragged him into some low-hanging tree limbs. Also at the Valentine Museum is an early model of the statue of Lee asleep on his cot. The original is on display at Lee Chapel in Lexington, Virginia.

3. Capitol Square ★★★

Tenth and Broad Streets.
Tours: 9 a.m.–5 p.m., every half hour (inside closed until December 2006).

Once visitors get past the magnificent statue of George Washington, which is faithfully reproduced as part of the Confederate seal, they can enjoy a number of other statues on the lawn of the capitol, including one of Stonewall Jackson and another of his doctor, Hunter Holmes McGuire, who founded the college of medicine at Virginia Commonwealth University. Inside the capitol, visitors can stand in the same spot in the General Assembly where Robert E. Lee was sworn in as general in charge of Virginia volunteers. Stonewall Jackson's body also lay in state in this room, draped by the Third National Flag. It was the first time "the stainless banner" had been used in an official government capacity. The flag consisted of the familiar square Confederate battle flag in the upper left corner with the rest of the flag a brilliant white.

4. St. Paul's Episcopal Church ★★

Ninth and Grace Streets
Self-tours during daylight hours.

This was the church for the leading citizens of Richmond, as well as President Davis and General Lee when he was in town for meetings. Davis was in church here on April 2, 1865, when he received a telegram from Lee telling him that the Federals had broken through the defensive lines at Petersburg and that he was being forced to abandon both Petersburg and Richmond. Davis caused a scene when he left the church to prepare to leave the city. Davis's pew is marked so visitors can sit in the same seats once occupied by President Davis and General Lee.

5. Lee House ★★

707 East Franklin St.
Private, but viewable from the street.

This is the house where Mrs. Lee lived during much of the war and the house to which General Lee returned just after his surrender at Appomattox Court House in April 1865. Within a few hours after Lee's arrival here as a defeated general, famed photographer Matthew Brady knocked on the door asking his permission to take some photographs to preserve that point in history. Lee agreed and a remarkable series of photographs was taken on the back porch of the house (not visible from the street). In one photograph Lee stands alone, unbowed and with fire still in his eyes. In another image, he is seated with one son and an aide at his side. (Brady's intentions with the photographs have been debated ever since because of the inclusion of a cross naturally formed by the panels of the door. In each image, Lee's

head is near the cross, making it unlikely that Brady did not notice the symbolism. Those images have comforted Southerners for generations in the belief that Lee performed his duty as a Christian soldier.)

6. Richmond National Battlefield Park Visitor Center ★★★

Tredegar Iron Works
490 Tredegar St.
Exit 74C from I-95
T: 804-226-1981
Daily, 9 a.m.–5 p.m.
Battlefields are open sunrise to sunset.

The National Park Service visitor center is located in one of the remaining buildings of Tredegar Iron Works, the vast manufacturing facility that forged everything from the iron plating that was installed on the *C.S.S. Virginia* to thousands of cannons used by Confederate armies in the field. Interpretive signs explain the process of how iron ore was brought to Tredegar, then refined until molten and poured into a cannon or rail molds. The factory was equipped with a rolling mill so that the iron could be rolled flat into plates used to arm Confederate Navy ironclads. Other exhibits are scattered over three floors. An interpretive film plays every half hour.

The National Civil War Center is scheduled to open in 2007 in the gun foundry building on the same general site. This will be a museum with a foundation promising to interpret the war fairly through the experience of the Confederacy, the Union, and free and enslaved blacks.

Across from Tredegar Iron Works, accessible by a pedestrian bridge, is Belle Isle. During the war this was the location of a prison camp for captured Union soldiers. There is little to see on Belle Isle today, though descendants of the 30,000 men who were kept here might want to stand on the same ground as their ancestors.

7. Hollywood Cemetery ★★★★★

412 South Cherry St.
T: 804-648-8501
Gate hours: Monday–Friday, 8:30 a.m.–
4:30 p.m.
Free admission. Tour map of famous
graves $5.

Still an active cemetery, Hollywood
Cemetery is the final resting place of
many famous Confederates. A map shows
the location of those graves, but most can
be found by following a blue line painted
in the road. The first interesting Confederate encountered is Private Henry Wyatt
of North Carolina, the first Confederate
soldier killed in the war. Wyatt was killed
at the Battle of Big Bethel. After him, visitors can find General George Pickett, one
of the generals leading the Pettigrew-
Pickett-Trimble Assault on the third day of
Gettysburg; General J.E.B. Stuart, the
famous cavalry chief who was killed north
of Richmond in 1864; General Joseph
Anderson, the president of Tredegar
Ironworks; and President Jefferson Davis
and his family. Across from Davis is the
grave of Fitzhugh Lee, Robert E. Lee's
nephew and one of Stuart's most trusted
subordinate generals in the cavalry.

Hollywood Cemetery has many sad stories.
The blue line passes the graves of John
and Willie Pegram. John was killed just
three weeks after his wedding in St. Paul's
Episcopal Church. His funeral was conducted in the same church by the same
pastor who had married him. Brother
Willie, a bespectacled artillery genius, was
killed just ten days before the war ended
at the Battle of Five Forks. Further along
is a triple tombstone over the graves of
General James Longstreet's children. Over
the course of several days, Longstreet
watched three of his children die from
scarlet fever. The general was so dis-
traught that his friend George Pickett handled all of the arrangements for the burial.

8. Monument Avenue ★★★

Use a city map to find Monument Avenue
in the northwest quadrant of downtown
before passing I-195 on the north side of
downtown. Watch for one-way streets.

The houses here are among the most
exclusive in Richmond. Parking is difficult. Walking is the best way to see the
statues of Confederate heroes, in addition
to the modern-day statue of Richmond
native and tennis star Arthur Ashe. Found
along Monument Avenue are statues honoring Matthew Maury, the commander of
the Confederate States Navy; Stonewall
Jackson; Robert E. Lee; and J.E.B. Stuart.

9. Virginia Historical Society ★★★★★

428 North Boulevard St.
T: 804-358-4901
Monday–Saturday, 10 am.–5 p.m.;
Sunday, 1–5 p.m.
Closed major holidays.
Admission: $5

One of the most poignant displays in the
Civil War section is the bloodstained uniform worn by J.E.B. Stuart when he was
mortally wounded at the Battle of Yellow
Tavern. The display also shows the pistol
he was carrying that day. Also visible is
the wheelchair used by Mrs. Robert E. Lee
after her limbs were crippled by rheuma-
toid arthritis. One of the most valuable
collections shows an example of every
firearm manufactured by the Confederacy.
Above those weapons cases is a series of
four paintings based on the seasons of the
year and the fortunes of the Confederacy.

Seven Days Campaign Driving Tour
★★★★★

National Park Service Driving Tour U.S.
360 at Mechanicsville and S.R. 156

A driving tour map can be picked up at
the visitor center at Tredegar Ironworks.

The Seven Days tour begins at
Chickohominy Bluffs, a high piece of
ground just outside Mechanicsville and
just before U.S. 360 intersects with S.R.
156, also called Cold Harbor Road. The
Seven Days battles ran from June 25
through July 1 in 1862. They were the
culmination of Union General George
McClellan's march up the Virginia
Peninsula in an attempt to capture
Richmond. When J.E.B. Stuart's cavalry
rode around McClellan's army a week earlier, he discovered that one Union corps
was north of the Chickohominy River and
isolated from the rest of the Union army.
Lee reasoned that if his larger force
destroyed that smaller Union corps, he
could whittle the rest of the Union army
down over time.

The Seven Days opened here, but Lee's
plan had trouble from the start. Stonewall
Jackson's small army of 17,000 men was
late in arriving on the field, so the entire
attack was held up. When Jackson's men,
exhausted from fighting in the
Shenandoah Valley the previous month,
finally arrived, an equally exhausted
Jackson did not press the attack. The
Federals tactically won first at Beaver Dam
Creek, then at Gaines Mill, but then had
to retreat in the face of superior numbers.

Not far from the June 1862 battlefield of
Gaines Mill, and still along S.R. 156, is
the June 1864 battlefield of Cold Harbor.
This was one of General U.S. Grant's worst
defeats, when he ordered a frontal assault
against Lee's entrenched positions. Grant's

army suffered 13,000 casualties in a matter of minutes, while the Confederates lost
only 2,500. After the battle, Grant lied
about his losses to Lincoln.

The Seven Days tour resumes along S.R.
156. The tour changes roads, but the
brown National Park Service signs are easy
to follow to White Oak Swamp, Glendale,
and the best-known of the Seven Days
battles, Malvern Hill. The Park Service has
set up several cannons on the slight hill
pointing in the direction in which Lee
ordered a tragic charge on July 1, 1862.
The concentrated fire of 100 Federal cannons cut down hundreds of Confederate
infantry—one of the few battles where the
primary weapons were cannons against
muskets. When the carnage ended, more
than 5,500 Confederates lay dead and
wounded, compared to only 3,200 Federal
losses. Lee ordered the same type of
charge just over a year later at Gettysburg.

Though he once again won a Seven Days
battle, McClellan retreated to the James
River, leaving Lee in possession of the
field. Lee thought about attacking the
Federals at Harrison's Landing to try and
push them into the James, but decided
his own army was too badly mauled.
McClellan loaded his men on board transports and sailed away. Though he had suffered 16,000 casualties to Lee's 20,000,
McClellan is considered the loser of the
Seven Days because he left the field.

Battle of New Market Heights ★

Historic marker 2.4 miles north of the
intersection of Va. 5 and S.R. 156
(approximately 3 miles from Malvern Hill).

On September 29, 1864, six regiments of
U.S. Colored Troops took New Market
Heights in a fierce battle with
Confederates. The black troops, fighting
more than a year after the 54th

Massachusetts had been the first black unit to engage the Confederates in the eastern theater, crossed an open field and a ravine before getting close to the slight hill of the Heights. The black troops suffered almost 40 percent casualties, but the Confederates pulled back. Of the sixteen Congressional Medals of Honor awarded to black troops during the Civil War, fourteen of them came from actions reported during this battle.

Berkeley Plantation ★★★

12602 Harrison Landing Rd. (off Va. 5), Charles City
T: 888-466-6018
Daily, 9 a.m.–5 p.m.
Admission: $10.50

Home to two presidents, this 1726 plantation on the James River was the headquarters for McClellan during the Seven Days. The Confederates missed a golden opportunity to catch the Union Army in a trap here after Malvern Hill when cavalry General J.E.B. Stuart found some high ground and fired a six-pounder cannon into the milling Yankees. The Federals responded by rushing Stuart and driving his men away. Had Stuart not tipped off the Federals to his cavalry's small presence on the high ground by firing on them, Lee could have brought his entire army to the same spot and smashed the remaining Federal forces. That conceivably could have ended the war or changed it, as McClellan's army was the main Union army in the East. Lee could have marched toward Washington with only a single Union corps at Fredericksburg in his way. There is a six-pound cannon ball from Stuart's guns lodged in the wall of an outbuilding at the plantation.

Fort Harrison ★★★★

From Va. 5, Kingsland Road to right on Hoke-Brady Road.

This dirt fort and three others along this road (Forts Johnson, Gregg, and Gilmer) represent the Confederate defenses in the summer of 1864. By this time Lee had shifted most of his men to defend Petersburg, so these forts were easily taken.

GETTING TO AND AROUND RICHMOND

Richmond International Airport is just east of the city, served by seven airlines.

Visitors will need a vehicle to get to all of the Civil War sites in the area. Even those in downtown Richmond require a car. It is possible to leave the car at the Museum of the Confederacy and hike to Tredegar Iron Works, but it takes thirty minutes to walk, and the hike back is all uphill.

Richmond is a big metropolis without a contained historic district. The best bet is to obtain a map of Civil War attractions from the Museum of the Confederacy, and drive from site to site.

ACCOMMODATIONS

Grace Manor Inn

1853 West Grace St., Richmond
804-353-4334
www.bbonline.com/va/gracemanor
3 suites
$150–$175

Built in 1910 as a fiftieth wedding anniversary gift, it opened as a B&B in 2003.

William Miller House

1129 Floyd Ave., Richmond
804-254-2928
www.bbonline.com/va/williammiller
2 rooms
$145–$165

Built in 1869, this Fan District house was built by the owner of a marble works.

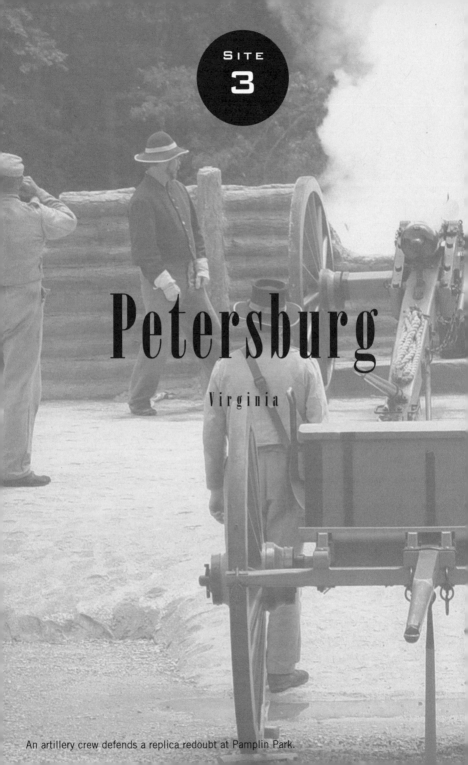

Petersburg

Virginia

An artillery crew defends a replica redoubt at Pamplin Park.

THE WAR YEARS

By the end of the war Petersburg was ringed with defensive (Confederate) and offensive (Union) forts and trench lines, a harbinger of the way war would be fought fewer than sixty years later in World War I. Many of those forts still exist. Just outside Petersburg is one of the best museums on the life of a common soldier ever designed. It is located along the Confederate line that broke, leading to the abandonment of Petersburg. All these factors make this a great place to spend at least a day and maybe several.

Petersburg was second only to Richmond in population in the state and among the largest cities in the Confederacy when the war began. Strategically, it was key to the effort to keep the Army of Northern Virginia supplied. Five different railroads converged downtown. The Southside Railroad ran westward and stretched all the way to Tennessee. The Weldon Railroad ran south to North Carolina and connected with a railroad running from Wilmington, North Carolina, so supplies run through the blockade could be sent to the front. The Norfolk & Petersburg Railroad had been important until Norfolk was captured early in the war. The Richmond-Petersburg Railroad ran directly north twenty-three miles to the center of Richmond. A shorter line ran to City Point where the Appomattox and James Rivers converged.

Because it lay directly south of Richmond, Petersburg was sheltered from any combat for most of the war until the summer of 1864. After failing to destroy Lee at several battles north of Richmond, George Meade's Army of the Potomac, with overall commander U.S. Grant in nominal command, began a strategy of searching for weak points under Richmond—which finally made Petersburg a target.

Grant separated the 18th Corps from his army and sent it up the James River to make a rapid march toward Petersburg. At almost the same time Grant ordered an even bolder move. On June 15, much of the Union army crossed to the south bank of the James River over a pontoon bridge that stretched nearly a half mile over the deep water. The engineering feat was so spectacular and unexpected that most Confederates, including Lee, refused to believe it was even possible.

The 18th Corps, under General William F. "Baldy" Smith, rushed the trenches on the east side of Petersburg. To Smith's surprise, he captured the lightly defended trenches, plus 200 prisoners and several cannons. The Union army now had a toehold in the city. But Smith was so suspicious at the ease of the trenches' capture that he refused to advance further out of fear that his corps had been sucked into a trap. There was no trap. The trenches were lightly defended because most of the troops were elsewhere fighting Grant. There simply were no Confederate reinforcements at all in the area, and Smith's lightning advance had caught the Confederates by surprise. Petersburg commander General P.G.T. Beauregard recalled some brigades he had stationed elsewhere and pleaded with Lee to send reinforcements as the major attack was coming on his front, not Lee's front in Richmond.

Lee did not believe Beauregard at first and did not send reinforcements until three days later when he confirmed that the Federals had indeed crossed the James. Thanks to

Beauregard's initial quick action and some desperate fighting by his men, Petersburg was saved by the time Lee's men arrived. Had Smith acted boldly on June 15, the capture of the city would have come swiftly. Instead, one Union corps commander's nervousness resulted in a siege that would stretch the war out for another ten months.

The war around Petersburg from June 1864 through April 1865 consisted of a series of small battles on the outskirts of the city with the Federals occasionally tossing shells into the populace in hopes of demoralizing the civilians trapped inside the city. The citizens did not react as the Federals had hoped. Instead of petitioning the Confederate government to surrender, they became more supportive of their own government and angry at their attackers, who were trying to kill them. At one point, the Federals used a huge sea coast mortar to throw shells into the city. Rather than cowering in fear, the citizens of Petersburg took bets on where the shells would land.

The railroads became frequent targets of the Federals, but Lee's forces adapted. When one part of the railroad was captured or cut, they simply ran wagons further down the line and picked up supplies there. In one bold raid, Confederate cavalry rustled an entire herd of Union beef cattle kept near City Point and brought them back to the starving city. An amused Lincoln applauded the Beef Steak Raid, asking his commanders if any of them had any ideas such as those held by the Confederates.

For ten months Grant ground away with attacks at points east of Richmond and south of Petersburg. His goal was to wear down the Confederates man by man. He could replace lost men. They could not. As 1865 arrived, it became obvious to Lee that his only hope was to link with General Joseph E. Johnston's Army of Tennessee in North Carolina. On March 23, Lee boldly struck at Fort Stedman, a Union dirt fort, with the goal of making some Union forces pull out of line in order to strengthen that fort. That would open a hole through which Lee hoped his army could slip unnoticed. But there were just too many Federals. They easily recaptured Fort Stedman, and the hole never opened.

On April 1, Federals captured Five Forks, a road junction south of Petersburg that was very close to the Southside Railroad. On April 2, the Federals captured part of the Southside Railroad at Sutherland's Station. The same day, General A.P. Hill, one of Lee's hardest-fighting generals, though one who also often made mistakes, was killed riding back to his headquarters. With the Weldon Railroad cut in many places and now the Southside Railroad cut, Lee's means of resupply was gone. He had to break out of Petersburg or his army would starve.

On April 2, Lee started marching west, seeking food and an open route where he could turn south to link with Johnston. He found neither. On April 9, he surrendered his army at Appomattox Court House.

The siege around Petersburg cost the attacking Union about 62,000 men and the defending Confederates around 40,000.

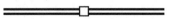

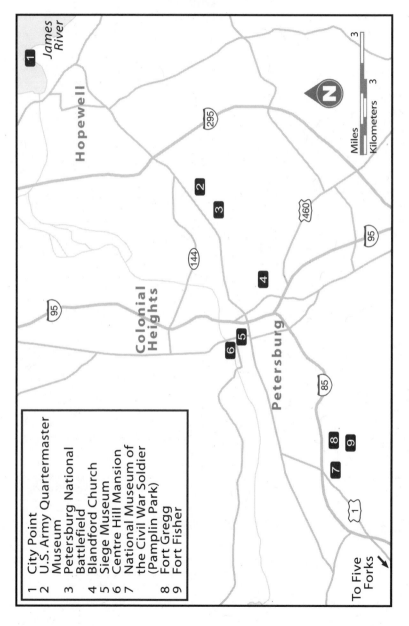

1 City Point
2 U.S. Army Quartermaster
  Museum
3 Petersburg National
  Battlefield
4 Blandford Church
5 Siege Museum
6 Centre Hill Mansion
7 National Museum of
  the Civil War Soldier
  (Pamplin Park)
8 Fort Gregg
9 Fort Fisher

James River

Hopewell

Colonial Heights

Petersburg

To Five Forks

Miles

Kilometers

Petersburg today, though it is larger in population than it was during the Civil War, is a shadow of its former self. Statistically and economically, it has been absorbed by greater Richmond. The downtown has not been abandoned, but the city once teeming with activity is no longer. Still, downtown Petersburg has a number of Civil War sites and museums that demonstrate what life was like during the war.

Petersburg is wealthy in Civil War defenses, including one Union fort from which the final attack that broke the Confederate defenses' back was launched, and the corresponding, nearby Confederate fort whose fall signaled the coming collapse of the defense. These forts are scattered around the outlying parts of the city. Some of them are on national park land, but others remain unprotected on private property. Some are so well preserved that they look like the soldiers are just out for lunch and will return any moment.

Petersburg also has a number of private citizens interested in preserving the city's heritage. Foremost among them is the Pamplin family, now Oregon residents, who spent millions of dollars in buying up property, collecting artifacts, and then building the National Museum of the Civil War Soldier.

POINTS OF INTEREST

1. City Point ★★★★

Hopewell (at intersection of Va. 10 and Appomattox Street about nine miles east of Petersburg; follow signs).
Daily, 9 am.–5 p.m.
Admission: Included in Petersburg National Battlefield admission of $5.

The reason Grant could sustain a siege of Petersburg can be found here at the confluence of the James and Appomattox Rivers. Here was the best organized supply depot of the entire Civil War—perhaps any war. Ships would dock at City Point and unload everything from ammunition to horses. An infrastructure grew up here on the land, including a huge bakery that could turn out loaves of bread for unloading on the Union lines still warm from the oven. Grant spent the winter of 1864 here in a cabin that is today more a facsimile than original. A clever Confederate spy fashioned a time bomb from a windup clock and successfully planted it aboard a Union barge here in 1864. Grant was showered with body parts, but the Confederates' hoped-for destruction of the supply base by chain-reaction explosion did not occur. The house at this site was the quartermaster's headquarters. Grant refused to displace the quartermaster, saying his job was more important and the generals were used to living in tents. Grant's cold staff members constructed the cabin while he was away at meetings. A model of the ingenious Confederate bomb is on display in the house. President Lincoln visited City Point for a meeting with Generals Grant and Sherman just a few days before his assassination.

2. U.S. Army Quartermaster Museum ★★

Building 5218, A Avenue and 22nd St., Fort Lee (quarter-mile east of Petersburg National Battlefield on Va. 36).
T: 804-734-4203
Tuesday–Friday, 10 am.–5 p.m.; Saturday and Sunday, 11 a.m.–5 p.m.
Free admission.

Be prepared to present a photo identification and state that your destination is the Quartermaster Museum, as this museum is located in Fort Lee, an active U.S. Army post under new security watches. This museum has some interesting exhibits focusing on how armies receive and distribute equipment and supplies. It covers all of the nation's wars, but includes some Civil War–related items such as General Grant's horse saddle and a variety of other saddles used by the U.S. Cavalry.

3. Petersburg National Battlefield ★★★★★

Va. 36 East 2.5 miles from I-95 or one-quarter mile west of Quartermaster Museum.
T: 804-732-3531
Daily, 9 a.m.–5 p.m.
Admission: $5

This 2,659-acre park encompasses only a small part of what was the entire Petersburg battlefield for ten months of 1864 and 1865, but it would have been impossible to have preserved all of the scenes of fighting, as that would have meant the National Park Service would have had to buy up virtually all of the land surrounding present-day Petersburg. Hardly an acre of ground surrounding the town to the east and south did not see fighting.

The park does include two of the more important parts of the battlefield; the trenches that were originally captured by Federal forces by the 18th Corps, and the Crater, the site of the desperate battle in 1864 during which Union forces destroyed a portion of the Confederate defensive line by tunneling under it and blowing it up with black-powder mines.

Stop 1 on the four-mile driving tour is behind the visitor center. Here is Battery #5, part of the trenches captured by General William "Baldy" Smith on June 15, 1864. Smith was a brilliant man who graduated fourth in his West Point class. The smartest graduates were always assigned to the engineering corps. It was the nature of an engineer to be cautious. When he first saw the deep trenches around this part of Petersburg, Smith believed they had to be heavily manned, which was just what the Confederates intended. They didn't have enough men to defend all of Richmond and Petersburg, so they dug deep trenches to make it look like they did.

When Union General Winfield Scott Hancock arrived on the scene, he started to advance toward the rest of the city's defenses, but Smith, his superior, stopped him. Smith still believed the easy capture was some sort of trap. For days Smith refused to move, enabling Lee to send in reinforcements to shore up the rest of the line. Had Smith advanced from these trenches in back of the visitor center, Petersburg would have been captured and Lee would have been forced to abandon Richmond ten months earlier than he did. Smith was relieved of his command once Grant realized the error he had committed in not advancing.

At **Stop 3** visitors can often watch reenactors performing living history during the summer months. This was a Confederate battery position before it was captured.

Stop 5 is Fort Stedman, one of the advance forts that the Federals built to keep an eye on the Confederates during the siege. On March 25, 1865, it was attacked in the predawn hours by Confederate forces with the goal of forcing the Federals to peel off men from other defensive positions in order to seal up the breakthrough at Fort Stedman. Lee hoped to be able to slip through the holes left by the absence of those Federal units. Fort Stedman did briefly fall, but Federals rushed in and captured nearly 2,000 Confederates. This failed attack proved to Lee that there were simply too many Federals on his front. He would not be able to break out to the south. The only way left for him was to march west and look for a chance to turn to the south.

Stop 8 is the Crater, the location of one of the strangest battles of the war. During the early summer of 1864, a regiment made up of Pennsylvania coal miners convinced their immediate commanders that they could dig a horizontal shaft from their lines to under the Confederate lines. They would then dig a chamber, fill it with gunpowder and blow a hole in the Confederate lines. On July 30, 1864, they blew the shaft and obliterated more than 200 South Carolinians, leaving behind a pit 30 feet deep by 200 feet long.

Two white brigades rushed into the pit—which was exactly the wrong thing to do. Both brigades should have gone around the crater, as the two black brigades that were supposed to have led the attack had been trained to do. At the very last minute, Grant pulled the black brigades of the U.S. Colored Troops from leading the attack because he feared charges of racism if the attack failed and the black men were killed.

As the Federal brigades floundered at the bottom of the muddy pit with sides too steep to climb, the stunned Confederates recovered from their shock. They ran to the sides of the pits and began shooting down at the trapped men, who were literally stuck like fish at the bottom of a barrel. The black regiments, which had been shuffled to the rear of the attacking column, were now ordered into the pit. Some followed their original training and marched around the crater. For several hours the Confederates shot every Federal they could see. The Crater turned out to be one of the worst Federal disasters of the war. The Confederates lost over 300 men—most of whom had been blown up in the explosion. The Federals lost more than 4,000 killed, wounded, and missing, with most of them left at the bottom of the Crater.

Erosion and time have collapsed the Crater today, so it is much less impressive than it was in the summer of 1864. Visitors have to use their imagination to picture what it must have been like at the bottom of the muddy, bloody pit.

4. Blandford Church ★★★★★

319 South Crater Rd. Leaving the Crater, turn right onto Crater Rd. (U.S. 360/U.S. 469). Turn right into the cemetery.
T: 804-733-2396
Daily, 10 a.m.–5 p.m.
Guided tours every 45 minutes.
Admission: $5 (combination tickets for Blandford Church, Siege Museum, and Centre Hill Mansion are $11).

First built in 1735, Blandford Church is one of the oldest churches in the nation. Somewhere in the graveyard is the body of a British general who died of disease during the American Revolution. He was buried secretly and is the highest-ranking British general still resting in foreign soil. In 1901, the City of Petersburg charged the Ladies Memorial Association with the task of turning Blandford Church into a memorial to the Confederates killed at Petersburg. The association commissioned thirteen stained-glass windows (eleven Confederate and two border states that contributed large numbers of men) that were personally designed and manufactured by Louis Comfort Tiffany of New York City. Eleven of the windows are fashioned after eleven of the twelve disciples of Christ (Judas is understandably left out of the church). Two state windows are based on the Confederate seal. When some of the states were unable to pay the modest fee that he had requested for each window, Tiffany created the windows anyway and asked that the states pay him what they could, when they could. He also gave the church a window he designed, which he called "Cross of Jewels." Tiffany was quoted as saying he saw his windows as a chance to promote healing between North and South.

5. Siege Museum ★★★★★

15 West Bank St. (downtown)
T: 804-733-2404
Daily, 10 a.m.–5 p.m.
Admission: $5

This museum, housed in the 1839 Exchange Building, concentrates on what happened inside the city during the ten-month siege. There is a film narrated by Petersburg native and actor Joseph Cotton. Among the displays is a porcelain doll that was decapitated by a Federal shell, which left the body of the doll intact. Price lists preserved from the period show that chickens cost $50.

6. Centre Hill Mansion ★★★

One Centre Hill Ct. (downtown)
T: 804-733-2401
Daily, 10 a.m.–5 p.m.
Closed major holidays.
Admission: $5

Built in 1824, this house belonged to one of the leading families of Petersburg. Although it has no particular military importance, its furnishings reflect the time period. The family was able to get a set of dishes through the blockade in time for Christmas in 1864, but by the time the dishes arrived, there was little food to serve on them.

7. National Museum of the Civil War Soldier (Pamplin Park) ★★★★★

6125 Boydton Plank Rd. (Exit 63-A to U.S. 1 South from I-85 south of Petersburg).
T: 804-861-2408
Daily, 9 a.m.–5 p.m. with summer hours extended to 6 p.m.; closed major holidays.
Admission: $13.50 (yearly pass $30).

Constructed where the Federals broke through the Confederate line south of Petersburg, the National Museum of the Civil War Soldier uses both the latest in audiovisual technology to bring static displays to life, and living-history reenactors to show visitors what life was like where history happened. There is no museum that tells the story of the Civil War soldier any better. Allow at least two hours, maybe three, to see all that Pamplin Park has to offer. Because the park offers a Civil War camping experience for kids and families, visitors with children might consider spending two days here.

This museum is free of bias. It simply concentrates on trying to tell the story of what each man (and some women) went through on the battlefield and in camp. The story is told through seven large galleries that hold more than 1,000 artifacts, sometimes arranged in life-size dioramas in which the visitor stands. Visitors pick up headsets at the beginning of the tour and also select an individual character (a real person) who tells his or her own story. Visitors do not know until the voice tells them the eventual fate of the person to whom they are listening. One of the more interesting displays allows visitors to stand in a firing line watching the other side fire at them and then hearing the Minie balls whizzing past their ears.

After leaving the museum, visitors can tour the battle line. One worthwhile detour is the individual rifle pits. These pits were occupied by pickets whose assignment was to watch and listen for enemy movements. It must have been lonely, dangerous duty. A reconstructed winter quarters is open for viewing. Tudor Hall, a house that was a Confederate headquarters, is open for touring, as is the Banks house, which Grant briefly used as a headquarters. One of the newest attractions is the Hart Farm, where visitors can participate in a "Civil War immersion" experience, a two-day Civil War camp for children and families where they learn some drills, eat food prepared using period recipes, and camp overnight in period tents.

8. Fort Gregg ★★★★★

Simpson Road off U.S. 1, just northeast of Pamplin Park.
Daylight hours.

Fort Gregg was a Confederate fort held by 600 men. On April 2, when Grant ordered a massive assault against the entire Confederate line, those men held off close to 5,000 Federals, giving Lee's army time to escape. Visitors can walk around this fort and read the interpretive signs. (This fort is visible from I-85.)

9. Fort Fisher ★★★★★

Intersection of Flank Road (C.R. 676) and Church Road (C.R. 672) directly east of Pamplin Park.
Daylight hours.

This massive Federal fort proves that not all hurricane damage is bad. After a hurricane blew down most of the trees in this fort, which kept it virtually hidden in plain site, the National Park Service went ahead and cleared out the dead wood, revealing this incredibly well-preserved earth fort,

the largest the Federals constructed during their ten-month siege. The Federals pushed out from here and broke through the Confederate lines at what is now Pamplin Park.

10. Five Forks ★★★★

Intersection of C.R. 613 and C.R. 627 nine miles southwest of Pamplin Park area. Access is from U.S. 1 South to White Oak Road (S.R. 613). Right on White Oak Road and then five miles to Five Forks Battlefield. Along the way, visitors will pass the White Oak Road battlefield.

Robert E. Lee entrusted the protection of the five-road intersection of Five Forks to General George Pickett. Holding the crossroads was vital because of the nearby Sutherland Station on the Southside Railroad. On April 1, 1865, while Pickett was away attending a fish dinner held by another general, the Federals attacked and overwhelmed the Confederates. The fish-hungry Pickett had ridden away without even designating a general to remain in command of the crossroads. By the time he discovered that the Federal attack was under way and returned to his post, the battle was over. With the loss of Five Forks, Lee's last lines of supply were now cut off. He would have to leave Petersburg. Willie Pegram, one of the last of Lee's best artillery commanders, was killed here. His brother, John, had been killed the previous month at Hatcher's Run. It was at Five Forks that Union General G.K. Warren, the hero of Gettysburg, was relieved of command by his superior, General Phil Sheridan, who believed Warren had moved too slowly in attacking. Lee never forgave Pickett for the loss of Five Forks, just as Pickett never forgave Lee for ordering the attack at Gettysburg that bears his name.

Getting To And Around Petersburg

The nearest major airport for Petersburg is Richmond International, east of the capital city, thirty miles from Petersburg via I-95. It is served by most major airlines.

One will need a car to get around Petersburg as the sites are far apart. It is thirty miles between City Point and Five Forks. Walking-tour maps of the national battlefield should be available from the National Park Service office, which is located near the trenches the 18th Corps captured, but the driving tour takes visitors to the same key points.

Though they are outside the main holdings of the national park, there are dirt forts scattered around the city. Most of them are marked on the Park Service–issued tour map of the battlefield. Some forts are readily visible and others are tucked away in residential areas. Keep a lookout for private-property signs to determine if the forts can be visited. Fort Gregg and Fort Fisher, mentioned in the Points of Interest, are two forts that are both on Park property. Unless visitors are on a quest to find where an ancestor may have fought, or want to understand how the city was encircled, one or two dirt forts is all one really needs to experience.

Accommodations

La Villa Romaine Bed & Breakfast
29 South Market St., Petersburg
T: 800-243-0860
www.lavilla.tierranet.com
4 rooms
$92

This 1858 house located in downtown Petersburg is furnished with handsome nineteenth-century antiques.

The Ragland Mansion
205 South Sycamore St., Petersburg
T: 800-861-8898
www.raglandmansion.com
9 rooms
$75–$85

This 1850s, 10,000-square-foot home was once the home of actor Joseph Cotton. World War I General John J. Pershing is also supposed to have stayed here. It is in the historic district.

Sources & Other Reading

The Last Citadel: Petersburg June 1864–April 1865, Noah Trudeau, Louisiana State University, 1993.

The Petersburg Campaign June 1864–April 1865, John Horn, DeCapo Press, 2000.

Richmond Redeemed: The Siege at Petersburg, Richard Sommers, Doubleday, 1981.

Beefsteak Raid, Edward Boykin, Funk & Wagnalls, 1960.

Death in the Trenches: Grant at Petersburg, William C. Davis, editor, Time-Life Books, 1986.

SITE
4

Fredericksburg

Virginia

Fredericksburg Wall.

THE WAR YEARS

ew other Civil War battles were fought as efficiently by the defending Confederates or as poorly by the attacking Federals as the Battle of Fredericksburg in December 1862. The urban battlefield itself has disappeared under residential development, but hardy tourists can still trudge up from the Rappahannock River to the stone wall at Marye's Heights to get a sense of the killing ground on which the bodies of more than 12,000 dead and wounded Federals were left. Fredericksburg's preservation of Chatham Manor, Marye's Heights, and the defensive line southeast of town, in addition to the rows of interesting shops in its vibrant downtown, make this a fine destination for the history traveler.

The 5,000 citizens of Fredericksburg knew by mid-April 1861 that their little town would be the site of a battle. It was inevitable because of where the town was located. Fifty miles to the north lay Washington, the Federal capital, where legislators and bureaucrats were shouting "On to Richmond!" from the safety of their office buildings. Fifty miles to the south lay Richmond, the Confederate capital, where legislators and bureaucrats were shouting "On to Washington!" from the safety of their office buildings.

By early November 1862, the time had come. The new commander of the Army of the Potomac, General Ambrose Burnside, had noticed some key flaws in Confederate defensive strategy, while Lee's Army of Northern Virginia was recovering from the wounds it had suffered at the Battle of Sharpsburg in September. By necessity, so as not to overload the demands on any one community gathering its fall crops, Lee had spread his army over a wide landscape in the central part of Virginia. Burnside's army, fed by a central commissary command, was much more contained and relatively intact. He would . be able to mobilize his men much more quickly than Lee.

Burnside convinced President Lincoln that he could strike out for Fredericksburg, cross the river, and be well on his way to capturing Richmond before Lee could gather his forces. Lincoln approved the bold move from this seemingly bold new commander who had just replaced the disgraced McClellan. Burnside's three corps began a swift march for Fredericksburg after their general confirmed with Washington war planners that they would rush a supply of pontoon boats to him so that he could cross the Rappahannock. Months earlier the Confederates had taken up the bridge planks to prevent an easy Federal crossing.

Just as Burnside had predicted, Lee was caught flat-footed by Burnside's swift march. The leading Union corps arrived on the north side of the river two days before Lee's leading divisions. To the Federals' pleasure, Fredericksburg seemed virtually undefended. All they had to do was get across the river. The pontoon boats were nowhere in sight, but in some spots the river was fordable, no deeper than to a soldier's knees.

To the surprise of his subordinates, Burnside refused to take advantage of this opportunity to cross unopposed. Burnside was a methodical man rather than the bold leader Lincoln thought he was. He had ordered those pontoon bridges from Washington, and he was determined to wait for them. He waited and waited some more. While they were waiting, Federal soldiers watched Lee's men arrive on the opposite side of the river and dig in on Mayre's Heights, ground that seemed to soar over the south part of the town.

The pontoons would not arrive for nearly three weeks. By the time Burnside was finally ready to attack on December 11, 1862, Lee's men had placed enough cannons in cross-firing positions so that one general confidently informed Lee that "a chicken cannot live on that field when we open up." Burnside never considered that Lee would have enough time to set up an impregnable defense as the result of his delaying the attack waiting for his precious pontoons. Lee's troops resisted the pontoon bridge construction for a while and then withdrew, allowing the Federals to cross into Fredericksburg. On December 12, Burnside allowed his men to pillage the town's civilian homes while the Confederates watched in seething silence from the high ground.

On December 13, more than 115,000 Federals began their attack on the Confederate positions in two huge, separate movements. On the southern outskirts of the town, the bulk of the Union soldiers moved across a broad plain toward a part of the line commanded by General Stonewall Jackson. In town, a smaller Federal force moved up the much higher ground held by General James Longstreet's men. For a brief moment, it appeared that the overwhelming Union attack on the south side of town was working, but a fierce Confederate counterattack sent the Federals streaming back the way they had come. Lee, watching the pageantry of the advancing Union flags on Jackson's position and then the panicked fleeing of those same flags, turned to Longstreet and said: "It is well that war is so terrible, least we grow too fond of it," meaning that the carnage of war kept generals from getting too involved with the beauty of well-executed counterattacks such as that just delivered by Jackson.

On Mayre's Heights, above the city, the carnage was staggering. The Confederates had taken cover behind a stone wall that ran along a sunken farm road. It was a strong, natural defensive position. There was no place to hide for the advancing Union soldiers, who were running uphill over land where the citizens of Fredericksburg grazed their cattle. With the exception of a few houses, there was no cover of any kind. Wave after wave of Union troops attacked, ignoring the fact that the previous charge had been stopped in its tracks by the converging cannon fire and can't-miss rifle fire coming from behind the stone wall. Not a single Union soldier touched that stone wall all day.

That night, many wounded Federal soldiers froze to death. The next day the Federals pulled back to count their losses—more than 12,500 men killed and wounded compared to fewer than 4,000 Confederates. Incredibly, Burnside mused about attacking again, but he was dissuaded by his subordinates. By December 15, the entire Union army was back across the Rappahannock.

The result of the battle was far reaching. The Federal army virtually destroyed the town. It was one of the first times in the war when total war would be practiced against civilians. It would not be the last. The Federal soldiers were disgusted with their commanders. Hundreds of them deserted and started walking back home. The Confederate soldiers were grimly pleased with the revenge they had on behalf of the civilians of Fredericksburg. Lee's reputation as a general who won battles was reinforced. Burnside was replaced within weeks, having served as Army of the Potomac commander for only a few months. As 1862 ended, the idea that the Confederacy might win its independence was on everyone's mind in both the North and South.

SITE
4

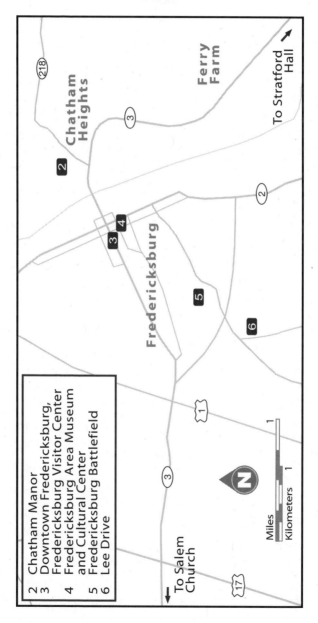

218

Chatham Heights

Ferry Farm

To Stratford Hall

3

2

2

4

3

Fredericksburg

5

6

1

3

17

To Salem Church

N

Miles

Kilometers

1

1

2   Chatham Manor
3   Downtown Fredericksburg,
    Fredericksburg Visitor Center
4   Fredericksburg Area Museum
    and Cultural Center
5   Fredericksburg Battlefield
6   Lee Drive

FREDERICKSBURG TODAY

The downtown remains compact and vibrant, with dozens of shops selling things like historic prints and books. Complementing those shops are small restaurants. Downtown Fredericksburg is a strolling kind of place where historians and their families can split their time between looking at museums and historic sites and shopping for items that will make the trip to this pre-Colonial town memorable. The visitor need not bother with the outskirts of town, which have succumbed to rampant commercialization.

Worst of all is what the developers have done to Salem Church, site of a crucial battle alongside Va. 3 just west of Chancellorsville that kept Federal reinforcements from attacking Lee at Chancellorsville. The church has been swallowed up by stores and signs. Only the most dedicated historian can even see the church located on the left as you're heading out of town, to know where to turn to visit its now cramped grounds.

POINTS OF INTEREST

North of the Rappahannock
1. Stratford Hall ★★★★

485 Great House Rd., Stratford
(42 miles east of Fredericksburg off Va. 3)
T: 804-493-8038
Daily, 9 a.m.–5 p.m.
Closed major holidays.
Admission: $10

Though Robert E. Lee left his birth house when he was three years old to move with his family to Alexandria, he always dreamed of buying this home once his military career was over. That never happened. His career in the U.S. Army and then the war and Reconstruction kept Lee from ever owning any home. Finished in 1738, Stratford Hall was considered one of the largest and finest houses in the colonies. The bedroom and the crib in which Lee was born are preserved, as are the fireplace angle irons embossed with images of angels. One legend of the house

is that when toddler Robert was missing just before leaving the house for the last time, he showed up and said he was just saying "good-bye" to the angels in the fireplace.

2. Chatham Manor ★★★★

120 Chatham Ln., north bank of Rappahannock
T: 540-654-5121
Grounds: 9 a.m.–4:30 p.m. House is closed on weekdays, but open weekends. Closed major holidays.
Admission: $4

As noted by the National Park Service, few houses have been visited by as many famous people as Chatham Manor. Finished in 1771, the house was a prominent fixture on the riverbank opposite Fredericksburg and was a popular destination for wealthy and powerful Virginians, including George Washington and Thomas Jefferson. The house was eventually purchased by the grandfather of Mary Custis, who would one day marry Robert E. Lee. Stories claim that a young Lieutenant Lee courted his future wife Mary on these grounds when both were young adults. It is one of the few homes in the nation visited by both George Washington and Abraham Lincoln.

During the war, Union troops occupied the north bank of the river as early as the spring of 1862, though they made no effort to cross the river. During that time President Lincoln visited the house to discuss plans for General Irwin McDowell's corps to help McClellan who was marching on Richmond from the Virginia Peninsula. That planned move across the Rappahannock never happened because Lincoln grew nervous that Stonewall Jackson might attack Washington. He ordered McDowell's corps to stay in place to defend Washington.

When Burnside came in force to Fredericksburg in the winter of 1862, Chatham Manor's grounds made a perfect artillery base, pointing at the town just across the river. Church steeples, providing perfect targets, were just hundreds of yards away. After the battle, the house was turned into a Union hospital, and nurses such as Walt Whitman, Clara Barton, and Dorothea Dix helped the wounded. Unknown Union dead are still buried in the yard. The house was willed to the Park Service in the 1930s. Five of the rooms are set up with public displays, and the rest of the rooms serve as office space.

Downtown Fredericksburg

3. Fredericksburg Visitor Center ★★★

706 Caroline St.
T: 540-373-1776

The track of the Federal soldiers once they landed on the south bank of the Rappahannock is well documented. The Fredericksburg visitor center should be

able to provide a map allowing visitors to follow which streets saw heavy fighting on December 11, 1862. Visitors with Federal or Confederate ancestors will be able to follow in their footsteps starting at the waterfront and going all the way to the stone wall at the National Park Service visitor center on Marye's Heights, a distance of about a mile. This author's ancestor, a sergeant with the 8th Florida Regiment, lost his left arm defending the south bank of the Rappahannock.

What became the Battle of Fredericksburg began with a clever ruse employed by Lee. Barksdale's Mississippi Brigade, reinforced by several companies of the 8th Florida Regiment, slowly fought their way through the streets and back toward Marye's Heights. It never occurred to the Federals that the Confederates had resisted, but then somehow melted away. The truth was that Lee was so confident in his high-ground defenses that he believed he could destroy the entire Federal army if he could only get them on the south side of the river. The resistance by the Mississippians and Floridians was designed to lure the Federals into the town and within rifle range rather than have them keep their distance and pound the Confederate positions with artillery.

Today, downtown Fredericksburg is lined with shops and restaurants and some museums focusing on the Colonial time period. The plantation once owned by George Washington's sister is open for touring. Just walking downtown Fredericksburg could take several hours.

The hardiest of hikers who want to experience what the Union soldiers experienced might choose to walk all the way from downtown up to the National Park Service visitor center on Marye's Heights, a distance of about a mile—all uphill. Use the map to follow the streets that the Union soldiers used. Along the way is a now-covered canal that provided cover. Also along the way are a few bullet-hit houses that provided some cover. During the war, this hillside consisted mostly of pastures, while the town itself hugged the river. If you walk this, remember that a mile up is also a mile back.

4. Fredericksburg Area Museum and Cultural Center ★★

907 Princess Anne St.
T: 540-371-3037
Monday–Saturday, 10 am.–5 p.m.;
Sunday, 1–5 p.m. Shorter hours in winter.
Admission: $5

This art and history museum covers the history of Fredericksburg from its founding through the present.

5. Fredericksburg Battlefield ★★★★★

The Stone Wall, Lafayette Boulevard at the Sunken Road.
T: 540-373-6122
Daily, 9 a.m.–5 p.m.
Closed major holidays
Free admission, but $2 charge to see the movie about the battle

In back of the visitor center is the Stone Wall, also called the Sunken Road, from behind which the Confederates inflicted so much damage on the Federals as they advanced up the hill. The wall protected a farm road that had been used so much since Colonial times that it had sunk below the surface of the rest of the hill. The wall made a natural defensive position. Confederates were packed tightly behind the wall; the best shots were assigned to man the wall while other men stood behind them, loaded the muskets, and then handed them forward.

More than 8,000 Federals fell in front of this wall, while fewer than 1,000 Confederates were wounded behind it. So devoid of cover was this pasture that

Federals took to piling the bodies of their comrades in front of them so they could make a human breastworks to stop Confederate Minie balls. That night, both Union and Confederate troops, keeping their positions on the slope and behind the wall, witnessed a display of the Northern Lights. A traditional tale of the Scots-Irish, from whom most Southerners could trace their ancestry, taught that seeing the Northern Lights foretold a great victory. The Irish Brigade, made up of Irish immigrants impressed into service by the Union, were also familiar with the same tale, and what they saw in the night skies dismayed them.

Walking the wall brings visitors to a bullet-pocked house and to the spot where General Thomas Cobb of Georgia was mortally wounded. Beyond that is a statue commemorating the Angel of Marye's Heights, Sargent Richard Kirkland of South Carolina. During the battle Kirkland ignored his own safety and jumped the wall to give water to wounded Federals.

The Stone Wall and the Sunken Road are beneficiaries of a recent push by the National Park Service to return battlefield features to what they were like during the war. Until recently the Sunken Road was an active city street. Now the pavement has been pulled up and visitors can walk in it just as the Confederates did.

6. Lee Drive ★★★★★

Half-mile south of the visitor center off Va. 3

Lee Drive follows the defensive line held by Stonewall Jackson down to Prospect Hill, where Confederate artillery was placed.

Stop 1 ★★★★★ shows where Lee watched the battle unfold and where he made his famous comment about war's terrible nature. He was almost killed here. Lee and his staff were standing near a heavy cannon that had just been delivered to the front from Tredegar Iron Works. As the gunners were firing it, the cannon, apparently made with poor-quality iron, exploded. Remarkably, not a single one of the high-ranking officers standing with Lee were injured, though the cannon crew was. After this incident Tredegar came under fire for quality-control problems, but the owner of the company fired back that he was being forced to make do with lower-quality iron ore because the Confederates could no longer protect his high-quality sources. The incident showed how early in the war the logistics capabilities of the South fell behind those of the North. The type of cannon that exploded, a thirty-pounder Parrott rifle, which should have been the South's best gun, can be seen on display nearby.

Stop 3 ★★★ marks where the Federals briefly broke through Confederate lines before being driven back. South Carolina General Maxcy Gregg was mortally wounded here with a ball to the spine. Gregg and Jackson had always feuded and did not like each other. Jackson went to visit him on his deathbed and told him to forget all their problems as he was about to die and meet the Lord. Gregg, who made a weak apology to Jackson that he was not a Christian, thanked the general for his forgiveness.

Stop 4 ★★★ is **Prospect Hill**, site of the Confederate gun emplacements. Young Major John Pelham, with two cannons, impetuously moved forward to fire on the advancing Federals. With just two cannons against thousands of Federals, he stopped

the advance cold until ordered back by his commander, J.E.B. Stuart. A marker at the spot to which Pelham advanced can be seen at the intersection of Business U.S. 17 and S.R. 608 just northeast of Prospect Hill. As Lee watched Pelham's movements with his two cannons, he remarked: "It is good to see courage in one so young."

7. Salem Church ★★★

Va. 3 and C.R. 639 (about 2 miles past I-95). After passing over I-95, stay in the left lane of Va. 3. Follow the brown National Park Service signs to the church.

As the bulk of the Army of Northern Virginia was engaged at Chancellorsville, Federal reinforcements under General John Sedgwick were on their way from Fredericksburg, which had been captured. Standing in their way at Salem Church were 10,000 Confederates under General Lafayette McLaws. McLaws and his men stopped Sedgwick's superior forces and held them in place until the Battle of Chancellorsville was over and Lee could rush him support. In less than three days, Lee's army had met and defeated two different superior Union forces. Visitors can walk around the church. The holes in the brick were made by Federal rifles.

Getting to and Around Fredericksburg

The closest major airports to Fredericksburg are Richmond International, one hour to the south, and Reagan International, one hour to the north. Dulles International west of Washington and Baltimore Washington might also be good choices depending upon the cost of tickets. One word of warning: getting to and from these airports is going to take visitors into heavy urban traffic, so it can take much longer than an hour during commuting hours.

A vehicle is necessary when visiting Fredericksburg. The battlefields of Chancellorsville, Wilderness, and Spotsylvania Court House are little more than a half hour away from downtown, but seeing them as they should be seen requires at least a two- or even three-day stay in the area. (See Site 5 for more information on these areas.)

Walking from downtown Fredericksburg up to the battlefield is possible, though walkers will have to be dedicated. (They don't call the area Marye's Heights for nothing.)

There is a trolley tour of Old Towne Fredericksburg leaving from the visitor center for a charge of $14.

Accommodations

La Vista Plantation

4420 Guinea Station Rd., Fredericksburg
T: 800-529-2823
www.lavistaplantation.com
2 rooms
$105–$150

This 1838 plantation-style home on ten acres is seven miles south of the city and on the same road that takes visitors to the Stonewall Jackson Shrine, where Jackson died after his accidental wounding.

The Richard Johnston Inn Bed and Breakfast

711 Caroline St., Fredericksburg
T: 877-557-0770
www.bbonline.com/va/richardjohnston
5 Rooms
$85–$185

Located in the heart of the Old Towne section of Fredericksburg, this inn was built in the 1700s and served as the home of a nineteenth-century mayor of the city.

Braehead Bed and Breakfast

123 Lee Dr., Fredericksburg
T: 540-899-3648
3 rooms
$90–$110

Owners of this bed and breakfast say that both armies occupied this 1859 mansion and that Robert E. Lee once actually ate breakfast here.

On Keegan Pond Bed & Breakfast

11315 Gordon Rd., Fredericksburg
T: 888-785-4662
www.bedandbreakfast.com/virginia/on-keegan-pond-bed-breakfast.html
2 Rooms
$85–$150

Located five miles from Fredericksburg, this 1870 farmhouse is located between several of the nearby battlefields. The owners have found Civil War artifacts on the grounds, leading them to believe it may have been a campsite.

SOURCES & OTHER READING

The Fredericksburg Campaign: Winter War on the Rappahannock, Francis O'Reilly, Louisiana State University Press, 2002.

Fredericksburg! Fredericksburg!, George Rable, University of North Carolina Press, 2002.

Marye's Heights: Fredericksburg (Battleground America Series), Victor Brooks, DeCapo Press, 2001.

Guide to the Battles of Fredericksburg and Chancellorsville, Jay Luvass, Harold Nelson, University Press of Kansas, 1996.

The Fredericksburg Campaign: Decision on the Rappahannock, edited by Gary Gallagher, University of North Carolina Press, 1995.

Chancellorsville, the Wilderness, and Spotsylvania Court House

Virginia

This stone Union soldier marks his regiment's advance at Spotsylvania Court House.

THE WAR YEARS

These three battlefields, arranged in a rough triangle no more than ten miles from each other, saw some of the most brilliant tactical maneuvers and some of the most savage fighting of the war. At Chancellorsville, the South's greatest hero fell. At the Wilderness, Lee almost sacrificed himself only to be saved by Texans—who sacrificed themselves. At Spotsylvania Court House, the battle raged for two weeks. This little triangle teaches history travelers a great deal about Civil War combat.

The Battle of Chancellorsville, fought on May 1–3, 1863, started to unfold the way Ambrose Burnside's Battle of Fredericksburg on December 11–13, 1862 should have occurred. The Battle of the Wilderness on May 5–6, 1864, one year after Chancellorsville, marked the first time that Grant and Lee clashed. The Battle of Spotsylvania Court House, a two-week-long orgy of death, started just two days after the Wilderness, and was fought because Grant wanted to prove to his Army of the Potomac that their new goal was to destroy Lee's Army of Northern Virginia.

All three battles shared several distinctions. They were fought on chance ground, meaning they were fought where the two armies found each other, as opposed to one army moving to a favored, selected defensive position, digging in, and then waiting for the other army to attack. All three battles were fought on unpopulated ground; no urban population was in the way, as was the case at Fredericksburg and Gettysburg. All three were fought on unfamiliar ground. So while Lee and his generals knew Fredericksburg's high ground and its river crossings from having visited there on occasion, the Confederate generals had no more idea of the geographical features of these battlefields than Hooker at Chancellorsville or Grant at the Wilderness and Spotsylvania.

CHANCELLORSVILLE

Union General Joseph Hooker, who replaced the disgraced Ambrose Burnside as head of the Army of the Potomac in January, did what Burnside should have done at Fredericksburg—he headed west about thirty miles. By April 30, Hooker had crossed the Rappahannock with his army of 130,000, and found himself on the same side of the river as Lee and on his left flank. Hooker started moving east, back toward Lee. The lead elements of Hooker's army were at a crossroads tavern called Chancellorsville when a small vanguard of Confederates led by Stonewall Jackson smashed into them.

After some fighting, Hooker lost his nerve. Without even checking the size of Jackson's force (his force outnumbered Jackson's by many times), Hooker backed away from the fight and had his men dig trenches. That allowed Lee time to leave behind a small force on Marye's Heights and move the bulk of his army out of Fredericksburg and rush them toward Chancellorsville to face this new threat.

On the night of May 1, Lee and Jackson were puzzling over how to attack a superior, dug-in force with a smaller, already-split force when J.E.B. Stuart rode up and announced that his cavalry had discovered that Hooker's far right flank was "in the air," meaning it had not dug any trenches. The men on that flank were simply in camps.

Lee and Jackson agreed on a bold move. Jackson's corps of 28,000 men would split from the main army, march around the front of Hooker and smash into that exposed right flank, then "roll up the Union line" (meaning force each regiment of Federals into the next until the entire line collapsed in fear).

On May 2, Jackson's flank attack began in the late afternoon, and it worked just as Lee and Jackson had envisioned. The Federal Eleventh Corps on the flank fled in panic as 28,000 Confederates came rushing from the woods giving rebel yells. The fleeing Federals ran right over the regiments in line next to them and soon it seemed that the Union army was collapsing in on itself. That night, Jackson was accidentally wounded by a regiment in his own corps as he scouted the success of the attack.

The next day, Stuart, filling in for Jackson, captured some high ground and started shelling the Union army. Hooker himself was almost killed by an exploding shell. That was all it took for the commanding general to lose whatever courage he had left. He pulled his men back across the Rappahannock. In effect, an open-field attack by 28,000 Confederates had defeated a dug-in Union army of 130,000. It would be Lee's greatest victory of the war.

THE WILDERNESS

One year later the generals and the strategy had changed. U.S. Grant was now the overall commander of all Union armies in the field, and he was riding with the Army of the Potomac. Under generals McClellan, Pope, Burnside, Hooker, and Meade, the Army of the Potomac had always met Lee in combat, then retired from the field for a while whether they had won or lost the battle.

On May 5 and 6, 1864, Grant attacked Lee in the Wilderness, a vast expanse of land a few miles west of Chancellorsville that was so choked with undergrowth that it had never been cleared for farming. Grant attacked in two columns, which caused Lee to have to fight one column, and then the next. When night fell on that inconclusive first day of combat, the undergrowth caught on fire from cannon blasts. As both armies listened to their screams, hundreds of wounded men on both sides burned to death as the fire outran their ability to crawl out of its way.

The next day, a final Union push shattered the Confederate lines holding a crossroads, and sent the remnants of A.P. Hill's Third Corps streaming away from the battlefield. As Lee watched his army dissolving around him, elements of his First Corps arrived on the field for the first time. The charge of the Texas Brigade broke the Union advance, ending the Federal army's chance of swallowing Lee's army. The Wilderness ended in a draw. In the past, it had been the habit of Union generals to pull back and rest before tackling Lee again. This time, instead of turning left and heading to safety so his army could recuperate from its wounds, Grant turned his horse to the right, in the direction that Lee's army had taken. His goal was to grind Lee's army into dust and the only way to do that was to fight him again.

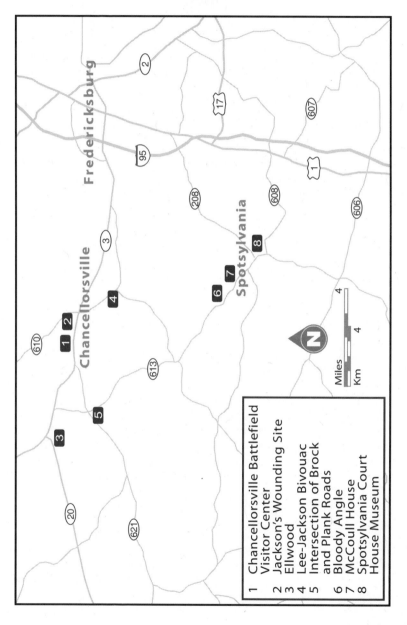

Chancellorsville Battlefield
   Visitor Center
2 Jackson's Wounding Site
3 Ellwood
4 Lee-Jackson Bivouac
5 Intersection of Brock
   and Plank Roads
6 Bloody Angle
7 McCoull House
8 Spotsylvania Court
   House Museum

SPOTSYLVANIA COURT HOUSE

The leading units of Lee's army were able to get in front of the leading units of Grant's army with barely ten minutes to spare just two days after the end of the Wilderness. Those ten minutes, during which Lee's men were able to throw up rudimentary earthworks just north of Spotsylvania Court House, would turn into a two-week battle fought constantly, day and night, in daylight and darkness, and in ever-deepening mud. The fighting here would be horrendous and unrelenting as Grant sought to destroy Lee with charge after charge. On several occasions Grant came close to his goal of breaking through the Confederate lines. Once, the Federals came within yards of capturing or killing Lee himself. Each time, however, the Confederates were able to fight back in hand-to-hand combat and push the Federals back. Nothing Grant tried, including an innovative method of charging trenches, worked. Each time Lee's Confederates tenaciously held their ground. The only thing Grant could do was disengage at Spotsylvania Court House and march around Lee to get closer to Richmond. Though capturing Richmond would have been a bonus, Grant's goal remained the same—to crush Lee's army. It would take him another eleven months to do so because he failed at the Wilderness and Spotsylvania.

SOURCES & OTHER READING

Chancellorsville, Stephen Sears, Mariner Books, 1998.

Chancellorsville 1863: The Souls of the Brave, Ernest Ferguson, Vintage, 1993.

The Battle of the Wilderness, Gordon Rhea, Louisiana State University Press, 2004.

The Battles for Spotsylvania Court House and the Road to Yellow Tavern, Gordon Rhea, Louisiana State University Press, 1997.

The Spotsylvania Campaign, Gary Gallagher, University of North Carolina Press, 1998.

If It Takes All Summer: The Battle of Spotsylvania Court House, William Matter, University of North Carolina Press, 1988.

THE AREA TODAY

In 1863, when Chancellorsville was fought, and in 1864, when the Wilderness was fought, this land ten to fifteen miles east of Fredericksburg was sparsely settled. The Wilderness, which included the land surrounding the Chancellorsville tavern, was not idly named. Scrub trees, briars, and vines covered vast acreage so thickly that farmers simply did not have the energy or the time to clear it to see if there was good ground beneath the mass of undergrowth. Instead, they just left it alone and farmed the acres around it.

Spotsylvania Court House, the county seat, was a thriving settlement in the center of two roads leading down from Chancellorsville and the Wilderness. That made it a place to protect for the Confederates, and a target to capture for the Federals. South of Spotsylvania lay Richmond.

Today, the Wilderness is no more. Long ago, its undergrowth was plowed under by home site developers. All along the edges of property owned by the National Park Service are subdivisions on which men burned to death because they could not escape approaching flames. Most of the site of the Battle of Chancellorsville is protected by the NPS, but some of the outlying parcels are under constant threat of residential development as Fredericksburg increasingly becomes a bedroom community for Washington. The village of Spotsylvania Court House remains small, somehow more resistant to the threat of development, likely because it is not along busy Va. 3 (wartime Plank Road), which leads directly to Fredericksburg and I-95.

POINTS OF INTEREST

Chancellorsville Battlefield Visitor Center
★★★★★
On Va. 3 seven miles from I-95.
T: 540-786-2880
Jackson's Wounding Site

Just to the east of the visitor center building along what was then the Mountain Road is the spot where General Thomas J. "Stonewall" Jackson was wounded at about 9 p.m. on May 2, 1863. A sign marks the spot. The road itself, more like a path, can still be discerned. At 8:30 p.m. that evening, Jackson and more than a dozen aides and scouts pushed through the Confederate lines at a point north of

here and rode forward (eastward) to determine the condition of the Federal army. Jackson wanted to find out if the Federals were still running or if they were starting to dig in and resist. As Jackson and his men quietly rode forward, they could hear axes felling trees. The Federals had recovered from their initial shock and were trying to set up a resistance. Jackson wheeled around and started back toward Confederate lines. He wanted to press the attack even in the dark.

Jackson had made a major mistake before venturing beyond his lines. He had not warned the commanders of his own outlying regiments that he would be scouting in front of them. He now made a second mistake. He and his staff started riding back toward their lines on a different road than they had taken on the way out. The regiments Jackson's party were now approaching at a trot had no idea that their commander was in front of them. They did know that 130,000 Yankees were in front of them.

As Jackson's party rode westward along the Mountain Road, a regiment opened fire, thinking they were being attacked by Yankee cavalry. One ball crashed through Jackson's right palm and two more through his left arm. Jackson's party were able to get him off his horse and moved him thirty to forty yards to the west to a spot now marked by a stone marker. From there he was taken by stretcher and ambulance several miles to the west where his arm was amputated at a field hospital.

Before leaving the visitor center, ask the ranger if Ellwood is open for visitation. This plantation house on the Wilderness battlefield cannot be seen from the road, but in its family graveyard is the buried arm of Stonewall Jackson.

Leave the visitor center by turning right on Bullock Road. Turn right at the intersection with Old Plank Road. Cross Va. 3 at the site of Chancellorsville and follow until turning right onto Furnace Road. Here at the intersection is the site of the famed "last meeting" of Lee and Jackson.

Labeled as **Stop 7**, or the Lee-Jackson Bivouac on the NPS map, it was here while sitting on cracker boxes that the two generals debated how best to attack Hooker. Hooker's left and center were both heavily entrenched. While they were puzzling what to do, Stuart rode up with news that Yankees on the far right were not entrenched, but were lounging around their tents. Lee suggested that Jackson

find a hidden road to the west and move against the flank. Jackson readily agreed, though he likely surprised Lee when he said he would take his entire corps, 28,000 men. That left Lee with just 10,000 men facing Hooker's entire army. Other elements of Lee's army were still back at Fredericksburg.

That night, as Jackson's aides discussed the attack the next day, his sword, which had been leaning against a tree, fell to the ground. The men glanced at each other. Since the days of knighthood, a falling sword had been a bad omen.

The next morning Jackson had a few words with Lee that were not overheard by anyone. Jackson pointed down the road and Lee nodded. It was the last time the two men would see each other. Continue on Furnace Road to Catharine Furnace and turn left onto a dirt-and-gravel road. This is the original road down which Jackson's corps marched. Follow this road until it intersects with Va. 613 (Brock Road). Turn left and watch almost immediately for a right turn onto another unpaved road. Union scouts perched in trees could see Jackson making the left turn onto what is now Va. 613, and they believed it meant some Confederate unit was leaving the battlefield. They could not see the turn to the right, as that little-used road was hidden from their view. Follow Jackson Trail West until it intersects again with Va. 613 and turn left.

The intersection of Va. 613 (Brock Road) and Va. 621 (Orange Plank Road) is an important feature of the Wilderness battle of May 6, 1864, and an important intersection for Jackson in May 1863. Jackson rode east until Orange Plank Road intersected with Plank Road (today's Va. 3). When he saw that he had not yet reached the end of the Union line, he quietly turned around and continued going north on Brock Road until it intersected with Plank Road.

One year later, this intersection was held by Confederate General A.P. Hill's Third Corps. Under heavy fire, Hill's men broke and went dashing west on Orange Plank Road. About one mile away was the Widow Tapp Farm where Lee was waiting for Longstreet's First Corps, which had not yet arrived on the battlefield. As Hill's men streamed past him, Lee tried to rally them, but to no avail. At that moment, the Texas Brigade, the leading brigade of Longstreet's corps, passed him, resolutely marching forward against the tide of Hill's retreating, panicked men. Lee pushed his horse Traveller into the ranks of the Texans and began to ride forward with them—right into danger. A huge sergeant took the reins of Traveller and turned him around and started walking an angry Lee to the rear. "Lee to the rear!" cried the Texans, meaning that they would lead a counter-charge against the coming Yankees, but only if their beloved general took himself out of harm's way. At that moment, Lee spotted Longstreet and he rode over to him. Longstreet made some joke about Lee's aggressiveness as they both watched the Texas Brigade disappear up the road. Within minutes, about one-third of the eight hundred men then in the Texas Brigade would fall dead or wounded, but they would hold up the Federal attack until the rest of the First Corps could arrive. Longstreet's men would prevail and Grant's men would pull back. The Wilderness would be considered a draw. A small stone monument etched with "Lee to the rear cried the Texans" stands beside Orange Plank Road on the Widow Tapp Farm.

Continue on Brock Road until it intersects with Va. 3. Turn right and drive about two miles, watching for a turnoff on the left that leads to a sign describing the start of Jackson's flank attack.

Backtrack west on Va. 3, turn left at the light, and head west on Va. 20. Watch for the left turnoff for Ellwood *only* if the rangers have given permission. If the gate is open, cars are allowed back to the plantation house. If the gate is closed but the rangers have given permission, park and walk about three-quarters of a mile to the house. In the family cemetery is a simple stone marker over Jackson's arm, which was buried here after it was amputated in a field hospital along Va. 3.

Leaving Ellwood, continue west on Va. 20, watching for the left turn onto Hill-Ewell Drive. This narrow piece of parkland runs through what was the main battlefield of the Wilderness. There is little to see here now as housing development has taken over the killing ground. Hill-Ewell drive is not a period road.

At the intersection with Va. 621 (Orange Plank Road), turn left and drive to the intersection with Va. 613 (Brock Road). Turn right and follow Brock Road for about eleven miles. Turn left onto Grant Drive at the Spotsylvania Court House NPS sign. At the head of the drive is a monument to Union General John Sedgwick. Sedgwick had just finished admonishing Union soldiers for ducking Confederate sniper fire by saying "They can't hit an elephant at this distance" when a Confederate, firing a British-made Whitworth sniper rifle, placed a single round under Sedgwick's left eye. Visit the exhibit shelter to get a sense of what happened here.

Follow Grant Drive around to the parking lot for the Bloody Angle. This was the scene of savage fighting for more than two weeks— one battle lasted twenty hours. Rifle fire was so intense in this area that a twenty-inch-diameter tree was cut down solely by rifle fire. One gruesome report by a Union soldier detailed how Federal bodies had been hit so many times by bone-breaking

Minie balls that picking them up was like trying to pick up large bags of jelly. The trenches in this area have been worn down by rain over the years.

Just south of the Bloody Angle is the site where Upton's Attack was staged. Union General Emory Upton convinced Grant that the proper way to attack the Confederate trenches was to line the men up in stacked brigades so long that they resembled long, thick arrows. The lead brigade would punch a hole in the Confederate line, and the following brigades would be able to move to either side behind Confederate lines. A skeptical Grant, who believed in long waves of men moving forward, rather than long, thick arrows of men, still allowed the young officer to try his radical approach to fighting. When Upton's attack worked and the Confederate line was pierced, Grant was surprised, so surprised that he had not even planned to send Upton supporting troops. When no supporting troops came to their aid, Upton's men were forced back to their own lines. The attack, planned by a young, modern-thinking officer had worked, but because his older superior had not reacted quickly enough to its success, it ultimately failed. Grant's mistrust of his talented subordinate would cause the battle to last much longer.

It was at the McCoull House, **Stop 15** on the NPS map, that Lee once again planned to personally lead a counterattack. A subordinate general, John B. Gordon, realized what Lee was thinking and convinced him to go to the rear while his Georgia troops fought back the encroaching Yankees. The Federals got so close that scores of them likely saw and recognized Lee. He could have been killed but was not.

The killing at Spotsylvania Court House went on for two weeks until a weary Grant simply pulled his men back and started marching them south, once again in the direction of Richmond.

From the end of the park road, turn right onto Va. 208 and head into the town of Spotsylvania Court House. After turning left onto Va. 608, the Spotsylvania County Museum will be on the right. It has some artifacts and a diorama of the battle. Drive three-quarters of a mile, and look for Va. 608 on the left (Massaponex Church Road), which will also be labeled with a sign following "Route of Jackson's Ambulance." Follow Va. 608 for about eight miles. Turn right onto U.S. 1 at Massaponex Church. During the war Grant and his generals were photographed in the church courtyard holding a staff meeting. Drive just three-quarters of a mile on U.S. 1 and turn left onto Va. 607 (Guinea Station Road). This road intersects with Va. 606. Turn left, cross the railroad tracks, then make another left onto another NPS site, the Stonewall Jackson Shrine.

Jackson died in this plantation foreman's office house on May 10, 1863, eight days after his wounding at Chancellorsville and the amputation of his arm. He died of pneumonia, which likely had taken root before he was even wounded. When he was accidentally shot, Jackson was wearing a black raincoat on a day that was otherwise mild. He may have been already suffering chills. The house itself is open most weekends. Inside is the bed in which Jackson died. The clock on the mantle is also original to the office.

GETTING TO AND AROUND CHANCELLORSVILLE

The instructions are the same as for touring Fredericksburg; fly into Richmond International to the south or Reagan International to the north, rent a car, and head for I-95. Both airports are about fifty miles away and both pass through congested traffic, though Washington's traffic will be heavier than that found in Richmond. Once at the battlefields, auto tours take visitors to most of the major sites, but there are walking trails to places that cannot be seen from the road.

The only staffed ranger station is at Chancellorsville, so inquire there for hiking maps to all of the battlefields. Be sure to take water on these hikes as there are no water fountains or other facilities. The main walking trail at Chancellorsville is four miles long. The Gordon Loop Trail beginning at the Wilderness Exhibit Shelter on Va. 20 runs for about two miles and crosses from Confederate to Federal positions. This battlefield is not visited nearly as much as Fredericksburg and Chancellorsville, so history tourists at Spotsylvania Court House often find themselves alone as the sun is going down. It is easy to imagine movement in the shadows. It is also easy to remember that so much lead was flying on this field that men's bodies turned to jelly and thick trees were felled after being hit multiple times by lead musket balls.

ACCOMMODATIONS

1859 Mayhurst Inn

12460 Mayhurst Ln., Orange
T: 888-672-5597
www.mayhurstinn.com
8 rooms
$140–$175

This inn, when it was a private house, hosted Robert E. Lee and Stonewall Jackson and was the headquarters for A.P. Hill when Orange was the winter quarters for the Army of Northern Virginia.

Holladay House Bed & Breakfast

155 West Main St., Orange
T: 800-358-4422
www.holladayhousebandb.com
6 rooms
$150–$190

This circa-1830 house is one of the oldest buildings in downtown Orange.

The Inn on Poplar Hill

278 Caroline St., Orange
T: 866-767-5274
www.innonpoplarhill.com
6 rooms
$125–$165

This inn is set on twenty-eight acres so it feels like a private park.

The Inn at Meander Plantation

2333 N. James Madison Hwy., Locust Dale (U.S. 15 north of Orange)
T: 800-385-4936
www.meander.net
8 rooms
$150–$250

Dinner is served by reservation Thursday through Saturday nights at this inn set on eighty acres.

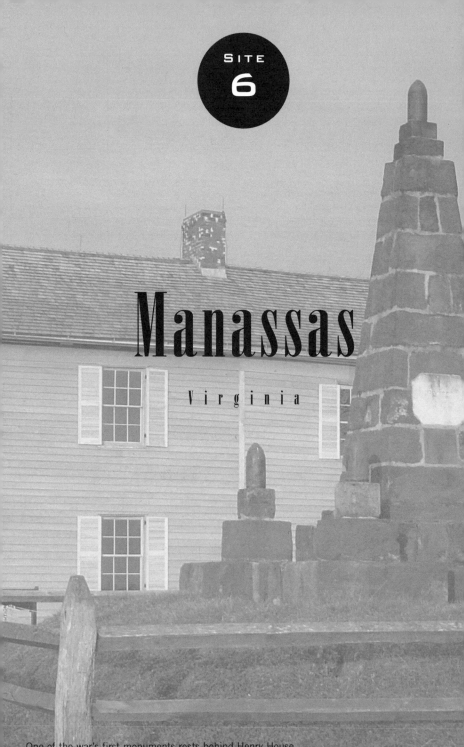

Manassas

Virginia

One of the war's first monuments rests behind Henry House.

THE WAR YEARS

The battles for First and Second Manassas (as the Confederates called them) or Bull Run (as the Union called them) greatly encouraged the South because both battles were routs in their favor. Though crowded by Washington's encroaching traffic and population, most of these battlefields have been preserved. Studying them can show how much Civil War field leaders, particularly the Confederates, learned about combat between the first, sloppy battle and the second, well executed battle.

Other than a minor battle on the peninsula of Virginia (Big Bethel on June 10) and a minor battle in far western Virginia (Rich Mountain, July 11), the war between North and South (which officially began on April 12, 1861) had consisted of little more than politicians on either side daring each other to make a move. The uniformed generals on both sides were busily training their uniformed men for combat they hoped would never come, while the politicians in their finest suits were looking at maps trying to figure out where to stage one big battle that they had convinced themselves and their citizens would cause the other side to give up. The North believed that the South would come skulking back into the Union as soon as it lost that battle, while the South believed the North would let the South leave peacefully after a single defeat.

When the nominal Union commander of the army, General Irwin McDowell, complained to President Lincoln that the pressure to invade the South was overwhelming his ability to train civilians into soldiers, Lincoln replied: "You are green, it is true, but they are green also. You are all green together." Lincoln wanted that battle.

Against his better judgment, McDowell, who had never before commanded more than a squad of men, finally began marching his 35,000-man army out of Washington toward a known Confederate force of 22,000 that was guarding Manassas Junction, the intersection of two rail lines about thirty miles west of Washington. There was an additional 11,000-man Confederate force in the Shenandoah Valley under Joseph E. Johnston near Martinsburg, but the Federals expected to strike before those men had a chance to march to the aid of P.G.T. Beauregard, the Confederate general in command at Manassas. This would be the knock-out blow Lincoln wanted.

Just as McDowell feared, his army was a motley assortment of amateurs. Whole regiments pulled out of the march to pick berries. Men dropped out from the heat and fatigue of walking more than a few miles. A march that should have taken no more than a day and a half wound into three. The result was that the Confederates had plenty of warning that the Federals were on their way.

At dawn on July 21, the Federals began firing on Confederates on the opposite bank of a stone bridge over a little creek called Bull Run. The commander of those men, Confederate Colonel Nathan Evans, was suspicious that the fire was so slow. His hunch proved correct when he received a signal that the bulk of the Union army was crossing Bull Run a few miles to the north. He took part of his command and rushed to his left to oppose the crossing. The big battle was finally starting.

All morning the Federals crossed Bull Run at Sudley Ford in numbers that could not be matched by the Confederates. The Confederates started falling back, first over Matthews Hill and then up the slope of Henry House Hill. McDowell failed to rush his infantry forward, but he did send two batteries of artillery forward to start shelling the retreating Confederates. This was a fundamental error in military judgment—artillery is never sent in advance of infantry. But McDowell had never been more than a minor staff officer. He did not know any better. He was as green a commander as his troops were green as soldiers.

As the Confederates fell back in the face of superior Federal numbers, one general named Bernard Bee spotted a Virginia brigade lying in the grass on the reverse slope of Henry Hill. He rode up to the general and asked for help. That officer said the Virginians would wait for the Federals to advance on them and then they would be given "cold steel." Bee returned to his own command at the base of Henry House Hill and shouted: "Rally round the Virginians. There stands Jackson like a stone wall!" Thomas J. Jackson's brigade rose up from their grassy hiding place and began pouring fire into the surprised Federals. From that moment on, the First Virginia Brigade was the Stonewall Brigade and its commander was Stonewall Jackson. Historians have never agreed whether Bee was calling Jackson "Stonewall" as a measure of esteem because he was not budging in the face of oncoming Federals, or whether he was calling him "Stonewall" because Jackson refused to come down off Henry House Hill to help the outnumbered Confederates under Bee's command. Bee was killed not long after making his famous pronouncement.

The two batteries of advanced Union cannons began firing on Jackson's artillery. One battery of Union guns then moved closer so they could fire at Jackson's infantry. As the battery was about to shoot at a regiment advancing on them coming from Jackson's direction, a Union major rode up and demanded that they not fire on the regiment because the blue-clad men were their long-awaited artillery support. The suspicious artillery commander did as he was told, with the result that most of his command was cut down. The blue-clad men were really the 33rd Virginia Regiment, still wearing their prewar blue militia uniforms. At that point, Jackson's men rushed forward and captured the Federal guns. They then began a counterattack that panicked the once-confident Union line. Within minutes, Jackson's attack had crushed the spirit of the Federals, and they began rushing back toward Washington.

The total losses on both sides were about 900 men killed and 2,700 wounded. Judged against later battles such as the Battle of Shiloh, Tennessee, in April 1862, First Manassas was a minor battle. But in July 1861, it was a disaster. Still, Lincoln refused to let the South go its own way, and the South now knew it would be a much longer war.

The next battle on the same ground came on August 30, 1862, after the Confederates won the August 9 Battle of Cedar Mountain, Virginia, which was on the edge of the Shenandoah Valley about thirty-seven miles to the west. The Battle of Second Manassas came about after Cedar Mountain when Union General John Pope of a newly consolidated Union Army of Virginia foolishly put his army in a natural trap formed by the Rapidan and Rappahannock Rivers. Lee planned to attack Pope and crush him using the two rivers as walls. Pope discovered the trap when some Confederate dispatches outlining the plan were captured, and he moved his army out of harm's way.

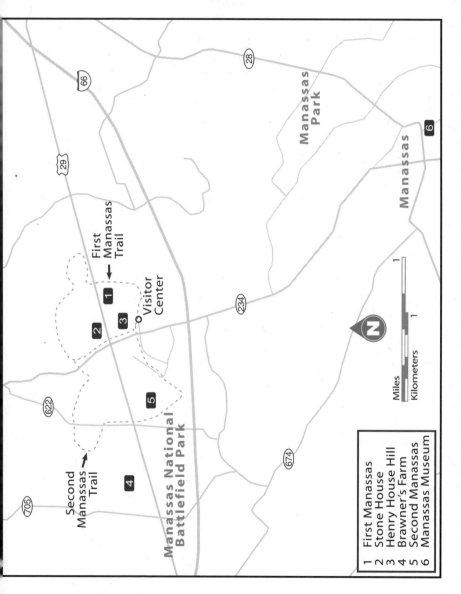

Lee, disappointed that the capture of the dispatches had spoiled his chance to destroy the new Union army, then decided to entice Pope into chasing him. He split his army and sent Jackson rushing toward Manassas Junction to capture supplies and draw Pope off from in front of Lee. Pope, whom Lee called "a miscreant" for his threats against civilians, fell for the trap. Pope started marching after Jackson, unaware that the second half of the Confederate army, under Longstreet, had started marching in his rear. When Jackson chose ground to give battle, Pope would find himself in a vise with Jackson on one side and Longstreet on the other. That vise began to close at Second Manassas on ground just west of the original battlefield of thirteen months earlier.

Pope never seemed to understand that he was only seeing Jackson's half of the army on August 29. He even refused to believe reports that Longstreet's half had arrived on the battlefield and would threaten the Federals in the morning. Though bolstered by a corps from the Army of the Potomac, Pope never organized his army to take on the threat of Longstreet, who was now on his flank. When Longstreet's men burst out of trenches and woods that Pope had assumed to be empty, the Federal army virtually dissolved. Only a last-minute last stand by a mixed collection of forces on Chinn Ridge (also part of the First Manassas battlefield) saved the Federal Army of Virginia from total destruction. Within days, Pope, who had only been in a major command for a matter of months, would be replaced. Officially, 1,700 Federals were killed, and an abnormally high number of 6,000 were missing. Many of those must have been killed, and another large portion captured. Lee lost about the same numbers of killed soldiers, but fewer than 100 were reported missing.

After the win at Second Manassas, Lee sent Jackson after Pope in hopes of crushing what was left of Pope's army, but Pope's rear guard successfully stopped Jackson cold two days later at the Battle of Chantilly on September 1. Lee had come very close to totally destroying the only army standing in defense of Washington. Had Jackson won Chantilly, Lee might have spent the next day negotiating with Lincoln for the surrender of the Federal government.

SOURCES & OTHER READING

Battle of Bull Run: A History of the First Major Campaign of the Civil War, William C. Davis, Louisiana State University Press, 1981.

Donnybrook: The Battle of Bull Run, 1861, David Detzer, Harcourt, 2004

Baptism at Bull Run, James T. Reger, Harbor House, 2004.

Return to Bull Run: The Campaign and Battle of Second Manassas, John Hennessey, University of Oklahoma Press, 1999.

The Second Bull Run Campaign: July–August 1862, David Martin, DeCapo Press, 2003.

Second Manassas, 1862: Robert E. Lee's Greatest Victory, John P. Langellier, Mike Adams, Osprey Press, 2002.

MANASSAS TODAY

Most of the battlefields of First and Second Manassas (or First and Second Bull Run if you prefer the Northern name of the battles) are preserved to look the way they did in 1861 and 1862. It is unfortunate that a modern-day intrusion of nearby I-66 running from Washington to the east to I-81 to the west creates a constant, loud hum that cannot be ignored while you try to think about the fighting that took place here.

Over the past few decades the growth of Washington bureaucracies and the private companies that feed on those bureaucracies have steadily spread to the west along I-66, the main commuting artery into the nation's capital. This sprawl has gobbled up land adjoining the national park that once served as staging areas and camps for both armies. Only the establishment of the national battlefield in 1940 has kept this particular land from being developed. A few years ago a Virginia developer started bulldozing land immediately adjacent

to the national park that had been Lee's headquarters during Second Manassas. To stop the developer from putting in a strip mall on the very edge of the Second Manassas battlefield, preservationists had to buy and add it to the national park. Even the park itself, though it can never be developed into strip malls and houses, is under development pressure. Part of the battlefield was paved over in 2003.

Other battlefields in this sphere of development around Washington are likely destined to be lost. Not far away from Manassas, the battlefield of Bristoe Station, where Confederate forces were cut down in a surprise volley of Federals hiding behind a railroad embankment on October 14, 1863, is in danger of being developed into housing. On this site, right where hundreds of houses are planned, are the unmarked graves of hundreds of those men who never made it back to their own homes.

POINTS OF INTEREST

Manassas National Battlefield Park
★★★★★

12521 Lee Hwy. (Exit 47B off I-66)
T: 703-361-1339
Site open in daylight hours daily. Visitor center 8:30 a.m.–5 p.m. Closed major holidays.
Admission: $3

1. First Manassas

Manassas is unique among the battlefield parks because visitors really get three bat-

tlefields for the price of one: First Manassas on July 21, 1861; Brawner's Farm on August 28, 1862; and then Second Manassas on August 30, 1862. Though they were fought in the same vicinity and involved many of the same troops, Brawner's Farm and Second Manassas were two separate battles with two different sets of objectives and entirely different tactics.

Visitors should start their tour of First Manassas at the visitor center to view the movie explaining the battle and to tour the recently renovated museum with its artifacts from the battle. Most of the important portions of this battlefield can be seen on a one-mile walking tour that begins at the rear, or north side, of the visitor center. Visitors who want to see all of the important sections of First Manassas will want to take the five-and-a-half-mile walking tour. Note that this tour goes over hilly terrain. Take water on both tours. The longer tour includes a stop at the reconstructed Stone Bridge where the battle started with a feint, or false attack, on entrenched Confederates.

As with most trails at national parks, this one does not follow the battle in chronological order. To trace the advance of the Federals at the beginning of the battle, drive north on Sudley Road for just over two miles, park near Sudley United Methodist Church, find Bull Run, then walk back south toward the visitor center. This can be done on parkland, but there is no marked trail, so be careful if walking along the road. The marked trail begins at Matthews Hill, the point where the Confederate resistance began to grow after minor fighting at Bull Run itself. Heading south, visitors will want to stop at the Stone House, which was a field hospital during both battles.

2. Stone House ★★★★

Built as a stagecoach tavern, the Stone House located at the intersection of U.S. 29 and Sudley Road was a private home at the time of the first battle. It is one of only three wartime structures still standing from the battle (the Brawner House and the Dogan House at the intersection of Groveton Road and U.S. 29 being the other two). During Second Manassas, Pope set up his headquarters on a hill just north of the house. He likely chose not to stay in

the house itself as it was a prominent feature of the landscape and might have drawn fire had the Confederates discovered he was using it. Both sides used the house as a hospital during both battles, depending upon the way the battle flowed, and it is still the subject of ghost stories today. It was along the small creek across U.S. 29 from the Stone House that Jackson had a wounded hand bandaged after the battle. He also met President Jefferson Davis in this vicinity to discuss the matter of marching on Washington.

3. Henry House Hill ★★★★★

Continue heading south toward Henry House Hill. This is the same direction in which the Federals were advancing and from which the Confederates were retreating when General Bee went in search of Jackson's Virginians, whom he knew were on the reverse slope of Henry House Hill. Note how Henry House Hill's slope is very gradual, but the reverse slope is entirely hidden from view. Coming up the hill, one can only gradually see the Stonewall Jackson statue emerging just below the crest of the hill.

The Henry House is being rebuilt. During the battle, old Mrs. Henry was bedridden and resisted her family's urging her to leave. She was killed by a Union artillery round that struck in her bedroom. Behind the Henry House is one of the nation's oldest Civil War monuments, a stone pyramid erected during the war by some of the units who fought here. There is an interesting photograph of the men present at the dedication of the monument. A close examination of the photograph shows the soldiers wearing a variety of hats and expressions. One man is flashing a fraternal or Masonic secret sign.

Follow the trail back toward the visitor center, where you'll find cannons representing Rickett's and Griffin's U.S. batteries, which dueled with Jackson's guns. The Federal guns were higher-quality rifled guns while Jackson had supposedly lower-quality smoothbore cannons. At this close range, the Confederate smoothbores were more effective because they threw a wider arc of canister, a can filled with loose lead balls that turned a smoothbore cannon into a large shotgun.

Walk over and examine the statue of an unrealistically muscular Jackson and the enormous biceps given him by a sculptor in the 1930s. As you continue walking south, turn around to look north toward the direction of the approaching Yankees. The front slope of Henry Hill begins to disappear, demonstrating how easy it was for Jackson's men to stay hidden from the advancing Federals by lying down in the tall grass. Jackson's tactic of staying hidden until the last moment was the key to winning the battle. Jackson's wartime success was always tied to his belief in hitting hard and fast before his enemy had a chance to evaluate his strength.

Walk to the cannons in front of the visitor center. These guns represent Griffin's battery, which Griffin had moved in order to get a better bead on Jackson's infantry. As Griffin was about to fire down Jackson's line, a direction known to the military as enfilading fire, he saw a blue-clad regiment advancing on him from one side, but from the same general direction as Jackson's men. Griffin re-aimed his cannons at those men, but before he could fire, a superior officer rode up and told Griffin that the advancing regiment was his long-anticipated artillery support. They were not, and Griffin knew that even as the regiment was advancing from the south and his artillery support would have been coming from the north. He knew the blue-clads had to be Confederates, but, ordered not to fire, Griffin's battery was decimated when the blue-clads marched

to within fifty yards before leveling a devastating volley on the artillery. The regiment, the 33rd Virginia of Jackson's First Virginia brigade, then charged the cannons. They led a sweep down the Union right flank. The entire Union line began to crumble. Jackson's charge, starting from this point, was the beginning of the end of the First Battle of Manassas.

4. Brawner's Farm ★★★

Brawner's Farm is not part of the Park Service's marked, general tour of the Second Manassas campaign, but the Park Service does not bar visitors from following the battle here. Drive west on U.S. 29 from the intersection with Sudley Road, past the intersection with Groveton Road and past the sign for Battery Heights. Watch on the right for a turnoff toward a field closed off by an iron gate. Park and walk through the opening beside the gate.

As they walk north, visitors are duplicating the 6 p.m. July 28, 1862, path of a green brigade of Wisconsin and Indiana soldiers wearing tall black hats who would become known as the Iron Brigade after battles like this one. Stonewall Jackson's men had been hiding in the woods to the north, behind the Brawner farmhouse (straight ahead), when they noticed the Black Hat Brigade marching by in column. Jackson intentionally attacked the column, which had not seen him, in order to bring the Federals to combat. For two hours, the two sides blasted away at each other until darkness came and the fighting was broken off with the battle ending in a draw. There is a well-marked loop trail through the woods marking both the Confederate and the Union positions. At some points the two sides were no more than sixty yards from each other. The most famous casualty of this battle was General Richard Ewell, Jackson's subordinate, who was wounded in his knee. His leg was amputated, and in the future he would often go into combat driving a carriage or strapped into the saddle of a horse. Ewell would replace Jackson as Confederate Second Corps commander after Jackson's death following Chancellorsville.

5. Second Manassas ★★★★★

Ambitious hikers can start their Second Manassas tour by walking the trail from Brawner's Farm to the Unfinished Railroad Cut, the natural trench in which Jackson hid his men while waiting for Union General John Pope to appear. Others may want to return to their vehicle, drive east for a quarter mile, turn left onto Groveton Road, and drive to the Park Service parking area for the Unfinished Railroad Cut (**Stops 5** and **6** on the National Park Service map). Jackson's men held this portion of the battlefield for several days through vicious attacks by Pope's army and an attack by the newly arrived corps from the Army of the Potomac.

Trails leading both northeast and southwest from the parking lot show how deep this cut still is and why it made such a natural defensive position for Jackson. At one point during the battle, Jackson's men ran out of ammunition and started throwing rocks at the advancing Federals. The Federals, either because they were also running out of ammunition or because they got into the spirit of that type of fighting, began throwing rocks back at the Confederates. For a while, the battle on that portion of the battlefield became a contest to see who could hit each other on the head with a rock.

It was against the southwestern (or right) side of Jackson's line that a Union controversy took place. Arriving on the field in the morning of August 30 was Union General Fitz-John Porter's corps, an advance element of the Army of the Potomac, which was still on its way. Pope

ordered Porter to attack immediately, an order at which Porter balked because he had not had time to see the battlefield. In addition, Pope's abilities were unknown to Porter, and he had no confidence in this stranger who was ordering his men into combat. Porter did not attack as ordered, which enraged Pope.

Later in the day Pope again ordered Porter forward, and this time Porter reluctantly attacked, only to be hit with a galling fire from Jackson's line. Pope had told Porter that the attack would be easy because Jackson was retreating. Jackson was most certainly not retreating, since Confederate General James Longstreet's Second Corps had arrived on the field and was now organizing itself in the trenches beside Jackson. The key was that Pope still did not know Longstreet had arrived. As Porter was falling back, Longstreet's corps climbed out of the trenches and attacked the already-confused wing under Porter. Longstreet pushed the Federals back toward Chinn Ridge, which had been part of the First Manassas battlefield. There, a last-ditch stand by a few stalwart Federal units saved the rest of the Union army from being overrun.

Stop 8 of the NPS driving tour, just south of Stop 7, the Confederate Cemetery, has two interesting stone monuments to the 5th and 10th New York Regiments, two units that did their best to stop Longstreet's Corps. In five minutes, 123 men were killed in the 5th New York. The 5th and the 10th were dressed in red pantaloons, red and blue jackets, and red turbans—dress patterned after that of French Moroccan Zouave troops, who were considered the most colorful troops in the world. (Both sides had regiments who enjoyed the colorful Zouave dress.)

Stop 9 is Chinn Ridge, the location of the Federals' last stand, which allowed Pope's army to form on Henry House Hill, then start an orderly retreat toward Washington.

6. Manassas Museum ★★★

9101 Prince William St.
T: 703-368-1873
Tuesday–Sunday, 10 a.m.–5 p.m.
Closed major holidays.
Admission: $3

Although this museum has some displays on the war, it contains many more on the

history of the town itself. Interestingly, one of the town's favorite mayors was a Yankee officer who returned to the South after the war with a dedication to rebuild what he had helped wreck. Ask for a map showing a driving tour of the Civil War sites in the area, including a house called Liberia, which was General P.G.T. Beauregard's headquarters. The house is currently undergoing renovation.

GETTING TO AND AROUND MANASSAS

Dulles International Airport is no more than fifteen miles from Manassas. One of the southern approaches to the airport passes through Blackburn's Ford, the site of a small skirmish that tipped off the Confederates to the approach of the Federals. Getting from the airport to the national park requires a car as there is no public transportation.

Getting to other Civil War sites in the greater Washington, D.C., area, can be difficult due to heavy traffic near Washington. Tourists driving north along I-95 toward should take the Va. 234 exit. This shortcut increases the accessibility of the national park for those visiting the Petersburg, Richmond, and Fredericksburg area battlefields.

ACCOMMODATIONS

Bennett House

9252 Bennett Dr., Manassas
T: 800-354-7060
www.virginia-bennetthouse.com
2 rooms
$95–$140

This Victorian-era home is located in the historic district of downtown.

The Grey Horse Inn

4350 Fauquier Ave., the Plains
T: 877-253-7020
www.greyhorseinn.com
6 rooms
$105–$195

The Plains is a small village with a completely different feel from urban Manassas, but close by. Many residents in this town are wealthy horse-farm owners.

Briar Patch Bed & Breakfast

23130 Briar Patch Ln., Middleburg
T: 866-327-5911
www.briarpatchbandb.com
6 bedrooms
$125–$195

This farm house was built in 1805. Some bullet holes left from a cavalry battle that swirled around the house in 1863 remain. The battle was part of the campaign that culminated in the Battle of Gettysburg.

Shiloh Bed and Breakfast

13520 Carriage Ford Rd., Nokesville
T: 703-594-2664
www.shilohbb.com
2 suites
$185–$205

This bed and breakfast in the area of the Battle of Bristoe Station is just eight miles from Manassas Regional Airport.

Appomattox
Court House

Virginia

The McLean House at Appomattox Court House.

THE WAR YEARS

T his national historic site in southwestern Virginia is where two nations fought, one small nation died, and the larger nation remerged united and stronger than ever. This site is quiet, reverent, and respectful of the 620,000 men and women who died in the service of their country. No other Civil War site can match the feel of Appomattox Court House.

Lynchburg lay twenty-three miles west of the village of Appomattox Court House and Lexington was just forty-five miles northwest of Lynchburg. Both had been attacked in June 1864, and Union forces had burned both the Virginia Military Institute and the home of the governor. The cities of Petersburg and Richmond were less than one hundred miles to the east and both of them had been under attack for nearly nine months. Tens of thousands of soldiers were dead from battles that had taken place barely five days' march away. Thousands more civilians were sick and starving, trapped inside their besieged homes.

Yet Appomattox Court House sat untouched by war. Far from having vital converging rail lines like those in Petersburg and Lynchburg, the village had no military significance. Other than being a dot on a map in a section of the state Union generals had not yet invaded, the county seat of Appomattox County was of no interest to them.

One fifty-one-year-old man living in a large house in the village had moved there for just that reason. Wilmer McLean had been a merchant in Manassas, Virginia, in July 1861, when Confederate forces began occupying his fields bordering Bull Run creek. Within a few days a general had appropriated his house as a headquarters. A few days later a shell went crashing through his home, and the great battle that ensued—the Battle of First Manassas—left behind unexploded shells and bodies on his property.

McLean was too old to fight in the war as a foot soldier, and his politics tended toward the indifferent. He did not want to take either side. Rather than rebuild his Manassas property, which was now on the front lines, he looked on a map of Virginia for a place far removed from anything of vital military interest. Appomattox Court House, with a population of fewer than a hundred people, fit that bill. He bought the finest house in the village, a two-story brick house built in 1848, confident that the brush with war he had experienced at Manassas would be his last.

McLean's personal peace plan worked for nearly four years. Then on April 2, 1865, Robert E. Lee was forced to abandon the trenches of Petersburg and Richmond. Lee and his exhausted, starving army began an overland march toward the west, the only direction that was still open for them. Hoping at some point that he could turn south and link up with General Joseph E. Johnston's Army of Tennessee, then in North Carolina, Lee kept his army marching westward, staying just ahead of the pursuing Federals. But Federal cavalry could move faster than Lee's trudging, hungry men. On April 7, Lee heard that Union horsemen were converging on Appomattox Depot, the small rail station three miles south of Appomattox Court House. The food he had been expecting to distribute to his debilitated army was about to be captured. Lee then received a note from pursuing General U.S. Grant asking for the surrender of the Army of Northern Virginia.

For a day Lee resisted the idea of surrender, telling Grant in a note back that no "emergency" requiring surrender had yet arisen. Lee changed his mind on the night of April 8 when it became obvious that more Federals were arriving to surround him. A quick count of effective soldiers showed Lee that he had fewer than 10,000 armed men. The Federals likely had at least six times that many already on the scene. On the morning of April 9, a brigade of North Carolinians cleared the Lynchburg Road of Federals, a final skirmish victory, but the Confederates could see more Yankees gathering in the distance. Lee, after rejecting some advice to encourage his army to scatter into the mountains and act as guerrillas, sent a note to Grant asking for a meeting to discuss surrender.

As Lee and his aide slowly rode into Appomattox Court House, they encountered McLean. They asked him for a suitable house for a meeting of several men. When Lee rejected the shabby house McLean pointed out, the merchant reluctantly offered his own house. The man who had seen the first major battle of the war start in his fields had just invited the generals who would end that same war into his parlor.

At 2 p.m., Grant and his staff arrived to meet with Lee and his one aide. It was an interesting scene. Lee was dressed in a fine, hand-tailored dress uniform that he had worn expecting to be taken into custody. Grant was dressed in a muddy private's sack coat with major general's shoulder bars sewn on the shoulders. For a few minutes, the two men chitchatted, and Grant reminded Lee that they had met once in Mexico when both had been lowly staff officers.

Within minutes the simple, direct surrender was drafted and signed by the two generals, who saw no need to inject politics into the proceedings. Lee's aide wrote later: "It was in itself perhaps the greatest tragedy that had ever occurred in the history of the world, but it was the simplest, plainest, and most thoroughly devoid of any attempt at effect that you could imagine."

However, the war was not over. Only Lee's Army of Northern Virginia had surrendered. Despite Grant's suggestion that Lee promote himself as a symbol, Lee reminded Grant that he was just one general and not a political leader. Lee said that he had no authority to surrender any army other than his own. It would take another month before all of the Confederate armies would surrender and for all fighting to cease.

Though Appomattox Court House had become the most famous spot in all of Virginia, the village virtually died within three decades. The train line was more than three miles away at Appomattox Depot, so what little growth occurred during Reconstruction came along the line. When the courthouse burned down in 1892, the county seat was moved.

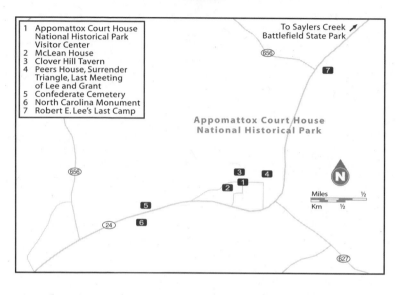

1 Appomattox Court House
  National Historical Park
  Visitor Center
2 McLean House
3 Clover Hill Tavern
4 Peers House, Surrender
  Triangle, Last Meeting
  of Lee and Grant
5 Confederate Cemetery
6 North Carolina Monument
7 Robert E. Lee's Last Camp

To Saylers Creek
Battlefield State Park

Appomattox Court House
National Historical Park

Miles ½
Km ½

APPOMATTOX TODAY

The village of Appomattox Court House, mostly reconstructed in the 1930s by the National Park Service, looks like it should have people from the 1860s walking its gravel and dirt streets. Other than the modern conveniences in the rebuilt courthouse that serves as a visitor center, and a bookstore and restroom building on the outskirts, the village looks as it must have looked during the war. Extensive archaeological work allowed the Park Service to accurately re-create the village.

Still far from major population areas and set back from a road that is not heavily traveled, the historic park offers visitors a quiet place to contemplate the end of the war. It is unfortunate that it is frequented by a relatively small number of visitors, as this is where the modern U.S. was stitched back together by the even-handedness and clear thinking of both Grant and Lee. More people should visit and think about how these two conscientious soldiers did all they could to make peace in a wartorn land. Because it is quiet, it is a good place to reflect upon the turning point of history that took place here.

This is a historic park where slow strolling comes naturally. Visitors with time and good walking shoes will want to walk the two miles along the grassy path from the spot where Lee rested on Appomattox Creek to the Confederate Cemetery where several Confederates and two Union soldiers killed during the last days of the war are buried.

POINTS OF INTEREST

1. Appomattox Court House National Historical Park Visitor Center ★★★★★

Va. 24 three miles north of its intersection with U.S. 460 in Appomattox
T: 434-352-8987
Daily, 8:30 a.m.–5 p.m.
Closed major holidays.
Admission: $4

This is not the original courthouse, which burned in 1892. But this building houses some interesting artifacts and dispenses some worthwhile information. At least thirty black men acting as teamsters for the Army of Northern Virginia were paroled here at Appomattox. Federal accounts of attacks on those wagons earlier in the week told of how black soldiers, possibly these same men, put up a fight for their wagons. On the second floor are artifact displays, including items that were in the parlor of the McLean House on the day of the surrender. Among the most poignant is a doll that a Federal officer found in the room and nicknamed "the witness doll." After the surrender, Federal officers descended on the McLean House and appropriated the furniture as souvenirs.

An entertaining display shows the many versions of the surrender as imagined by artists who were not there. Some men are painted in who were not even in the room, such as George Armstrong Custer. Curiously, Custer got the best artifact from that day. General Phil Sheridan bought the table on which Grant wrote out the surrender terms and presented it to Libby Custer, the general's wife.

2. McLean House ★★★★★

About 150 yards west of the visitor center.

The original house was taken apart brick by brick by Yankee speculators with the intention that it be reassembled at the World's Columbian Exposition in Chicago in 1893. The house was packed up for shipping when investors' money ran out. Nothing was done for nearly fifty years until Congress voted to create the historic park. Held up for another four years by World War II, the house finally was reconstructed in 1947. While the house is a reconstruction, it is a faithful one because the 1893 investors took careful measurements and documentation so they could rebuild the house in Chicago.

Inside, the parlor just to the left of the front door is furnished just as it was on April 9, 1865, with reproduction furniture. The two men sat several yards apart at two different tables as Grant's aides hovered in the background. Grant tried to put Lee at ease by mentioning that they had once met in Mexico when Grant had been a commissary officer and Lee an engineering officer. For a few moments, there was nothing but chitchat, until Lee reminded Grant that they were there to discuss his army's surrender. The only major point of discussion that Lee brought up during the meeting was that all Confederate cavalrymen owned their own horses, and he asked that they be allowed to keep their mounts so they could be used once they returned to their farms. Grant readily agreed. One clause in the surrender document Grant drafted would later anger Washington politicians who hungered for some type of public, legal revenge against the leaders and generals of the Confederacy. Grant promised Lee that his troops could go home and that they would not be further disturbed by the U.S. as long as they did not take up arms again. In effect, Grant had given blanket pardons for all men in arms and said that they would not be treated as traitors to the U.S.

Before he left the room, Lee shook hands with all of Grant's staff officers. He looked at Colonel Ely Parker, a Seneca Indian who had drafted the surrender terms for Grant. With a wry smile on his face, Lee commented that there was "at least one native American" in the room.

As Lee mounted his famed and favorite gray horse Traveller, Grant walked out onto the porch and raised his hat in a kind of salute to Lee. Lee returned with a hand salute and rode away from the house at 3 p.m. to break the news to his soldiers.

3. Clover Hill Tavern ★★★★

Just west of the visitor center.

Built in 1819 as a way station and overnight lodging for stagecoach passengers on the Richmond-to-Lynchburg Pike, Clover Hill Tavern was restored in 1954. It is the oldest original structure in the village. On the day after Lee agreed to the surrender, he asked that Grant give all of his men some tangible proof of their surrender. A small printing press was found and placed in the tavern, and more than 28,000 paroles were issued. The small slip of paper, with a space to be filled in with the man's name, said that the bearer "is a paroled prisoner of the Army of Northern Virginia, has permission to go to his home and there remain undisturbed." Today, displays describe how the parole process worked.

4. Peers House, Surrender Triangle, Last Meeting of Lee and Grant ★★★★

North, along the gravel path.
Private residence, not open for touring.

The Peers House, with a cannon in its front yard, was the site from which the Army of Northern Virginia fired the last cannon on the morning of April 9, the same day Lee and Grant were talking surrender. The end of a war is always confusing for both sides. Both were trying to sort out the latest rumors, including whether surrender talks were really occurring or were just a cover so that the other side could move up men and guns. The commander of this artillery battery saw Federals moving in the distance, and he fired, killing at least two men. They were among the last to die from hostile action in the eastern theater.

Next to the Peers House is the Surrender Triangle, named for the odd-shaped piece of open ground formed by the gravel paths. The formal surrender of arms and battle flags took place here on April 12. Lee had already started riding back to Richmond, so he was not present for the stacking of arms. Grant also skipped the ceremony.

Lee and Grant met briefly on April 10 on a knoll just past the Surrender Triangle. On that day, Grant made another subtle plea to Lee that he send word through the lines that he had surrendered and was asking other Confederate forces in the field to also surrender. Lee rejected the idea again, saying that he was responsible only for his own army and not those of other generals. It was what Grant had expected him to say, so the two men saluted each other, and Lee began riding toward Richmond. He and Grant would meet once more in 1869 when Lee dropped in on President Grant at the Executive Mansion in Washington.

The road leading down to Appomattox Creek was the supposed scene of an incident that is still shrouded in controversy. According to postwar accounts, Union General Joshua Lawrence Chamberlain had his division come to "port arms" as the Confederates arrived to surrender, which was a minor form of salute to the Confederates whom the Union Fifth Corps had fought for four years. Confederate General John Gordon, seeing this gesture, touched his horse, causing it to rear on its hind legs as he swept his sword downward in a return salute to Chamberlain. Some historians have claimed that Chamberlain made up the account and that Gordon went along with it.

Walkers who walk down the pathway to Appomattox Creek and across the bridge will find a plaque on the opposite side describing the spot where Lee rested.

5. Confederate Cemetery ★★★

Visitors in a walking mood can follow the grassy path from the visitor center for about a half mile to the southwest, back toward Appomattox, to find the fenced Confederate cemetery. Here are men who had the misfortune to be among the last killed in the last campaign in the last battle of the Army of Northern Virginia. Also buried here are two Union soldiers.

6. North Carolina Monument ★★★★★

East side of Va. 24 across from Confederate Cemetery.

Across the road from the Confederate cemetery and 200 yards into the woods is a Confederate memorial erected in the early twentieth century by the North Carolina legislature. Follow the mulch path to the marker erected near the site where a North Carolina regiment fired the last shots on April 9, just before the surrender took place. The volley cleared the road of Federals, giving the Confederates a brief, if ultimately pointless, victory. The memorial notes that North Carolina gave more fighting men than it had men of voting age, and that more than a third of those Tar Heels who went off to war died. North Carolina lost more men than any other state in the Union or Confederacy.

This is the only state monument at Appomattox.

7. Robert E. Lee's Last Camp ★★

About two miles north of the visitor center on Va. 24.

There is nothing to see aside from a historic marker, but the top of this wooded knoll was where Lee made his last camp before surrendering to Grant. It is a short but steep hike from the parking lot to the campsite. It was here that Lee donned his uniform for his meeting with Grant and here that he composed his famous farewell address to the Army of Northern Virginia. Lee also received two remarkable visitors here on the morning of April 10. One was Union General George Meade, commander of the Army of the Potomac. When Lee joked that Meade had more gray hair than Lee had remembered, Meade fired back: "You are the cause of that!" The other visitor was General Henry Hunt, the chief of artillery for the Union Army. It was Hunt who had accurately directed murderous artillery fire against Lee's men at Malvern Hill in July 1862 and then at Gettysburg in July 1863. If any one man was directly responsible for the most deaths suffered by the Army of Northern Virginia, it was Hunt. Hunt and Lee had served together at Fort Hamilton, New York. Their cordial meeting after the surrender reveals the bond that West Point graduates and military men had with each other.

OTHER AREA ATTRACTIONS

Saylers Creek Battlefield State Park ★★★

28 miles east of Appomattox near Farmville.

Park is at intersection of CR 617/CR 618 Watch for brown signs turning off from U.S. 460.

This was Lee's last, and worst, defeat. As

he watched the battle, fought on April 6, 1865, he cried out: "My God! Has the army been dissolved?" More than 8,000 Confederates and eight generals were captured in the battle as pursuing Federals caught up with and overwhelmed Lee's army, which was moving ever slower as its hungry men ran out of energy.

GETTING TO AND AROUND APPOMATTOX

Lynchburg Regional Airport, about twenty-five miles west of Appomattox, is the closest commercial airport. It is served by two commuter airlines. Three rental car agencies serve the airport.

Once visitors arrive at Appomattox Court House, they will need a car to visit General Lee's final headquarters, which is about two miles northeast of the visitor center. There is no designated path from the visitor center to Lee's campsite. While walking back to these two sites is worthwhile, the

Confederate Cemetery and the North Carolina monument are on Va. 24 and can be visited before reaching the visitor center if you're coming from U.S. 460. That would save time, but walking is part of the allure of Appomattox Court House. Following in the footsteps of men like Lee and Grant gives visitors time to contemplate all that happened here.

With the exception of Lee's final headquarters, all sites are easily negotiated on foot and by wheelchairs.

ACCOMMODATIONS

Spring Grove Farm Bed & Breakfast

C.R. 613, ten miles northwest of
Appomattox Court House
T: 877-409-1865
www.springgrovefarm.com
11 rooms, 1 cottage
$175–$250

This 1842 farmhouse looks like a plantation home. Bear in mind that it is out in the country, far away from restaurants.

Babcock House Bed & Breakfast

106 Oakleigh Ave., Appomattox
T: 804-352-7532
www.babcockhouse.com
5 rooms and 1 suite
$95–$120

The house dates back to 1884, but was converted to an inn in 1996.

Longacre Bed & Breakfast

107 Church St., Appomattox
T: 800-758-7730
www.lanierbb.com/inns/bb25879.html
5 rooms
$80–$120

This bed and breakfast breaks this book's unofficial rule that accommodations must have an 1860s-period look, as it is a Tudor-style mansion, but Appomattox is a small town with few bed and breakfasts, and this one is hospitable.

SOURCES & OTHER READING

Lee's Retreat: A History and Field Guide, Chris Calkins, Page One. 2000.

Battles for Appomattox Station and Appomattox Court House April 8–9, 1865, Chris Calkins, H.E. Howard, 1987.

The Appomattox Campaign: March 29, April 9, 1865, Chris Calkins, Combined Books, 1997.

A Place Called Appomattox, William Marvel, University of North Carolina Press, 2000.

Lee's Last Retreat: The Flight to Appomattox, William Marvel, University of North Carolina Press, 2002.

Shenandoah Valley

Virginia

The Battle of Cedar Creek is reenacted on its original ground every October

THE WAR YEARS

Y ou can't see this Civil War site in one day, but the Shenandoah Valley offers battlefields, historic towns, historic graves, and some of the most beautiful scenery
found in the nation, all of which combine to make this a great place to visit.

The Shenandoah Valley, roughly 180 miles long and fifty miles wide, defined on
the west by the Allegheny Mountains and on the east by the Blue Ridge
Mountains, was far more than a picturesque home to the Scots-Irish and German immigrants who settled the area in the 1700s.

This fertile bottom land was the perfect place for farmers. Sheltered from harsh winter
and sweltering summer weather by the mountains on either side and irrigated by
streams and rivers fed by water running down from the gently sloping tree-covered
mountains, the valley was Virginia's breadbasket before the war began. Wheat was the
crop of choice of most farmers.

By 1861, the valley was one long, bustling rural community, tied together by the valley
Pike, a 100-mile road between Winchester and Staunton paved with crushed stones.
This highway brought far-flung farming communities together, allowing trade both inside
and out of the valley to flourish.

Then Virginia seceded on April 17, 1861. The idyllic valley became both an asset for the
Confederacy and a military target for the Union. The valley itself was one huge strategic
tool. Shielded by mountains on both sides, the Pike could accommodate fast-marching
Confederate armies when they wanted to strike at important northern cities like the
United States capital of Washington, located a mere seventy-five mostly flat, marchable
miles east of the northern end of the Valley. Conversely, the Pike moved toward the southwest, away from Richmond, so the road itself, bordered on the east by 4,000-foot-tall
mountains, was useless for any Northern advance on the Confederate capital.

But it was not the Pike itself that both sides most wanted to protect or destroy. The real
value of the Shenandoah Valley lay in those hundreds of small farms raising wheat that
could be processed into bread to feed soldiers, and oats that could feed cavalry horses.
With scores of small towns acting as collection locations, the military on both sides
could easily gather the crops and put them to immediate use. Control of those farms
and towns was paramount to both sides.

General Thomas J. "Stonewall" Jackson, a resident of the valley since 1851, recognized
that fact just before launching a ten-week-long series of battles that drove the Federals
out of the Shenandoah. Jackson's Valley Campaign began on March 23, 1862, with the
Battle of Kernstown, just south of Winchester, near the northern end of the valley.
Jackson actually lost the battle, but gained a surprising strategic advantage. Frightened
by the thought of Jackson just five marching days from the Executive Mansion,
President Lincoln pulled back forces poised to strike at Richmond and ordered them to
protect the capital city.

Jackson, incredulous that the Union high command took his 17,000-man force so seri-
ously, promptly embarked on a cross-valley campaign that eventually resulted in victories

at McDowell in the Allegheny Mountains (May 8), followed by Front Royal (May 23), Cross Keys (June 8), and Port Republic (June 9) in the foothills of the Blue Ridge Mountains. Jackson had captured the public's attention and his nickname the summer before at the Battle of First Manassas, and his resounding defeats of three different, much larger Union armies under three different generals promptly made him a Confederate national hero.

The Federals were so bruised and embarrassed by the manhandling Jackson gave them in such a short time that they did not even attempt to enter the southern part of the valley for the rest of 1862 and most of 1863. In July 1863 Lee shielded his army between the two mountain ranges on his way north. His destination, though he did not know it, was a little town called Gettysburg.

Nature—rather than the Federals—began to bedevil the Confederate use of the valley. In 1862 there was a drought, followed by too much rain in 1863, conditions that cut crop production in half. That natural disaster played a major role in the future failure of the Confederate army's ability to feed itself.

By the end of 1863, Federals, buoyed by the Confederate loss at Gettysburg, began to creep back into the northern part of the valley. In 1864 Union Commanding General U.S. Grant began to focus on destroying Confederate General Robert E. Lee's army rather than capturing territory. To open up another front so Lee could not draw on reinforcements from the valley, Grant once again focused on operations in the region in the summer and fall of 1864.

Then the Federals suffered a setback at the Battle of New Market on May 15, 1864. In that battle, a small force, bolstered by teenagers from the Virginia Military Institute, beat back a superior Union advance. Two months later in July, a Confederate force slipped away from the Petersburg trenches and rushed down the Valley Pike toward Washington. Jubal Early's Confederates got within a few miles of the Executive Mansion before a thrown-together Union force stopped them from capturing Washington.

An angry Grant replaced the Union general who had let Early slip by with a general who had practiced a heavier hand against the South in campaigns in Mississippi and Tennessee. Phil Sheridan's name would be long remembered—and cursed—by the residents of the valley.

Under Sheridan, Union regiments did not focus on fighting the meager Confederate forces in the region. Instead, the Federals concentrated on destroying the civilian farms that had been so critical to the Confederacy as a food resource. For weeks, smoke from burning barns, homes, and fields hung over the valley. Sheridan quipped that he destroyed so much of the valley crops "that a crow flying over the region will have to pack his own provisions."

Sheridan finished off the bulk of the Confederate opposition in the Shenandoah Valley at the Battle of Cedar Creek, south of Winchester, on October 19, 1864. The South's Garden of Eden was in ruins. Offensive operations shifted back to the east around Petersburg. There was little left in the valley to fight or destroy.

SITE

8

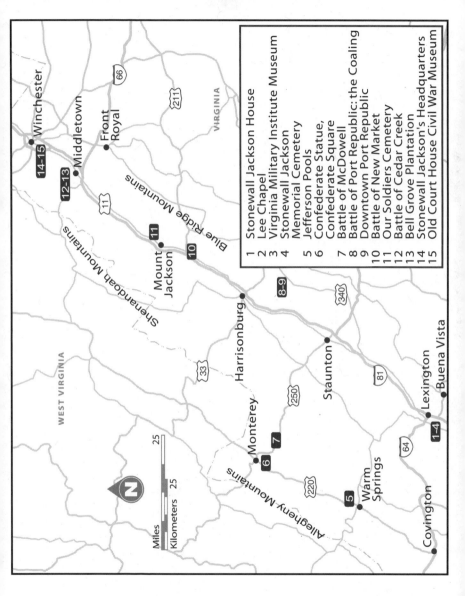

1 Stonewall Jackson House
2 Lee Chapel
3 Virginia Military Institute Museum
4 Stonewall Jackson
   Memorial Cemetery
5 Jefferson Pools
6 Confederate Statue,
   Confederate Square
7 Battle of McDowell
8 Battle of Port Republic: the Coaling
9 Downtown Port Republic
10 Battle of New Market
11 Our Soldiers Cemetery
12 Battle of Cedar Creek
13 Bell Grove Plantation
14 Stonewall Jackson's Headquarters
15 Old Court House Civil War Museum

WEST VIRGINIA

VIRGINIA

Winchester
Middletown
Front Royal
Mount Jackson
Harrisonburg
Monterey
Staunton
Lexington
Buena Vista
Warm Springs
Covington

Shenandoah Mountains
Blue Ridge Mountains
Allegheny Mountains

66
211
11
340
33
250
220
81
64

14-15
12-13
11
10
8-9
7
6
5
1-4

N

Miles   25
Kilometers 25

SHENANDOAH TODAY

The Shenandoah Valley today, with a concentration on Civil War sites, stretches from Winchester in the north to Lexington in the south, a distance of about 128 miles. Luckily, and somewhat unexpectedly, the construction of I-81 has helped preserve the Valley's beauty, quaintness, accessibility, and historical significance. Although most people properly view interstate highways as necessary modern eyesores, the interstate is actually a great help to the historic traveler because the four-lane interstate allows drivers to travel from one end of the historic valley to the other in the course of a day, even including plenty of time to stop and visit museums and battlefields.

At the same time, those travelers wanting to take a more leisurely approach can get off I-81 and drive two-lane U.S. 11, which was built on the original roadbed of the Valley Pike. Towns and villages crop up about every ten miles, so it definitely necessitates a more leisurely pace. That said, it offers worthwhile rewards. The towns along the route feature Confederate cemeteries to explore, Confederate statues to examine, and historic buildings that have been preserved.

The valley still retains its agricultural and rural character. The largest city is Harrisonburg, with 40,000 citizens and two universities, James Madison and Eastern Mennonite. The next most populous cities are Staunton with about 24,000 people, Winchester at 23,600, Waynesboro at 20,000, and Lexington with around 8,000.

POINTS OF INTEREST

1. Stonewall Jackson House ★★★★★

8 East Washington St., Lexington
T: 540-463-2552
Monday–Saturday, 9 a.m.–5 p.m.;
Sunday, 1–5 p.m.
The last tour begins at 4:30 p.m.
Admission: $6

The only home owned by Virginia Military Institute Professor Thomas J. Jackson and his wife Anna looks exactly the way it did when Jackson bought it in the mid-1850s. Some furniture is original to the house. Some items, such as Jackson's barbells, which he used to exercise, bring the man to life. Ironically, one of the South's greatest heroes never wore a Confederate uniform inside his own home. He left here in April 1861 leading the Corps of VMI cadets to Richmond to act as instructors for raw recruits pouring into the capital city, but he was wearing his old U.S. Army uniform. Jackson never returned to this house. The backyard reflects the fierce general's passion for vegetable gardening.

2. Lee Chapel ★★★★★

East side of Washington & Lee University Campus, Lexington
T: 540-458-8768
April 1–October 31, Monday–Saturday, 9 a.m.–5 p.m.; Sunday, 1–5 p.m.
November 1–March 31, Monday–Saturday, 9 a.m.–4 p.m.; Sunday, 1–4 p.m.
Free admission

Robert E. Lee had Custis, one of his sons, help design this chapel as a nondenominational meeting facility for Washington College, which Lee headed as president from 1865 until his death in 1870. When it was completed in 1868, Lee moved his office into a room on the lower level. Apparently the office is exactly as he left it on the day he became ill. On the main level is a white marble statue of Lee asleep in his tent. Carved by Edward Valentine, the detail is fine enough that the weave of Lee's blanket can be discerned. Lee and all of his immediate family are interred on the lower level, which also houses a museum holding many Lee family artifacts.

3. Virginia Military Institute Museum ★★★★

Jackson Memorial Hall (east side of campus), Lexington
T: 540-464-7334
Daily, 9 a.m.–5 p.m.
Free admission

The VMI Museum, normally housed in the basement of Jackson Memorial Hall, has been moved temporarily to the George Marshall Museum across campus until 2007 while a 13,000-square-foot expansion is completed. Only a small portion of the VMI Museum relates to the war, but among the artifacts are Jackson's trousers and the black rubber raincoat he was wearing the night he was accidentally shot. Close examination shows how bullet holes in the coat were repaired. Historians speculate that Jackson might have been wearing the raincoat on a warm, rainless day because he was already suffering chills from the onset of the pneumonia that would kill him.

4. Stonewall Jackson Memorial Cemetery ★★★★

South Main St., Lexington
Open dawn to dusk
Free admission

Jackson and his immediate family are buried under the bronze statue of the general. Nearby is his original grave with its tombstone still in place, and the family gravesite of his first wife, who died in childbirth. Several other Confederate generals and the inventor of the ironclad C.S.S. Virginia are also buried in this old cemetery. Check the map directory at the front of the cemetery for the locations of other famous graves.

5. Jefferson Pools ★★★

Warm Springs
At the intersection of Va. 39 and U.S. 220.
T: 540-839-5346
$12 per hour

Located forty-two miles west of Lexington are two wooden bathhouses (one for men and one for women), dating back to Colonial days. The spring-fed warm pools found inside the houses have soothed weary bones dating back to George Washington's. Lee, Jackson, and their wives have soaked in the waters. This simple relaxation may be the best $12 you ever spend in a historic site, but be forewarned—bathing is by Colonial custom, which means it is acceptable for the less inhibited to go "clothing optional."

6. Confederate Statue at Courthouse Square ★

Monterey
43 miles west of Staunton off I-81 on U.S. 250 and 30 miles north of Warm Springs on U.S. 220.

Although nothing significant happened in this little town at the intersection of U.S. 220 and U.S. 250 on the western slope of the Allegheny Mountains, it is worth the trip to see the Confederate statue downtown. The stone Confederate is holding a bolt-action, magazine-fed rifle, a weapon that was not invented until decades after the war was over. The stone carver created the statue in 1918 during World War I when bolt-action rifles were available for

models. It is certainly the worst mistake
made in a statue on any courthouse square.

7. Battle of McDowell ★★

11 miles east of Monterey on U.S. 250
and 34 miles east of Staunton off I-81.

One of Stonewall Jackson's 1862 Valley
Campaign victories came on May 8, 1862,
at McDowell, which was actually fought on
top of Stitlington Hill. It can be reached
by hiking up from the roadside stop on the
side of U.S. 250 just east of McDowell
itself. The hike is steep and not recom-
mended for anyone but the most dedicated enthusiast who carries water. It can
take an hour to complete the round trip.
Still, anyone who makes this trek will have
a better appreciation of how strenuous
fighting in the mountains was.

8. Battle of Port Republic: The Coaling ★★★★

13 miles east of Harrisonburg off I-81, 3
miles north of the village of Grottoes on
U.S. 340, and 1.5 miles north of the
intersection of U.S. 340 and C.R. 659.

Watch for historic markers beside Grace
Episcopal Memorial Church on U.S. 340.
The hill to the left of the church is the
Coaling, the high ground that was the
scene of desperate fighting on June 9,
1862. Perched on this hill was a Union
cannon battery that was eventually taken
by Louisiana troops. An eyewitness
described how the blood of screaming
artillery horses, their throats cut to keep
them from being used to move the cannons,
mixed with the blood of the men trying to
take the cannons. The blood of men and
horses ran down the hill in rivulets. More
than 300 men, mostly from Louisiana and
Ohio, died on this hill. Jackson was so
moved by the struggle of the Louisianans
to take the cannons that he ordered that
the guns be forever named the Louisiana
Battery. The Confederates won both this
fight and the main battle.

9. Downtown Port Republic ★★

Two miles west of the intersection of U.S.
340 (south from the Coaling) and C.R.
659 is the village of Port Republic, which
actually saw little fighting in its streets.
Stonewall Jackson was almost captured in
this tiny village when a Union cavalry
patrol successfully crossed the river during
a raid preceding the battle that would center around the Coaling.

The yellow house located on the right of
C.R. 659 just after you enter the village is
the Port Republic Museum, which is open
on Sundays from 1:30 to 4 p.m. If you
walk up to the porch and peer in the window, you will see the life-size photo blow-
up of Confederate General Turner Ashby
lying in a wooden casket. Jackson spent
considerable time in that front room praying over the body of Ashby, who had been
killed on June 6 just east of Harrisonburg.
His photo was taken soon afterward.
Ashby had been Jackson's chief of cavalry
and, like Jackson, was lost to the
Confederacy at the height of his career.

10. Battle of New Market ★★★

Exit 264 off I-81, then S.R. 211 West.
New Market State Battlefield State
Historical Park and Hall of Valor Museum
8895 George Collins Pkwy, New Market
T: 866-515-1864
Daily, 9 a.m.–5 p.m. Closed major holidays.
Admission: $8

This battlefield is sacred ground for the
cadets of the Virginia Military Institute.
Forced to call up the teenagers to repel a
strong Union force coming down the Pike,
Confederate General John C. Breckinridge,
a former U.S. vice president, reluctantly
threw the boys into combat on May 15,
1864. Of the 254 cadets engaged, ten
died (including a collateral cousin of this
author). They are still honored on the campus in Lexington. Preserved on this 300-
acre state park is the Bushong Farm,

behind which was a Union cannon battery the cadets attacked. Many boys lost their shoes in the soggy ground in front of the cannons—a field now known as the Field of Lost Shoes.

11. Our Soldiers Cemetery ★

Mount Jackson
North side of the town on U.S. 11.

This small Confederate cemetery where the dead from a nearby hospital are buried is not remarkable so much for size or the number of men who are buried here. Rather, it is worthwhile for the statue of the mourning soldier, his eyes downcast and his hat off his head in respect. This evocative marble tribute depicts the sadness that many Southerners still feel at the loss of the lives of so many during the war.

12. Battle of Cedar Creek ★★★★★

Middletown
Cedar Creek Battlefield Foundation Visitor Center
8437 Valley Pike, Middletown
T: 540-869-2064

In the 1980s this battlefield was going to be paved over and turned into an industrial park. Preservationists rallied and purchased several hundred acres of the battlefield, on which a reenactment takes place each October close to the original battle date of October 19, 1864.

Early that morning Confederate forces under General Jubal Early caught the Federals napping and completely routed them. Rather than pursue the fleeing Federals, hungry Confederates stopped to eat their cooking breakfasts. Later that day, Union General Phil Sheridan, who had heard the fighting, rallied his men and led them back onto the battlefield to defeat the Confederates in a second battle over the same ground. Although there is not a great deal to see at this battlefield (there are no monuments like those gener-

ally found at National Battlefields), purists will enjoy the opportunity to see the lay of the land just as the combatants saw it (if you can ignore the warehouses looming over the killing fields).

13. Belle Grove Plantation ★★★★★

336 Belle Grove Rd., Middletown
T: 540-869-2028
Daily, April–October;
Monday–Saturday, 10:15 a.m.–3:15 p.m.;
Sunday, 1:15–4:15 p.m.
Tours begin 15 minutes after each hour
Admission: $7

This 1797 plantation was the scene of heavy fighting during the Battle of Cedar Creek on October 19, 1864, when the Confederates swarmed out of the creek bottom to envelop the Federals camped around the house. The Federals ran from the house. Later in the day, Confederate General Stephen Dodson Ramsuer of North Carolina was severely wounded through the lungs and brought here. He died in the library, hours after he had learned his wife had given birth to their first child. At Ramseur's side at his death were his three best friends from West Point—all high-ranking Union officers, including General George Custer.

14. Stonewall Jackson's Headquarters Museum ★★★★★

415 Braddock St., Winchester
T: 540-667-3242
April–October, Monday–Saturday, 10 a.m.–4 p.m.; Sunday, noon–4 p.m.
November–March, Friday–Saturday, 10 a.m.–4 p.m.; Sunday, noon–4 p. m.
Admission: $5

This small, city-owned museum was Jackson's headquarters in the winter of 1861–1862. It was here that Jackson planned his infamous Romney campaign. Also, here on a table still in the house, is where he signed his week-long resignation from the Confederate army when the

Confederate Secretary of War criticized Jackson's conduct after the Romney campaign. That campaign, conducted in killing cold weather, snow, and ice storms, left officers and troops temporarily under Jackson's command exhausted and angry at the way he had used them in contrast to the way he handled his own beloved First Virginia Brigade. This simple, no-frills museum was restored thanks to help from actress Mary Tyler Moore, whose Confederate ancestor once owned it.

15. Old Court House Civil War Museum
★★★

20 North Loudoun St., Winchester
T: 540-542-1145
Friday–Saturday, 10 a.m.–5 p.m.;
Sunday, 1–5 p.m.
Admission: $3

Aside from the collection of artifacts, this relatively new museum has preserved graffiti on its walls written by both sides, including a curse written by a Union soldier directed at Confederate President Jefferson Davis.

GETTING TO AND AROUND SHENANDOAH

Roanoke Regional Airport on the south end, and Shenandoah Valley Regional Airport near Harrisonburg in the center, are the two best access points into the Shenandoah Valley. Washington's Dulles International Airport, about fifty miles east of Winchester on the north end of the valley, is the closest large airport.

The only logical way to see the valley and its battlefields is by car. Sports enthusiasts with a lot of time could do it on bicycles if they stick to U.S. 11, the former Valley Pike. U.S. 11 parallels I-81 from one end of the valley to the other. Rarely is U.S. 11 more than a mile from the · interstate, and the towns and villages are generally no more than ten miles apart.

Because it is a valley, the terrain is relatively flat, but there is the occasional steep incline. Most of the high-speed traffic sticks to the interstate.

If you tire of battlefields in the valley, climb up the Blue Ridge Mountains and drive along Skyline Drive, part of which is contained in the Shenandoah National Park. Admission to the Park is $10, essentially making the Skyline Drive a scenic toll road that is a continuation of the famous—and free—Blue Ridge Parkway, which starts in North Carolina. One disadvantage of driving the mountain road is that the valley is often obscured by pollution floating down into the region from Midwestern and Northeastern factories and population centers.

If you drive along the ridges, you will likely have to come back down to the valley for gasoline, food, and lodging. Speed limits are kept to 45 mph in most sections.

Accommodations

Alexander-Withrow House

11 North Main St., Lexington,
www.lexingtonhistoricinns.com/alexander.htm
T: 877-283-9680
7 rooms
$90–$175

The Alexander-Withrow House was a bank in the 1850s, on the board of which Professor Thomas J. Jackson served. It has suites, one with a Jacuzzi.

The McCampbell Inn

11 North Main St., Lexington
www.lexingtonhistoricinns.com/mccampbell.htm
T: 877-283-9680
16 rooms
$90–$180

Once known as the Central Hotel, the McCampbell Inn hosted both Professor Thomas J. Jackson and former General Robert E. Lee when they first moved to Lexington. The same company owns both the McCampbell and the Alexander Withrow House.

Killahevlin Bed and Breakfast

1401 North Royal Ave., Front Royal
T: 540-636-7335
www.vairish.com
4 rooms
$145–$185

This four-room, two-suite bed and breakfast is not from the Civil War period, but the ground on which it rests was the spot where a Union general hanged two partisan rangers under the command of the Gray Ghost, Confederate Colonel John Singleton Mosby.

Candlewick Inn, LLC

127 North Church St., Woodstock
T: 540-459-8008
www.candlewickinnllc.com
5 rooms
$100–$180

This inn is housed in a house built before the Civil War, and it is near the site of a cavalry fight that occurred near the end of the war.

Sources & Other Reading

Stonewall Jackson, James Robertson, Macmillan Publishing, 1997.
Stonewall in the Valley, Robert G. Tanner, Doubleday & Company, 1976.
They Called Him Stonewall, Burke Davis, Wings Books, 1988.
The Burning, John L. Heatwole, Rockbridge Publishing, 1998.
From Winchester to Cedar Creek, Jeffrey Wert, Stackpole Publishing, 1997.
The Life and Wars of General Phil Sheridan, Roy Morris Jr., Vintage Press, 1993.
Struggle for the Shenandoah, Gary Gallagher, Kent State Press, 1991.

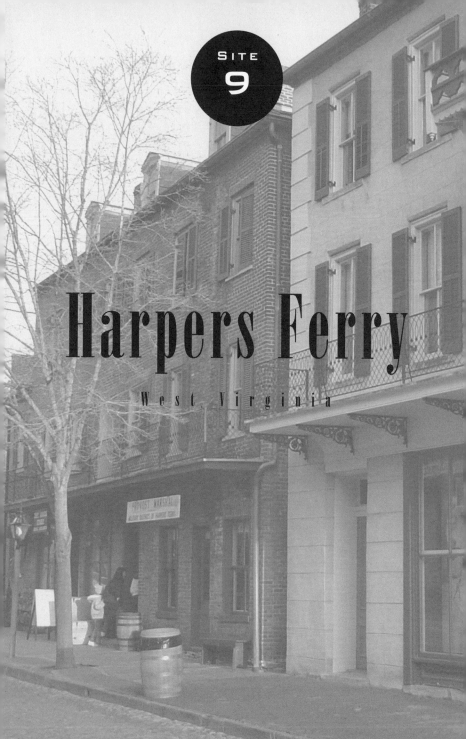

SITE
9

Harpers Ferry

West Virginia

Shenandoah Street in downtown Harpers Ferry looks as if it is still 1859.

THE WAR YEARS

E xcept for dodging the occasional car, walking the cobblestones of Harpers Ferry is like stepping back into 1859. This historic park tries hard to put visitors into the antebellum days when all the angry talk about secession was turning into a reality. It is like a living history park except without costumed interpreters.

Harpers Ferry, Virginia (West Virginia since that state was formed in 1863), was a town in the midst of experiencing how progress could kill one industry (river-barge shipping) while creating another (railroad shipping), when it was suddenly thrust into the national spotlight in October 1859. After a few months in the headlines that year it again faded from the public eye. Except for its one-day capture in September, 1862, the town would never again find itself in the national news. But what happened over two days in 1859 set the stage for the confrontation and conflagration that would come on April 12, 1861. Some might say that the American Civil War, at least the perception of war, started in Harpers Ferry a full one-and-a-half years before the real shooting started in Charleston, South Carolina.

Harpers Ferry is in a strange place for a town from a practical point of view and an absolutely horrendous place for a town from a military perspective. The town was founded in the late eighteenth century at the confluence of two rivers, the Potomac and the Shenandoah, both of which flooded on occasion then and still do now. Harpers Ferry residents just live with the understanding that sometimes the two rivers that flow on either side of the town actually come through the town itself.

Thomas Jefferson wrote that the area where these two rivers merge in this valley is one of the most beautiful places on earth, but that is not why there is a town at this most unlikely of spots. It was President George Washington in 1794 who insisted that a new national armory be built upriver from the new national capital. (It may not have been pure coincidence that the father of the country was a stockholder in a company that held development rights to just the spot of land where Harpers Ferry was surveyed.)

Investor Washington may have liked the site of Harpers Ferry, but General Washington would have hated it. It was built on a triangle of land jutting into the confluence of the rivers. On all three sides were heights looking down on the town, heights that enemy artillerymen would love to use as gun emplacements. Those same mountains kept the town isolated except for the mule-barge traffic passing by on the Chesapeake and Ohio barge canal.

On October 17, 1859, Harpers Ferry found itself invaded by twenty-two men who occupied the United States Arsenal, then proclaimed that they were the first wave of a slave revolt that was about to erupt throughout Virginia. The white citizens of Harpers Ferry were puzzled at the claim. That part of the state had few slaves, as the rocky land was unsuitable for the large-plot cultivation of crops like cotton and tobacco. The black slaves who did live in the area were puzzled too. They were in no mood to revolt, so the raiders took some of them prisoner alongside some prominent white people, including the nephew of George Washington.

The attack was led by John Brown, a well-known radical and violent abolitionist who had murdered some proslavery settlers in Kansas a few years earlier in an attempt to influence Kansas citizens' vote on whether they wanted to be admitted into the Union as a slave or free state. Brown's attack did not go well. Instead of staying in the armory where they controlled plenty of weapons, the raiders ran to a fire-engine house, which had windows that were too high to use as gun ports. Citizens shot down several raiders as an act of revenge for their shooting of five Harpers Ferry residents, including a popular free black railroad stationmaster.

Alarmed telegraphs to Washington warning about slave revolts brought help in the form of a Lieutenant Colonel Robert E. Lee and Lieutenant J.E.B. Stuart, who rushed to the scene by special train. When local militiamen refused to fight, Lee, a regular U.S. Army officer, took over command of a detachment of U.S. Marines, who had no problems following orders from a rival service officer. The next morning Stuart approached the engine house. He recognized Brown from an earlier encounter with the abolitionist in Kansas when the U.S. Army had disarmed him.

At Stuart's signal, the Marines rushed the engine house and captured Brown and his remaining followers. Brown was tried and sentenced to death for treason in December of that year. On his way to the gallows Brown made a prophetic statement: "The crimes of this guilty land will never be purged away but with blood." Judging by his actions and words, it seems that Brown was more intent on creating an incident at Harpers Ferry to call attention to slavery and abolition than actually launching a major slave revolt.

Just as Brown predicted, the war came in April of 1861. As soon as Virginia seceded, the evacuating Federal troops posted to the Harpers Ferry arsenal set fire to it. At least 15,000 rifles were lost to the new Confederacy, but the equipment to manufacture the rifles was saved and shipped further south to form the nucleus of the Confederate arms-manufacturing industry. The Confederacy abandoned the town not long afterward.

Harpers Ferry figured prominently in 1862 when Union General John Wool ordered its garrison to defend the town to the last man rather than evacuate in the face of Lee's invasion of Maryland. The threat of the presence of that garrison at his rear forced Lee to split his forces and send Stonewall Jackson to capture the town. Jackson's men occupied the heights around the town and easily captured it after some shelling. Jackson took some supplies, paroled the captured Union garrison, and rushed off to rejoin Lee.

Wool's expectation that having to deal with Harpers Ferry would slow down Lee's invasion of the North was fulfilled. Harpers Ferry stopped Lee's progress for several days, allowing George McClellan's Army of the Potomac to catch up to him and forcing Lee to fight at Sharpsburg, Maryland, about twenty-two miles north of Harpers Ferry. Had the Harpers Ferry garrison not been a factor, Lee might have rushed deep into Pennsylvania, possibly capturing Philadelphia or Harrisburg.

Harpers Ferry would not play a major role for the rest of the war. It was indefensible and unimportant to both sides.

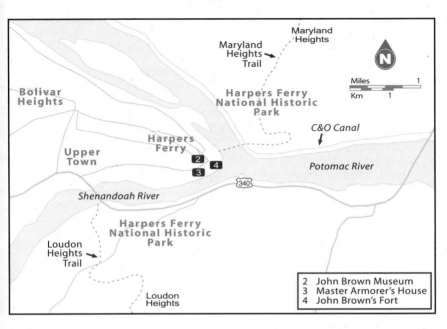

Maryland Heights

Maryland Heights Trail

Harpers Ferry National Historic Park

Bolivar Heights

Miles 1

Km 1

C&O Canal

Harpers Ferry

Upper Town

Potomac River

2
3 4

340

Shenandoah River

Harpers Ferry National Historic Park

Loudon Heights Trail

Loudon Heights

2   John Brown Museum
3   Master Armorer's House
4   John Brown's Fort

HARPERS FERRY TODAY

Harpers Ferry today is in a unique situation: it is a real town with a historic park at its core. Step a few blocks away from the National Park Service museums on Shenandoah Street and one finds shops and restaurants catering to tourists. Go a few more blocks and there are residents living in antebellum homes.

Traffic is light on the cobblestone streets, thanks to limited parking in the historic area and the convenience of the shuttle bus that runs from the visitor center on U.S. 340. This helps visitors appreciate the feel of the 1859-era town. Every sign on the historic buildings looks like it was designed in the antebellum period. It is not hard at all to imagine looking up and seeing John Brown and his raiders walking across the railroad bridge over the Potomac and coming into town. The armory, their target, is no longer standing, but the same streets on which the townspeople fought back until military help could arrive have not changed much at all.

POINTS OF INTEREST

1. Harpers Ferry National Historic Park
★★★★★

Shenandoah St.
T: 304-535-6029
Daily, 8 a.m.–6 p.m. Winter hours: closes
at 5 p.m. Closed major holidays.
Admission: $6

Obtain a map from the visitor center that
will describe what is found in each of the
historic buildings, most of which are along
Shenandoah Street. Be sure to take a walk
along the riverfront. There are a number of
historic markers explaining what used to
be in those spaces and what Harpers Ferry
was like both before and during the war.

2. John Brown Museum ★★★★★

Most of the buildings on Shenandoah can
be defined as museums, the most important and interesting of which is the John
Brown Museum. This museum traces the
origins of Brown's interest in abolition
right through his trial and hanging in nearby Charles Town. Photographs of each of
the twenty-two raiders are displayed with
short biographies accompanying them.
The museum includes some valuable artifacts, including the doors that were on the
firehouse in which Brown barricaded himself. Among the artifacts are some pikes,
long poles with iron knives attached to
their ends. Though Brown's raid was gen-
erously financed by the Secret Six abolitionists, who bought him the latest
breech-loading Sharps carbines, which
had not yet even been issued to most U.S.
cavalry units, Brown preferred arming
slaves with pikes. Of all the museums
found in Harpers Ferry, the John Brown
Museum is the best and a must for anyone
interested in the role the town played.

3. Master Armorer's House ★★★★★

This museum describes the armory at
Harpers Ferry, which Union troops burned

once Virginia seceded. The armory was
state-of-the-art for its day, turning out military muskets and pistols that were used
to arm the military and the militias scattered around the states. In its sixty years
of production before its destruction, the
armory produced nearly 600,000 weapons.
Another entrepreneur, John Hall, also
owned a nearby factory that produced Hall
rifles and carbines. It was Hall who perfected the idea of using interchangeable
parts to manufacture his rifles—the basis
for all of manufacturing today. During
John Brown's raid, Lieutenant Colonel
Robert E. Lee and Lieutenant J.E.B.
Stuart made this house their headquarters.

4. John Brown's Fort ★★★★★

Moved about 100 feet from its original
location and reconstructed, this building is
not from the Civil War period, but it is
close enough to merit study. After aban-
doning the armory when the townspeople
began to fight back, Brown and his surviving raiders barricaded themselves in the
town's firehouse—perhaps the most indefensible building in the whole town. The
windows in the firehouse are so high off
the ground that anyone inside would need
ladders just to see outside, not to mention
fire on any attackers. Common sense says
that the raiders should have stayed in the
armory with its unlimited supply of
weapons and gunpowder, but Brown
pushed them into the open to make a mad
dash for the tiny firehouse.

It has been thought by some that Brown's
tactics of purposefully telling a train crew
passing through town that he was leading
a slave revolt, splitting his meager forces,
taking prominent hostages, and then hol-
ing up in a place guaranteed to be overwhelmed indicate that he perhaps *wanted*
the raid to fail. Even his choice of Harpers
Ferry is suspect. There were few slaves in

that area of the state. Brown knew the raid itself would cause nationwide news, so one can speculate that the real purpose of the raid was to make himself and his men martyrs to abolition rather than to launch a real slave revolt.

5. Meriwether Lewis's Visit ★★★

While the park focuses on John Brown's raid in 1859, the town has other historical significance as well. Meriwether Lewis, one-half of the Lewis and Clark team assigned by President Thomas Jefferson to explore the Louisiana Purchase in 1803, picked up the expedition's weapons from the armory here. He also picked up the folding metal ribs of a collapsible boat he hoped to use for the many river crossings he knew lay ahead of the expedition. The iron-ribbed boat never worked, as Lewis could never stretch the animal skins around it tightly enough so it would not leak. But the idea of a collapsible boat shows that Lewis and Clark were both interested in testing new technology in a new territory. The exhibit room on Lewis's short stay in Harpers Ferry is designed to replicate what a storage room of the supplies he gathered might have looked like.

6. Niagara Movement ★★★

In 1906 the town hosted the first meeting of the Niagara Movement, a forerunner of the NAACP, where prominent black people came to a conference held at Storer College. The result of the conference was a call for equal treatment for blacks and whites, a cause that was made better known by the NAACP, founded in 1909.

7. Upper Town ★★★

If your heart and knees are up for it, a very steep sidewalk leads to the "upper town," the second tier of the historic district, where a Catholic church is under restoration. Continue walking past the church to find Jefferson Rock. Tradition says that Jefferson sat on the rock and contemplated the confluence of the two rivers, which, he thought, made the valley one of the most beautiful spots on earth, one so beautiful that "it is worth a trip across the Atlantic" just to see it. (The road noise from U.S. 340 was not present in Jefferson's day, but it is distracting enough now that any thought of this being the quietest spot on earth is dispelled.)

8. Maryland Heights ★★★

The most common photograph of Harpers Ferry is taken from Maryland Heights, the high ground directly across the Potomac River from the town. Get a map of the trail from the rangers and take a bottle of water. The trail to the top of Heights is reached by crossing the railroad bridge, then turning left and following the remnants of the C&O Canal. Watch on the right for the trail. The trail is not particularly steep, but it is best undertaken by people used to walking. The hike can take forty-five minutes, but once you're at the top, the view of Harpers Ferry is spectacular, as one can see the Shenandoah and Potomac Rivers flowing from the distance and then meeting at the point where the town was built. One word of warning: The weather in Harpers Ferry may be mild, but the weather atop Maryland Heights may be damp and windy. If you're going in the fall or spring, take a jacket.

During the war both Union and Confederate armies had forces up here. In fact, Stonewall Jackson put cannons and men on the Heights very early in the war without orders. He was questioned about his actions by Richmond politicians who were worried that putting Confederate forces into Maryland would anger the residents of that state. At that time, the Confederacy was still hoping that Maryland would see itself as a Southern state and secede, so they did not want to anger the locals with a premature Southern "invasion." President Lincoln took care of the possibility of the state seceding by jailing a large portion of the Maryland legislature so they could not meet for a secession vote. It was also up this same trail that a number of Union cavalrymen were able to escape capture when Jackson took the town in September 1862. A loop trail on top of the Heights leads to some of those still-existing Union emplacements.

9. C&O Canal ★★★★

T: 301-739-4200

One of the most popular parks in the Washington, D.C., area is this gravel path running along the Potomac and what is left of the C&O Canal. This path runs 185 miles from downtown Georgetown, the tony part of Washington, out to Cumberland, Maryland, the end point of the canal. The C&O was finally killed off by the efficiency and superior freight-hauling capacity of the Baltimore & Ohio Railroad. Use of the canal peaked in 1871, though it was still used into the 1920s. On any spring, summer, or fall weekend, hikers share this path with bicyclists, many of whom set out with a goal of biking the whole canal length in one day. Call the C&O ranger office to check on conditions before setting out. Sometimes sections of the canal are closed for repairs.

10. Bolivar Heights ★★

Located just across the road from the visitor center, Bolivar Heights is where many of the Union troops were when Jackson's guns opened up. The Union commander of the town, Colonel Dixon Miles, was killed here by a Confederate shell just after he had made the decision to surrender the town. Miles remains a controversial figure. Some historians believe he was a hopeless alcoholic who poorly managed his command; rumor has it that Miles was drunk when he was killed. Others think of Miles as a man who realized he could not win against overwhelming forces, so surrender would save the lives of his garrison. This part of the park is a flat walking tour outlining artillery positions.

11. Loudon Heights ★

A trail leads from Harpers Ferry up to the top of Loudon Heights. The Appalachian Trail also comes down off the ridge and continues through Harpers Ferry. It is not uncommon to see men and women with huge packs on their backs in the streets of Harpers Ferry. Jackson also captured this ridge. The cannon shot that killed Miles was fired from here.

GETTING TO AND AROUND HARPERS FERRY

The two nearest major airports are Dulles International and Washington Reagan National, with dozens of flights operating in and out of both. Dulles is closer by about thirty miles to Harpers Ferry. Washington's notoriously snarled traffic might also make Dulles a better choice. Another nearby airport is Baltimore Washington Airport. Be aware that all of the airports are located near heavily congested interstate highways.

Harpers Ferry may be the only national park that can be reached easily by train. A commuter station sits beside the his-

toric downtown. The park is about a one-hour train ride from Washington's Union Station, which also connects with Reagan National Airport by Metrorail. That means an airline passenger could pick up the subway, then a commuter train for a weekend at Harpers Ferry (if arriving on a Friday and leaving on a Monday). Midwestern tourists could board the train in Chicago and get off in Harpers Ferry.

The only practical way to get around Harpers Ferry is to walk. However, even though the bed and breakfasts in Harpers

Ferry are within walking distance of the historic district, the hills on which the houses are located are steep. It might be better to drive to the visitor center, pay the entrance fee, and ride the bus down to the historic site. All of the restaurants and tourist shops are on side streets away from the historic district.

Day packs and water bottles will be necessary for hikers who want to explore the heights above Harpers Ferry. One could spend several hours hiking on the Appalachian Trail, which passes through town, and then taking side hikes up to Maryland Heights and Loudon Heights. Maps are available at the ranger station.

ACCOMMODATIONS

The Jackson Rose Bed & Breakfast

1141 Washington St., Harpers Ferry
T: 304-535-1528
www.jacksonrose.com/index.htm
3 rooms
$95–$115

The owners believe this building dating back to 1795 was Stonewall Jackson's headquarters when he was assigned to defend Harpers Ferry in April 1861. He wrote his wife a letter describing the garden's beautiful roses. This house is within walking distance of the historic downtown.

Biscoe House Bed & Breakfast

828 Washington St., Harpers Ferry
T: 304-535-2416
www.bbonline.com/wv/briscoe/index.html
2 rooms
$100–$110

You can see mountains from this bed and breakfast in a 100-year-old house half a mile from the historic district.

Harpers Ferry Guest House

800 Washington St., Harpers Ferry
T: 304-535-6955
www.harpersferryguesthouse.com
3 rooms
$95–$110

This house was only built in 1992, but was constructed to look like a nineteenth-century house so that it blends into the neighborhood.

The Angler's Inn

867 Washington St., Harpers Ferry
T: 304-535-1239
www.theanglersinn.com
4 rooms
$85–$165

The name says it all. Fishing in streams and rivers is the focus of this property, though it is located just blocks from the historic area. The bed and breakfast will arrange fishing guides if guests would like to head out.

SOURCES & OTHER READING

Six Years of Hell: Harpers Ferry during the Civil War, Chester Hern, Louisiana State University, 1999.

John Brown and His Men, Richard Hinton, Ayer Company Publishing, 1968.

The Secret Six: The True Tale of the Men Who Conspired with John Brown, Edward Renehan, University of South Carolina Press, 1997.

To Purse This Land with Blood: A Biography of John Brown, Stephen Oates, University of Massachusetts Press, 1984.

John Brown: The Legend Revisited, Merrill Peterson, University of Virginia Press, 2002.

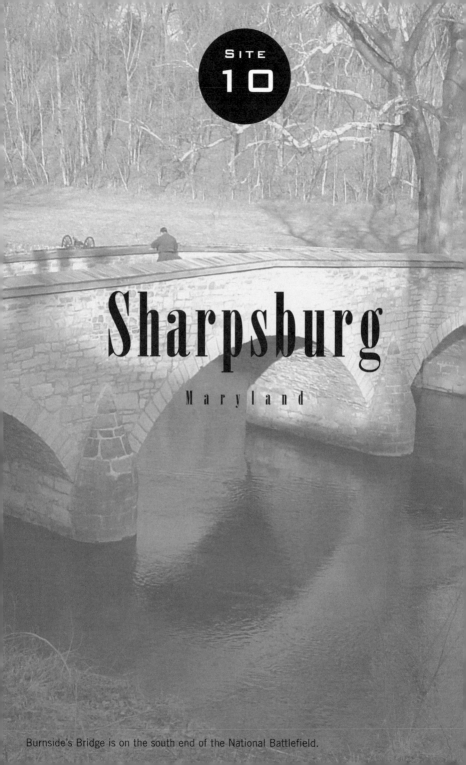

SITE
10

Sharpsburg

M a r y l a n d

Burnside's Bridge is on the south end of the National Battlefield.

THE WAR YEARS

T here is no better Civil War battlefield to study than Sharpsburg (Southern name) or Antietam (Northern name). Most of the compact battlefield is on National Park land. The battle took place in three stages at three different places on the field and at three different times of the day, making it easy to follow and understand.

Sharpsburg, a tiny farming village four miles north of the Potomac River, had absolutely no military significance, so its residents were stunned on the evening of September 16, 1862, as they watched thousands of Confederate soldiers forming battle lines east of the town. What in the world did they have that was worth defending? The citizens were right. Sharpsburg had nothing of monetary value that the Confederates would want. All the town had was woods, hills, sunken farm roads, and Antietam Creek. Actually, Lee wanted to defend his 40,000-man army from the onrushing 87,000-man Army of the Potomac under General George McClellan.

The Battle of Sharpsburg never should have happened. In early September, immediately after he had trounced Union General John Pope at Second Manassas, Lee proposed taking his army through Maryland and into Pennsylvania. The plan had many goals: remove any threat that the Union army might march into Virginia during the fall harvest; prove to skeptical foreign leaders that the Confederacy could launch major offenses on northern soil other than its own; and perhaps influence the upcoming November 1862 Congressional elections once the Northern populace saw war on its own doorstep.

The plan was simple. First, rush through Maryland, a slave-holding state forced to stay in the Union by Federal intervention in its state affairs. Second, plunge deep into the heart of Pennsylvania and capture some major city like the state capital of Harrisburg. Along the way, the Army of Northern Virginia would recruit new troops from among thousands of sympathetic Marylanders who had not had the chance to express their loyalty to the South.

Lee's plan started unraveling when an unexpected development materialized as he gathered his generals for a strategy meeting in Frederick, Maryland. Against all military logic, the isolated Union garrison at Harpers Ferry had not been withdrawn by its commander, General John Wool, who was back in Washington. Lee could not leave the Federal garrison at his rear to attack his supply lines as he ventured into Pennsylvania. He would have to stop his advance and take it out. To eliminate Harpers Ferry without forcing his entire army to backtrack, Lee split his forces into four parts: two parts to surround Harpers Ferry, one part to protect the passes on South Mountain through which McClellan would eventually pursue him, and one part around which the other three would gather once they'd accomplished their mission.

Disaster now struck. Union soldiers discovered an extra copy of the order splitting the army left on the ground several days after Lee had broken camp. History has never determined who lost the order, but it wound up in the hands of McClellan, who waved it around, saying that now he could defeat "Bobby Lee." Lee learned the same day that McClellan had the order, from a loyal Southerner who had been in McClellan's camp when the "Lost Orders" were delivered.

It was now too late for Lee to stop the splitting of his army, because Jackson and McLaws were already on their way to Harpers Ferry. Lee sent word to D.H. Hill, ordered to watch South Mountain's passes, that he would have to fight until he could hold no longer. Everything depended on Hill's buying time so that Jackson and McLaws could return from capturing Harpers Ferry. Once that was accomplished, Jackson and McLaws and a retreating Hill would be able to re-form with Lee east of Sharpsburg where Lee had found the hills and Antietam Creek, which would form the anchors of his lines.

It was a dangerous strategy. Once Lee realized that McClellan had his complete campaign strategy in front of him, Lee could have retreated immediately back across the Potomac River before McClellan's forces arrived. Instead, Lee chose to do battle in hopes of slapping the Federals on northern soil. But that meant that if McClellan breached Lee's lines, there was no escape. The Potomac River was at Lee's back. McClellan's army, twice the size of Lee's, had more than enough men to push Lee's into the water.

Before Sharpsburg, there was the Battle of South Mountain, Maryland. Fought on September 14 to slow McClellan's advance on the rest of Lee's army, the battle pitted D.H. Hill's five-brigade division holding two mountain passes against four Union corps, consisting of thirty-two brigades arranged in twelve divisions. The eventual winner of the battle was never in any doubt, but Hill's men, consisting mostly of North Carolina regiments, put up an all-day, last-stand defense that bought Jackson and McLaws time to capture Harpers Ferry and Lee time to scout out the potential of setting up defenses at Sharpsburg. Jackson would arrive to join Lee on the afternoon of September 16. McLaws would arrive on the morning of September 17.

When McClellan was finally ready to fight on the morning of September 17, Lee had most of the four pieces of his army in place. The only piece missing was the 3,000 men of General A.P. Hill's Light Division. Hill had stayed behind in Harpers Ferry to gather supplies. Just as the battle was starting at dawn, Hill and his men were beginning a seventeen-mile march to join it.

The Battle of Sharpsburg began on the Confederate left flank with two corps of Federals rushing from the East Woods with their march aimed at the little white Dunker Meeting House in front of the West Woods. Midway across the field was Miller's Cornfield, which was almost ready for harvesting. Back and forth the two sides fought through Miller's Cornfield until every stalk was stomped flat or cut down by musket fire. At several points the Federals pushed deep into the West Woods, but each time fierce Confederate counterattacks pushed them back. Though outnumbered on the left by at least three to one, the Confederates held and the Federals withdrew. The battle went into a lull.

The second phase of the battle now began in the center, as Federals began marching toward a farm road that had been used so much it had sunk below the ground surface. The Confederates, perhaps unwisely, posted themselves down in the road, using it as a trench, but the advancing Federals were able to fire down into the road, giving them some advantage. A mistaken order pulled some Confederates out of the Sunken Road, which opened the way on the left for Federals to climb into the road and shoot down its length. With their left now gone, the Confederates finally abandoned the Sunken Road,

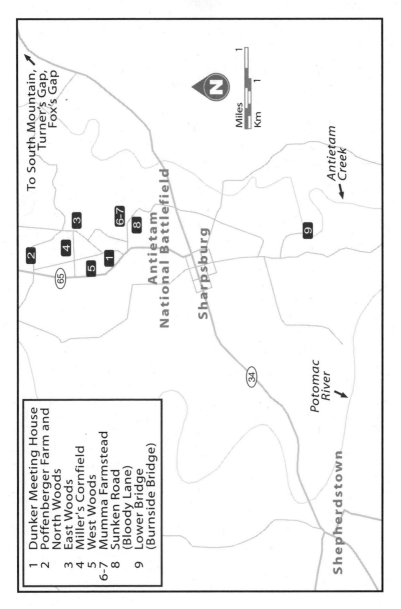

To South Mountain, Turner's Gap, Fox's Gap

Antietam Creek

Antietam National Battlefield

Sharpsburg

Miles
Km

Potomac River

Shepherdstown

1 Dunker Meeting House
2 Poffenberger Farm and North Woods
3 East Woods
4 Miller's Cornfield
5 West Woods
6-7 Mumma Farmstead
8 Sunken Road (Bloody Lane)
9 Lower Bridge (Burnside Bridge)

which history would remember as the Bloody Lane. Confederate bodies would be so plentiful that one Union officer demonstrated he could walk the length of the road without actually stepping on the ground. The battle now went into its second lull.

With the day moving into the afternoon, the battle shifted to the Confederate right flank. There was a stone bridge over Antietam Creek that the Ninth Corps under Ambrose Burnside wanted. All afternoon, Burnside tried to take that bridge. Defending it were no more than 500 Georgians, who were facing Burnside's 12,000 men. Ignoring pleas to look for another crossing, Burnside stubbornly kept after the bridge until the Georgians finally retreated. Burnside had wasted hours in taking a bridge. After the battle, angry soldiers demonstrated that the creek was no more than knee deep in most places.

With Burnside's corps finally over Antietam Creek, Lee's army was in deep trouble. McClellan's superior numbers were finally coming to bear on his thin line. As Burnside bore down on the remainder of Lee's battered army, the Federals ignored a blue-clad column coming at the double-quick from the south. The Yankees assumed it was another Federal unit wanting in on the kill. Within minutes, that column had arrived and the blue-clads leveled 3,000 muskets at the Federals and let fly with several deadly volleys. The men in blue were A.P. Hill's Light Division, who were wearing Federal-issued overcoats in anticipation that they would need warm clothing for the coming fall. A stunned Burnside broke off his attack. Dusk had arrived. That day's battle was over.

In twelve daylight hours, the Federals had lost more than 2,000 killed, and the Confederates had lost 1,600. Total casualties of killed, wounded, and missing on both sides numbered more than 23,000, the highest total for any single-day battle in American history.

Lee stayed in place one more day, but McClellan did not attack. McClellan did not fight again until the last of Lee's units was crossing the Potomac at Pack Horse Ford. The bloodied but angry veterans of Lee's army virtually destroyed the green Union unit that was ordered to attack Lee's rear guard.

On paper, McClellan should have won Sharpsburg. He had at least twice as many men as Lee before the battle even began, but he had not even engaged two corps, more than 20,000 men. On September 18, McClellan could have fielded a fresh 50,000-man army, many of whom had fought very little the day before, against Lee's army, which had been reduced to 30,000 effectives. McClellan made no effort to make such an attack. It was this lack of action that caused Lincoln to replace McClellan in November.

SHARPSBURG TODAY

Sharpsburg today is not much larger than it was in September 1862, and the town itself did not see any fighting. Lee had his headquarters on what is now a small open park in the town, but there is little that is battle-related to see in the town itself. There are some bed and breakfasts in town, but visitors looking for a wider selection of restaurants will have to go to nearby Shepherdstown, Harpers Ferry, Charles Town in West Virginia, or Frederick, Maryland. Downtown Sharpsburg has a nice relic and art shop, but the shopping opportunities are few.

The National Park encompasses 3,200 acres just one mile east of town. All of the major landscape features of the battlefield are preserved or re-created with the exception of the thick East and West Woods, which are much smaller than they were at the time of the battle. In most years the famous Miller's Cornfield is planted and the stalks are just as high as they would have been on that bloody day.

Sharpsburg is one exception among National Parks in that the driving tour offered closely matches the chronological progress of the battle. (At most other parks the driving tour starts closest to the visitor center, and the battle usually cannot be followed chronologically.) This driving tour, sometimes matched by a ranger giving a personal talk about each phase of the battle, gives most visitors all they need to know to understand how the battle progressed throughout the day.

POINTS OF INTEREST

1. Antietam National Battlefield
★★★★★

1 mile east of downtown Sharpsburg
T: 301-432-5124
Daily, 8:30 a.m–6 p.m.
Winter hours shortened to 5 p.m.
Closed major holidays.
Admission: $4

Antietam's visitor center is perched on a hill overlooking the major portions of the battlefield, and its outside porch is an excellent place to get a sense of the land that Lee selected to defend his army. The only part of the line that cannot be seen from this vantage point is the far right where the stone bridge crosses Antietam Creek. While in the visitor center, look at the photos on display. Taken by Alexander Gardner, they can be matched up with battlefield features, a sobering link between the nineteenth and twenty-first centuries. One shot showing several Confederates beside a fence was taken on the Hagerstown Road near the turnoff for the visitor center parking lot. Another showing the Dunker Meeting House in the background was taken just west of the visitor center. When Gardner displayed all of his photographs in a New York City storefront, the populace was shocked. It was the first time any of them had seen a combat photograph.

Stop 1 ★★★★ is the Dunker Meeting House, which served as a church for a religious sect. Its whitewashed walls were prominent in the predawn darkness, and the Federals who were advancing from the north used it as a goal. The Federals advanced to this spot, virtually into the Confederate lines, before they were pushed back in savage fighting. The building actually survived the fighting, only to be brought down in a storm in 1928. The Park Service reconstructed it in 1962. Its simple wooden benches make a good place to contemplate the bloody battle visitors are about to tour.

Stop 2 ★★★★ is the Poffenberger Farm and the North Woods, where Joseph Hooker's First Corps launched its attack to open the battle.

Stop 3 ★★★ is the East Woods, where Joseph Mansfield's Twelfth Corps opened its attack. Both corps were aiming south through Miller's Cornfield toward the Dunker Meeting House. Luckily for Lee, the movement of both corps had been detected the previous night, so he was able to transfer some troops to bolster the Confederate left flank. That would be the key to Lee's success at Sharpsburg: being able to move troops from one end of the line where nothing was happening to another part of the line where combat was fierce. Mansfield, one of the oldest active generals in the field at 61, was killed early in the attack. Mansfield had been the boss of a young Lieutenant Robert E. Lee when Lee was assigned as an engineer at Fort Pulaski, Georgia.

Stop 4 ★★★★★ is Miller's Cornfield. Scores of men on both sides were cut down in this field, including General John Bell Hood's Texas Brigade, whose monument of red stone stands here.

Stop 5 ★★★ is the West Woods. Union General John Sedgwick lost more than 2,000 men when he advanced into these woods and discovered that he had Confederates on three sides of him. Sedgwick himself would be wounded in three places from three different directions. Sedgwick's men had been ordered to attack in the belief that the Confederates were on the run.

Stops 6 ★★ and **7 ★★** begin the second phase of the fighting. The Federals began advancing on the center of the Confederate line past the Mumma Farmstead. Many of the Yankees were city boys who had rarely been in the country. As they passed some large objects in the Mumma farmyard, they playfully knocked them over. It was only then that the city slickers realized what beehives look like. Much of the Federal line broke up until they could get out of range of the bees.

Stop 8 ★★★★★ is the center of the Sunken Road or Bloody Lane. Southern troops, mostly from Alabama and North Carolina, secured this part of the line, but they should have been lying in front of the road, not in the lower part of the road where the Federals were able to aim down at them. A walk up and down the road gives visitors a sense of how little the Confederates could have seen until the Federals were right on top of them. An observation tower at the southern end gives a bird's-eye view of the battlefield. Right outside the tower is a monument and history of the Irish Brigade, several brigades from New York and Massachusetts that were made up of Irish immigrants forced into service by the Union in exchange for promises of citizenship. The Irish Brigade fought well here and three months later at Fredericksburg, where they were badly cut up.

Stop 9 ★★★★★ is the Lower Bridge, now known as Burnside Bridge. It was there that a hardy little band of 500 Georgians, apparently all of them good shots with a rifle, held off an entire corps of Federals from taking the bridge. It was not until a general promised the corps a ration of whiskey for each that the Federals were motivated enough to rush across the bridge. Satisfied that they had held up the Yankees as long as possible, the Georgians left with few losses. A walk leads to a ford that Burnside's men could have easily crossed without even having to take the bridge. (Burnside would repeat his single-mindedness in trying to take this bridge in December when he insisted on taking Fredericksburg, Virginia by marching over pontoon bridges. Just like here, soldiers could easily have forded the Rappahannock River in several places without waiting for the pontoons.) One interesting monument here is to Sargent William McKinley, a future president of the U.S.

Stop 10 ★★ is the last stop at Sharpsburg. It was in this area that Burnside's corps was hit by A.P. Hill's Light Division, which was able to advance close to the Yankees because the men were wearing blue overcoats captured from Federal stores at Harpers Ferry. Burnside's corps, which had taken so long to cross Antietam Creek, took no time in retreating back across it.

2. South Mountain Turner's Gap ★★

From downtown Sharpsburg, head east on Md. 34 to Boonesboro. In Boonesboro, turn right onto Alternate U.S. 40 or Old National Pike. Follow it to the top of the mountain, which is the gap that Lee had to defend. Daylight hours.

Across from a stone restaurant are signs describing the fighting at Turner's Gap.

3. Fox's Gap ★★★★★

Daylight hours

From Turner's Gap, continue on Old National Pike toward Middletown, watching

on the right for a road called Reno Monument Road. Follow this road until it runs into Fox Gap Road. Turn right. Watch on the left for a clearing with a wrought-iron fence around a monument. This is Fox's Gap, where some of the heavier fighting occurred. Here Union General Jesse Reno and Confederate General Samuel Garland fell mortally wounded. Walk down the paved blacktop road for about seventy-five yards, following the wooden signs pointing to the North Carolina monument. Watch on the left for a path. About thirty yards off the road is a spectacular monument depicting a fallen Confederate color-bearer representing all of the Tar Heel troops who fought to defend the two gaps. The stone wall was a defensive position for the Confederates.

4. Shepherdstown ★★★

Retrace the route back to Sharpsburg, then head southwest on Md. 34. Downtown Shepherdstown is about five miles from Sharpsburg.

Just before crossing the Potomac River, you'll see the National Park headquarters for the C&O Canal on the right. It is really an office now, with nothing to see on the inside, but before the war, this was the home of Henry Kyd Douglas, a staff officer for Stonewall Jackson. Douglas wrote a memoir of his months with Jackson titled *I Rode With Stonewall.* While the book is a colorful look at Douglas's wartime career, it has been criticized as fanciful. Some historians believe it was Douglas who made a copy of—and then lost—the famed "Lost Orders" Lee drew up for the dividing of his army in order to capture Harpers Ferry just before the Sharpsburg Campaign. The circumstantial evidence does point to Douglas, but he never admitted to being the culprit.

Across from the headquarters is a road down to the C&O Canal, which sits beside the Potomac. Visitors with time will want to walk along the canal to think back on the early part of the nineteenth century when the canal was alive with activity. The path on which they now walk was the path on which mules pulled small barges up the river. The C&O is now one of the nation's most popular parks for bikers and runners.

Cross the river and park in downtown Shepherdstown. Most of the buildings date back to before the war and are now retail establishments and restaurants.

Follow the main street through Shepherdstown until it begins to hug the Potomac. Continue for several miles until coming on a historic marker for Pack Horse or Boetler's Ford. Here is where most of the Army of Northern Virginia crossed on its way to Sharpsburg. The army used the same ford again when it went to and from Gettysburg. This was the scene of a sharp fight after Sharpsburg when a very green Union unit attacked Lee's rear guard as it was crossing the river. The Confederate unit turned on the Yankees and cut them up.

GETTING TO AND AROUND SHARPSBURG

Dulles International, Baltimore Washington International, and Reagan National are the three major commercial airports near Sharpsburg, with Frederick Municipal Airport in Frederick, Maryland, being the closest private aircraft airport. As noted in other entries about Civil War sites in the sphere of Washington, D.C., the large commercial airports are served by traffic-choked interstates and highways.

When arriving at Antietam National Battlefield, walking or riding a bike are good ways to see the park, though the auto tour is in chronological order. The first two parts of the battlefield are flat for easy walking or biking. The third part is somewhat hilly, but doable if you are fit. During busy months rangers drive golf carts to three different spots on the battlefield, asking visitors to follow them in their own private vehicles. These personalized tours give visitors a chance to ask questions. One problem is that the pull-over parking at all of the specified stops on the tour is limited.

While Sharpsburg does have a good number of monuments on its grounds, it is not crowded with monuments like Gettysburg and Shiloh. This economy of monuments allows visitors to see the field the way it was in 1862. The only changes have come about from regular farming, as much of the land is leased to farmers.

Unfortunately for the history traveler who likes to walk in historic towns, Sharpsburg has only a handful of shops downtown, so there really is no place to walk.

ACCOMMODATIONS

The Inn at Antietam

220 East Main St., Sharpsburg
T: 877-835-6011
www.innatantietam.com
6 rooms
$110–$175

Located next to the Antietam National
Cemetery, this site had some Confederate
cannons firing onto Federals from its hill-
top overlooking the battlefield. The house
was built in 1908.

Jacob Rohrbach Inn

138 West Main St., Sharpsburg
T: 877-839-4242
www.jacob-rohrbach-inn.com
4 rooms
$140–$150

This inn in downtown Sharpsburg offers
bicycle rentals by the hour or all day to
bike to the battlefield, the C&O Canal, or
even to Harpers Ferry, twelve miles away.

Thomas Shepherd Inn Bed and Breakfast

Corner of Duke Street and German Street,
Shepherdstown
T: 888-889-8952
www.thomasshepherdinn.com
6 rooms
$110–$150

This inn was built in 1868 and has been
operating as an inn since 1983. It is close
to the live music scene in the quaint
downtown.

SOURCES & OTHER READING

Landscape Turned Red: The Battle of Antietam, Stephen Sears, Mariner Books,
2003.

*The Gleam of Bayonets: The Battle of Antietam and Robert E. Lee's Maryland
Campaign, September 1862,* James Murfin, Louisiana State University Press,
2004.

Antietam: The Soldiers Battle, John Priest, Oxford Press, 1993.

Guide to the Battle of Antietam, Jay Luvass, Harold Nelson, University Press of
Kansas, 1996.

*Taken at the Flood: Robert E. Lee and the Confederate Strategy in the Maryland
Campaign of 1862,* Joseph Harsh, Kent State University Press, 1999.

*Confederate Tide Rising: Robert E. Lee and the Making of Southern Strategy,
1861–1862,* Joseph Harsh, Kent State University Press, 1998.

*Sounding the Swallows: A Confederate Companion for the Maryland Campaign of
1862,* Joseph Harsh, Kent State University Press, 2000.

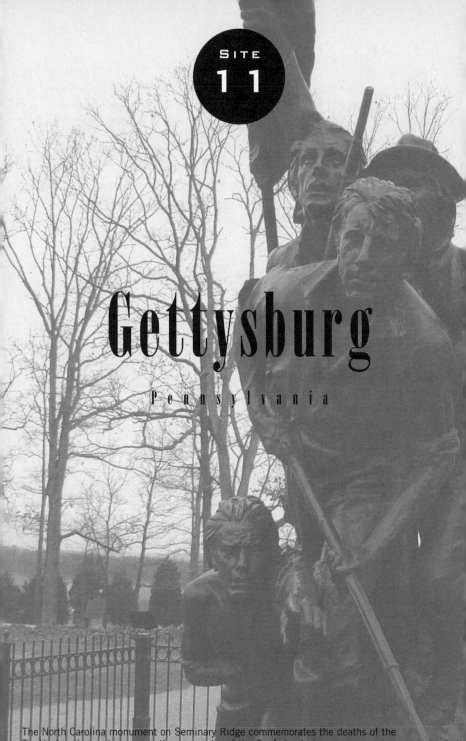

Gettysburg

Pennsylvania

The North Carolina monument on Seminary Ridge commemorates the deaths of the
Tar Heels, who made up more than a quarter of the Confederate losses.

THE WAR YEARS

Gettysburg was the largest and northernmost battle of the entire war. Had Lee won a major battle on Northern soil, Europe might have been persuaded to officially recognize the Confederacy. Had he won it, Northern citizens, disturbed that war had come to their doorstep, might have pushed their politicians to let the South go its way. The battle was grandly complicated, fought over three days over all types of terrain and directed by some of the most colorful generals in American history. It is without a doubt one of the best Civil War sites in the nation.

Had Robert E. Lee been able to get another day's jump on the Army of the Potomac before Union General Joseph Hooker discovered the movement of the Army of Northern Virginia, the small town of Gettysburg would never have become famous. Had Lee been granted that extra day, he might have captured and ransomed Harrisburg, the capital of Pennsylvania, before moving in any number of other directions. He might have turned south toward Washington. The key was marching time. When Lee's departure from Virginia was discovered sooner than he had expected, Lee had to change his strategy.

Instead of forming a series of brigade-size arrows aimed at the heart of the industrial and agricultural North as he had originally planned, Lee was forced to form a solid defensive block of troops at a convenient place in Pennsylvania where his troops could quickly gather. With his divisions scattered in Chambersburg to the west, Carlisle and Harrisburg to the north, and York to the east, Lee chose a town where roads from all those places converged—Gettysburg.

Gettysburg was a prosperous farming town of 2,500 people in the summer of 1863. While some of its younger men were fighting in the Army of the Potomac, the town itself had been untouched by war until a few days earlier when a small scouting party of Confederate cavalry rode through the town. The Confederates did no damage, but alarmed telegraphers sent messages to Washington and Harrisburg announcing that the state had been invaded.

On June 30 the lead units of Lee's main body of troops arrived on the outskirts of Gettysburg. An infantry scouting party noted what it thought were Union cavalrymen west of the town. The general of the lead division, Henry Heth and his corps commander, A.P. Hill, dismissed that report, believing only local militia to be in the area. They did not believe that the Army of the Potomac was anywhere close. Heth said he would move on Gettysburg the next day to check out rumors that there was a warehouse of shoes in the town.

What neither Heth nor Hill realized was that rushing toward Gettysburg from the south-east was the Army of the Potomac, now under the command of General George Meade. Hooker had been replaced by Lincoln, who was still angry at him for losing the Battle of Chancellorsville in May.

On the morning of July 1, Heth's division started marching on Gettysburg in direct viola-tion of Lee's standing orders not to bring on a general fight until all of his army was con-centrated. The Yankees that the scouts had seen were two brigades of Union cavalry under General John Buford. These men, armed with repeating rifles, knew how to fight and hold the high ground on which they were posted.

When Lee heard the distant gunfire, he was astounded. His orders had been violated. His infantry was still scattered to the west and north of Gettysburg. He hoped that J.E.B. Stuart's cavalry was east of the town, but he had not heard from Stuart in days. As Heth stubbornly pushed from the west, General Richard Ewell's Second Corps, which had been commanded by Stonewall Jackson until his death in May, started arriving piecemeal from the north. The Yankee cavalry, now fighting on two fronts, did not give ground willingly.

As the day passed, elements of the Union First Corps infantry arrived on the field, spurred into double-quick marching by the sound of cannons that Heth's rash movement had brought about earlier in the day. As more Federal troops arrived, they fought well, but still had to fall back through the town and up onto high ground called Culp's Hill on the north side of the town and Cemetery Ridge on the east side. That night Ewell chose not to attack the Federals on Culp's Hill because of oncoming darkness and the fatigue of his men, who had been marching all day.

On July, 2 Lee's men attacked both ends of the Federal line. The Union line looked like a fishhook, running along Cemetery Ridge with the curved barb making a semicircle around Cemetery Hill and Culp's Hill on the north side and the straight end of the shank ending on high ground called Little Round Top at the south end of the field. The important thing was that the Federals were on higher ground than the Confederates. The Federals could see all movements of the Confederates from lookout posts, and the Confederates had to climb up steep hillsides to reach the Yankees posted at each end of the field.

At one point during the day, a Union general named Dan Sickles pushed his Third Army Corps out of line at the south end of the field and into the open, thinking he would occupy some higher ground. This immediately exposed his men to attack by putting them in the open, away from supporting fire. The Confederates attacked, and small battles occurred in memorable places now called the Wheatfield, the Peach Orchard, Devil's Den, and Little Round Top. The fighting was fierce, but at the end of the day, the Federals still held the high ground.

On the morning of July 3, Lee decided that since there had been such fierce opposition on both the northern and southern ends of the Federal line on the first two days, the center must be weak. He had no idea that the Federals had more than 120,000 men, 40,000 more than his own forces, so there were plenty of Federals to put in the middle. Lee ordered a charge of 12,000 men against the high ground at Cemetery Hill. If the infantry broke through, they would be supported by J.E.B. Stuart's cavalry, who had finally arrived on the field on the second day and were now several miles east of the Federals' battle line in their rear.

The troops who moved from Seminary Ridge came from a half-dozen states, and were not just the Virginians commanded by George Pickett. The proper name of the attack, if one calls it after all the major generals in command of it, should be the Pettigrew-

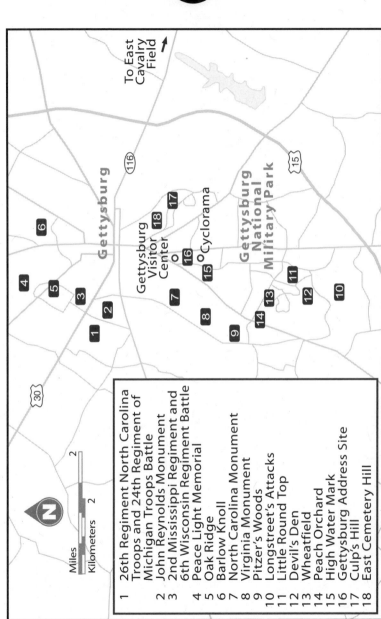

To East
Cavalry
Field

Gettysburg

Gettysburg
National
Military Park

Gettysburg
Visitor
Center

Cyclorama

Miles
Kilometers

1   26th Regiment North Carolina
     Troops and 24th Regiment of
     Michigan Troops Battle
2   John Reynolds Monument
3   2nd Mississippi Regiment and
     6th Wisconsin Regiment Battle
4   Peace Light Memorial
5   Oak Ridge
6   Barlow Knoll
7   North Carolina Monument
8   Virginia Monument
9   Pitzer's Woods
10   Longstreet's Attacks
11   Little Round Top
12   Devil's Den
13   Wheatfield
14   Peach Orchard
15   High Water Mark
16   Gettysburg Address Site
17   Culp's Hill
18   East Cemetery Hill

Pickett-Trimble Assault. The troops walked across a mile of open ground, under fire from cannons all the way. As they neared the Emmitsburg Road fences, Union muskets opened fire on them. Hampered by having to climb the wooden fences, the Confederate attack slowed, giving the Federals more time to fire into their ranks. In the end, only a few hundred North Carolinians and Virginians were able to breach the Union line before being killed or captured. Lee's belief that the center would collapse had proven untrue.

Three days of fighting left both sides with 7,000 killed, 27,000 wounded, and about 18,000 missing or captured. Meade's army could sustain those kinds of losses, as the North still had millions of civilians who had not yet volunteered or been drafted. Given the South's smaller population, Lee's army could not. His army would never again be as large or as fit as it was on July 1, 1863.

SOURCES & OTHER READING

Gettysburg, Stephen Sears, Houghton Mifflin, 2003.

Gettysburg: A Battlefield Guide, Mark Grimsley, Brooks Simpson, University of Nebraska Press, 1999.

Gettysburg: A Testing of Courage, Noah Trudeau, Perennial, 2003.

Gettysburg: The First Day, Henry Pfranz, University of North Carolina Press, 2001.

Gettysburg: The Second Day, Henry Pfranz, University of North Carolina Press, 1998.

The Gettysburg Campaign: A Study in Command, Edward Coddington, Touchstone reissue, 1997.

Pickett's Charge: The Last Attack at Gettysburg, Earl Hess, University of North Carolina Press, 2001.

GETTYSBURG TODAY

History travelers who enjoy seeing pristine, reverent battlefields like Shiloh may wince when they make their first trip to Gettysburg and see fast-food restaurants on the site where so many men died for their country. What has changed for the better is the determination of the National Park Service to restore the battlefield to its 1863 appearance. The process started several years ago when electric lines along Emmitsburg Road were buried. A few years ago a motel on the left side of the Pettigrew-Pickett-Trimble Assault was demolished and the land restored to the open field that it was in 1863. Today, chainsaws resound throughout the park on any given day as lumbermen remove the woods that are a modern-day aberration. Most of the expanse of land that became a battlefield for those three days in July consisted of fields of crops and grass. The heavy woods that have grown up around the monuments would never have been left standing by 1863 residents.

Despite the intrusions of twenty-first–century commerce on the killing grounds, Gettysburg, which has a central population just four times what it was in 1863, is a town that history travelers return to time after time. The downtown buildings are from the period. Some bed and breakfasts are located on the battlefield itself. The town and its merchants welcome both Yankee and Southern tourists. The question of who was on "the right side" of the battle and war is rarely heard. There is plenty to study and enjoy here.

POINTS OF INTEREST

1. Gettysburg National Military Park Visitor Center ★★★★★

97 Taneytown Rd.
T: 717-334-1124
Visitor center is open daily 8 a.m.–5 p.m.
Summer hours 8 a.m.–6 p.m.
Park is open 6 a.m.–10 p.m.

Visitors should stop at the National Park Service visitor center to obtain the tour road map. Far and away the most popular battlefield in the NPS system, the park is visited by nearly 2 million people each year. To handle traffic, the Park Service has made most of the roads one-way. The map is necessary to make the eighteen-mile road tour. Those who want to follow specific regiments or a chronological history of the battle can hire licensed battle-field guides, who will drive your personal vehicle, at the visitor center.

The visitor center offers two floors of displays, including two walls of sometimes haunting photographs of men who fought at the battle. The photos are rotated as visitors send pictures of their ancestors who served at the battle. In the basement in dimly lit display cases are uniforms, hats, shoes, weapons, and other accoutrements of both sides. All of the services are covered, including infantry, cavalry, artillery, and the navies. The uniform collections are valuable to reenactors (who can be identified by their intense interest in the types of buttons on a coat, or whether the buttonholes appear to be hand-sewn or machine-sewn). Also on the basement level is a display of cannon tubes, which are handy for helping to identify different types of cannons and their effective ranges.

The visitor center also houses a large electric map of the battlefield that is used to orient visitors to directions and actions during the larger fight. The charge for the electric map program is $4.

2. Cyclorama Center ★★★★★

97 Taneytown Rd.
Daily 9 a.m.–5 p.m.
Admission: $4
Closed November 2005–2008.

Just south of the visitor center is the Cyclorama Center, housing an 1884 painting of the battle that is presented with a twenty-minute sound and light show. This is one of the last surviving examples of the 360-degree paintings that were the rage in the late nineteenth century as entertainment. Painted by a Frenchman who did extensive on-site research, this twenty-seven-foot-tall copy was exhibited in Boston for years until waning interest closed its theater. An entrepreneur then purchased it in time to open for the 1913 fiftieth anniversary of the battle. The Park Service purchased it in the 1940s.

3. Driving Tour ★★★★★

Gettysburg was a sprawling, three-day battle with fights that took place simultaneously on many different parts of the battlefield. It is almost impossible to tour chronologically. Stops described here will skip some stops on the official NPS tour and add others.

Stop 1 ★★★

Here is the monument to First Corps Major General John Reynolds, the first Union infantry general to arrive on the scene.

As he was rallying his troops, a Confederate Minie ball entered his head, killing him instantly. Reynolds, a well-respected leader, would perhaps have gone on to command the Army of the Potomac had he survived Gettysburg.

Stop 1a ★★★★★

(not on the official NPS tour)

Starting on the western edge of the battlefield, from U.S. 30 turn south onto Meredith Avenue. Follow Meredith past the monument to John Burns, an elderly Gettysburg resident and a veteran of the War of 1812 who fell in with Union troops to fight the Confederates who were moving past his farm. Pull over between the monuments honoring the 26th Regiment North Carolina Troops and the 24th Regiment of Michigan Troops.

The placement of these two monuments shows how close the two regiments were as they shot into each other's ranks on July 1. The 26th North Carolina arrived on this spot on the afternoon of July 1 with 902 men. When they left the battle on July 3, fewer than ninety answered the roll. The rest had been killed, wounded, or captured. The 24th Michigan and the rest of the Iron Brigade to which it belonged were so shot up that the famed Brigade was disbanded and the remaining troops distributed into other regiments. Walk down to Willoughby Run, crossed by every Confederate soldier coming from the west.

Stop 1b ★★★

(not on the official NPS tour)

While passing over the railroad, note that this was the scene of heavy fighting, principally between the 2nd Mississippi Regiment occupying the natural trench formed by the railroad and the 6th Wisconsin Regiment of the Iron Brigade. The 2nd Mississippi was eventually overwhelmed.

Stop 2 ★★

This high ground, now the Peace Light Memorial dedicated by President Roosevelt, was the starting point for an attack by Confederate General Robert Rodes' division, which had just arrived from Carlisle, Pennsylvania.

Stop 3 ★★★★★

Hundreds of Union soldiers lay prone behind the stone wall on Oak Ridge (now Doubleday Avenue) as Rodes' men marched in the direction of some woods up ahead in their front. At a signal, the Federals rose and fired point-blank volleys into the Confederates, who fell in straight lines as if they were still marching. The sunken field to the west of the wall is Iverson's Pits, named after the Confederate general who failed to check out whether any Federals were behind this stone wall. The Confederates were buried in long pits in the field. For years ghost stories have been told about hundreds of dead Confederates haunting the pits.

Instead of continuing the NPS driving tour at this point, turn right at the observation tower onto Mummasburg Road, then left onto Howard Avenue to Barlow Knoll.

Stop 3a ★★★★

(not on the official NPS tour)

The fighting that took place here is still the subject of debate. General Francis Barlow positioned the First Division of the 11th Corps on this knoll. The 11th Corps, which had run at Chancellorsville when surprised by Stonewall Jackson's flank attack just two months earlier, put up a fight, but was eventually overwhelmed by Confederates rushing into the men's faces. Barlow himself was severely wounded. Legend says that he was personally attended to by Confederate General John Gordon, the commander of the troops that swept over this knoll. The controversy is over whether Barlow made a mistake in advancing his men too far to this knoll to fight in an exposed position. At any rate, the disgraced 11th Corps did slow the Confederate advance, which allowed other Federal units enough time to scamper up Culp's Hill and begin digging in before the Confederates could push them off.

Turn right onto Carlisle Road and go into town, go around the square, then turn right onto Middle Street, one block south of the square. Follow West Middle Street to the light at West Confederate Avenue. Turn left onto Confederate Avenue to rejoin the official NPS tour.

Confederate Avenue follows Seminary Ridge, the only high ground won by the Confederates at Gettysburg. The 12,000-man Pettigrew-Pickett-Trimble Assault was launched from here at 1:30 p.m. on July 3. The assault has long been misnamed Pickett's Charge, a trick of period Virginia newspaper editors who wanted to give credit for the attack to Pickett's Virginia brigades. Pickett's division had been the last to arrive on the field and had done little fighting over the previous two days as they were still marching toward Gettysburg. Pickett commanded only one-third of the men in the assault. The cannons that fired on the Union line on Cemetery Ridge were lined up here on Seminary Ridge.

Stop 4 ★★★★★

The North Carolina Monument, designed by Gutzon Borglum, the same man who carved Mount Rushmore, is dedicated to the forty-two regiments of North Carolina troops who fought at Gettysburg. Fifteen regiments from that state participated in the Pettigrew-Pickett-Trimble Assault under the command of North Carolinian General James J. Pettigrew. One-quarter of the Confederate losses suffered at Gettysburg came from North Carolina. The monument, erected in 1929, depicts four men in the charge. One is whispering encouragement in the ear of another. The faces show that all are determined to do their duty.

Stop 5 ★★★★★

Here, near the Virginia memorial, is where Lee watched the charge on the third day. The monument itself, like all of the Southern monuments found along Confederate Avenue, is a work of art with very realistic statues of Confederate soldiers. A path leading from the Virginia monument heads east. The path crosses the field and ends at the "High Water Mark" within the Union lines.

Stop 6 ★★★★

Here in Pitzer's Woods, General James Longstreet launched his attack on the second day. A statue of Longstreet is here. On some weekends, Confederate reenactors camp in these woods and give demonstrations for the public.

Stop 7 ★★★

It was from this area that Longstreet launched his July 2 attacks on the Union right flank. The Confederates who left this area swept to the northeast and into fights at Little Round Top, the Devil's Den, the Wheatfield, and the Peach Orchard. Longstreet's attacks came hours late as he maneuvered his men in an effort to find a road that the Federals could not easily see from the heights they held.

Stop 8 ★★★★★

Many historians believe that the Battle of Gettysburg was decided at Little Round Top. For a while the Federals had failed to recognize the value of this rock and had left it unoccupied. As soon as General G.K. Warren discovered it was unprotected, he commandeered several units and rushed them into place just minutes before Longstreet's Confederates attacked. The 20th Maine Regiment, led by Colonel

Joshua Lawrence Chamberlain, anchored the extreme right of the Union line here. The 20th Maine resisted every charge by the Confederates and then rushed down on their own bayonet charge to break up any more Confederate attacks. This spot on the battlefield is likely to be the most crowded because of the view and the statues honoring several Union heroes perched on the rock. Colonel Patrick O'Rorke's relief face on the 140th New York monument is shiny from people rubbing his nose. G.K. Warren's statue is perched on a rock as he stares into what would be named the "Valley of Death."

Stop 9 ★★★

After leaving Little Round Top, turn left onto Crawford Avenue and stop at Devil's Den, a cluster of huge rocks that hid Confederate sharpshooters firing at exposed Union soldiers on top of Little Round Top. A famous photograph of a dead Confederate sharpshooter was posed in the rocks here. The soldier's body was dragged to several locations on the battlefield and used as a prop. Across the road is the Triangular Field, a supposedly haunted part of the battlefield.

Stop 9a ★★★★★
(not on the official NPS tour)

Leaving Devil's Den, follow the road around and turn left onto Wheatfield Road and then left onto Ayers Avenue. This was the Wheatfield, a bloody field where first Confederates and then Federals charged each other. The fights here were set up when Union General Dan Sickles moved his corps off the line along Cemetery Ridge toward the Wheatfield. His exposed corps became the object of attack for the Confederates. Sickles would lose his leg for his rashness, but would visit his leg bone on occasion when it was on display at Walter Reed Hospital.

Stop 10 ★★★

The Peach Orchard was the furthest point Sickles' men reached and also the scene of heavy fighting on the second day. Turn onto Hancock Avenue; Catholics will be particularly interested in the statue of Father Corby, who stood on a rock and absolved the sins of the Irish Brigade just before they went into battle on July 2.

Stop 15 ★★★★★

This is the "High Water Mark," the furthest point in the Union line to which the Confederates advanced on the third day. The guns of Battery A 4th U.S. Artillery, commanded by Lieutenant Alonzo Cushing of Wisconsin, are here. Confederate General Lewis Armistead touched Cushing's guns just as he was mortally wounded after crossing the stone wall with a couple hundred Virginians. Forty yards to the north, the monument to the 26th Regiment of North Carolina Troops recognizes them for having penetrated deeper than any other Confederate regiment. Two color bearers of the 26th were not shot down by the Federals, who admired their bravery in continuing their march. Confederate reenactment units camping in the park make it a point to cross the same field and cross this same stone fence.

Stop 15a ★★★★

(not on the official NPS tour)

Park in the Cyclorama parking lot and tour the National Cemetery, where President Lincoln gave the famous Gettysburg Address in November 1863.

Stop 13 ★★★★

After leaving the cemetery, turn right onto Taneytown Road. Turn left onto Hunt Avenue. Turn right onto Baltimore Pike. Turn left onto Culp's Hill Avenue and follow it to Spangler's Spring. This was a desperate destination for many Union soldiers who needed water. Follow the signs to the Culp's Hill observation tower. This was going to be the focus of the attack by Ewell's men on the first day, but Ewell called off the attack because he believed his men were too tired. Historians have speculated that had Jackson been alive, he would not have stopped at nightfall but would have pressed forward and pushed the Federals off Culp's Hill. That would have put a Confederate stronghold on the high ground and might have changed the outcome of the battle, because the Federals would have had a strong Confederate force on their right flank.

Stop 14 ★★★

East Cemetery Hill was likely the real object of Lee's attack on the third day, rather than the fabled "copse of trees" back at the High Water Mark. This ground was more strategically important than Cemetery Ridge because it was higher. Had Lee's men gained control of the cannons here, they could have turned the guns and fired down the entire line of Federals strung along Cemetery Ridge.

Stop 16 ★★

(not on the official NPS tour)

From the square downtown, follow East York Street, then Hanover Road (S.R. 116) east for about five miles until you see the left turn for the East Cavalry Field. Here J.E.B. Stuart's cavalry fought George Armstrong Custer's cavalry—and lost. Had Stuart won, speculation is that he would have then advanced behind the Union lines in anticipation of a Confederate infantry breakthrough on Cemetery Ridge. Stuart acted oddly on this field. While most armies try to sneak up on their enemies, Stuart had a cannon fired in several directions before even engaging the Federals. He alerted them to his presence when it would have been more advantageous to have attacked before the Federals knew Confederates were in the area.

OTHER AREA ATTRACTIONS

Gettysburg offers a variety of attractions beyond the battlefield. There is the Lincoln Train Museum, the National Civil War Wax Museum, the Jennie Wade Museum (the house where the only civilian killed in the battle lived), Soldiers National Museum, the Hall of Presidents, General Lee's Headquarters Museum, and the Battle Theater, among others. Some Civil War sutlers (merchants to reenactors) have shops here and sell authentic (and sometimes not-so-authentic) uniforms and accoutrements. Civil War art galleries and gun shops deal in authentic, but expensive, weaponry. But these attractions must take a back seat to the real battlefield, and it can take up to two whole days to see it properly.

GETTING TO AND AROUND GETTYSBURG

The closest major airport to Gettysburg is in Harrisburg, about thirty-five miles north. Eight airlines serve it.

Of all the national battlefield parks, Gettysburg offers the greatest number of choices of how to see it. The best way for newcomers to the battlefield to learn about it is to hire the services of a licensed battlefield guide. Guides are found at the visitor center, or from April through November at a small stone building on U.S. 30 at the western edge of the battlefield when arriving from Chambersburg. The cost is $40 for a two-hour tour tailored to visitors' interests. In those two hours, the guide drives the visitors' car and gives a running commentary on the subject the visitors have requested. For instance, visitors might want to follow a famous regiment in which an ancestor served, or follow the battle's progress in chronological order, which is not possible if using the Park Service's tour map. Be sure to book guides early in the day during the busy summer months. Note that it is not possible to reserve a guide in advance of arrival.

Another choice is a four-hour bus tour (for $20), during which visitors listen to recorded accounts of the battle. There is also a nearby horse stable that rents out horses and allows visitors to ride portions of the battlefield while listening to a recorded tour.

For those visitors who already know the battle and are familiar with the layout of the battlefield, the best way to see it is on foot. Some lovers of the battlefield come with a compass and walk several miles a day, tracing the movements of various regiments. The rewards can be worthwhile, such as finding monuments deep in the woods that aren't accessible by car. The only way to experience the Pettigrew-Pickett-Trimble Assault is to walk it from the Virginia monument to the High Water Mark. Along the way, visitors can rest in the same swale described by veterans of the attack. It was the only time on the march across that mile-long open field where they felt safe from the eyes of the gunners atop the Round Tops. For the full effect, climb over the wooden fences lining the Emmitsburg Road. The soldiers could not knock down those sturdy fences, so each man had to climb over the fence, making himself an easy target.

Accommodations

Cashtown Inn

1325 Old Route 30, Cashtown
T: 800-367-1797
www.cashtowninn.com
7 rooms
$100–$130

Robert E. Lee first heard the guns of
Gettysburg, ordered by one of his generals
in direct violation of Lee's orders, while
standing in front of the Cashtown Inn.
Most of the Army of Northern Virginia
marched past the inn on their way to
Gettysburg, seven miles to the east. The
inn has a bar, a full-service restaurant,
and a book of ghost stories reported by
guests.

Farnsworth House Inn

401 Baltimore St., Gettysburg
T: 717-334-8838
www.farnsworthhouseinn.com
11 rooms
$105–$160

Located in a building that was occupied
by Confederate sharpshooters, the
Farnsworth House has a fine-dining
restaurant next to a bookstore with thousands of Civil War books. Four of the
rooms are nonchalantly billed as haunted,
though no explanation is given as to what
happens if guests are brave enough to
book those rooms.

The Doubleday Inn Bed and Breakfast

104 Doubleday Ave., Gettysburg
T: 717-334-9119
www.doubledayinn.com
3 rooms
$95–$130

Though the house is not period, it is located on Oak Ridge, directly across from the
supposedly haunted Iverson's Pits, so
nighttime finds guests walking onto the
battlefield in hopes that some of those
dead Confederates will put in an appearance.

Battlefield Bed & Breakfast Inn

2264 Emmitsburg Rd., Gettysburg
T: 888-766-3897
www.gettysburgbattlefield.com
4 rooms and 4 suites
$160–$250

Housed in an 1809 farmhouse just south
of the National Park, this inn is staffed by
reenactors who give regular programs on
what it was like to be a soldier back then.

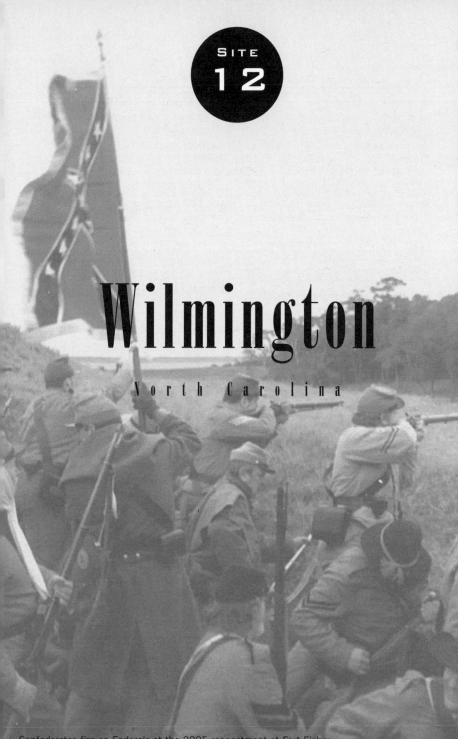

SITE

12

Wilmington

North Carolina

Confederates fire on Federals at the 2005 reenactment at Fort Fisher.

THE WAR YEARS

O f all the ports found in the South, Wilmington was the most hated by the Union because it was not able to stop the blockade runners from using it as home base until January 1865. Not until the Union captured the huge sand fort called Fort Fisher on Kure Beach near the mouth of the Cape Fear River was the final fate of the Confederacy sealed. Part of the formidable Fort Fisher still exists on the Atlantic, making Wilmington a great Civil War city to visit.

Before the war started, few people outside North Carolina had ever heard of Wilmington. Though it was the largest city in the state, this river port town thirty miles upriver from where the Cape Fear River flowed into the Atlantic still had a population under 10,000. Unlike much larger port cities like New Orleans, which shipped goods such as cotton all over the world, Wilmington concentrated on products made from the region's vast stretches of pine trees. Pine pitch and turpentine were the area's principal products, and the city shipped these to Northern cities to help build other ships.

North Carolina, reflecting its strong Unionist views, was the last state to leave the Union. Angered by President Lincoln's demands for the state to supply regiments to attack South Carolina, the state seceded on May 20, 1861, nearly six months after South Carolina had left and more than a month after the bombardment of Fort Sumter. One of the first installations captured by the secessionists was Fort Caswell, an old brick fort that had been built to defend the mouth of the Cape Fear River from invasion—by British, not U.S., ships.

Wilmington's importance as a blockade-running port was immediately recognized by the Confederacy and the entrepreneurs who would own and build the ships that would attempt to slip past the Union warships. The best advantage the city had was what nature had created. At the mouth of the Cape Fear River were two islands, Bald Head and Oak, on which batteries could be placed to protect the two approaches to the river, named, simply enough, Old Inlet and New Inlet. To further protect New Inlet, Confederate forces started to build an L-shaped fort that they would name Fort Fisher.

As the war progressed, blockade runners grew more confident and Union blockaders more frustrated. Thanks to Frying Pan Shoals to the southeast, Union ships could not lay a close blanket of ships around the inlets. The blockaders had to remain further at sea, which meant an increased number of angles from which blockade runners could approach the inlets. With each trip, the blockade runners learned more about how to evade the warships. They built their ships with hulls that were low to the water; painted the hulls slate gray; developed retractable smokestacks so the ship's profile could be lowered; used coal that burned with little smoke; even blew smoke off under water. On foggy or moonless nights, the best blockade runners were almost invisible and silent. Figures show that 75 percent of the blockade runners based in Wilmington made suc-cessful voyages into and out of the port, the highest percentage for any Southern port.

The goods brought in by blockade runners included English-made Enfield muskets, lead, tin, black powder, uniforms—all items that Southern armies could certainly use. The same ships usually found room for civilian goods such as ladies' hats and dresses, even straight pins. Once in port, the military goods were loaded on train cars and sent to armies in the field, usually Robert E. Lee's Army of Northern Virginia. The Wilmington & Weldon Railroad connected Wilmington's waterfront to the Weldon & Richmond railroad near the North Carolina and Virginia border.

As the Northern armies and navies captured New Orleans and shut down Savannah in 1862, negated Charleston in 1863, and captured Mobile in August 1864, Wilmington became ever more important to the Confederacy. Lee himself said that if Wilmington fell he would not be able to maintain his army, which was entrenched in the summer and fall of 1864 around Richmond and Petersburg. Lee knew that it was only a matter of time before the slowly advancing Federals turned their attention to Wilmington.

The only reason the Federals had not tried to capture Wilmington earlier in the war was because of their fear of Fort Fisher, located on the beach a short distance from New Inlet. The L-shaped fort had a land face that stretched a third of a mile between the Cape Fear River and the Atlantic Ocean. The sea face stretched more than a mile down the Atlantic beach. In some spots the sand walls were topped by flat-topped gun emplacements that soared more than sixty feet in the air, an altitude that greatly increased the range of the fort's cannons. Some of the best cannons ever manufactured were in place here, including an Armstrong cannon imported from England. There was also a battery of horse-drawn British-made Whitworth cannons, highly accurate breech-loading guns that could be quickly moved to any point on the beach. Any Union blockading ship trying to pursue a blockade runner too closely ran the risk of coming within range of Fort Fisher's well-trained and eager gunners.

As the war wound down, it was obvious that Fort Fisher would become a target. On December 23 and 24, 1864, dozens of ships shelled the fort, but the sand walls absorbed the shelling without much effect. A Union force landed and was forming to attack the fort when the army commander, Ben Butler, had a change of heart and called off the attack. Butler even sailed away before his men were back on board the ships, leading U.S. Grant to relieve him of command in capturing Fort Fisher.

Nearly three weeks later, an even larger fleet returned to drop even more heavy shells. This time the Federal Navy, under Admiral David Porter, wanted to share in the glory of capturing the fort. Porter foolishly ordered a landing party, armed with pistols, sabers, and short carbines, to attack the land face at the apex with the sea face—the strongest part of the fort. Not a sailor made it to the top of the sand walls. Many of the wounded were drowned when they were washed out to sea at high tide.

The new Union general in charge of the ground attack was Alfred Terry. Terry ignored Porter's disastrous, uncoordinated attack and placed his men, nearly 10,000 in all, closer to the Cape Fear River, away from the strong sea face. After a day's fighting, Fort Fisher, literally the last bastion protecting the blockade runners, fell to Terry's soldiers. Over the next five weeks, the Federals crossed over to the west bank of the Cape Fear River to slowly beat out all resistance, particularly at Fort Anderson, another dirt fort halfway up the river on the way to Wilmington. On February 23, Union troops marched into the city.

With the fall of Wilmington, the city became a forward supply base for Sherman's army, which was then marching through North Carolina.

Left to right, top to bottom:

1. Grave of unknown soldier
   at Corinth

2. Artillery demonstration
   at Petersburg

3. *Cairo* at Vicksburg

4. Fort Jackson Museum

5. Warren statue at Gettysburg

Left to right, top to bottom:

1. John Brown's Fort at
   Harpers Ferry

2. Cushing Battery
   "High-water mark"
   at Gettysburg

3. Bloody Lane at Sharpsburg

4. Robert Smalls' bust
   at Beaufort

5. Torpedo in Columbus

Left to right, top to bottom:

1. Jackson Square in
   New Orleans

2. Cannon at Little Round Top
   at Gettysburg

3. Cedar Creek Battlefield

4. Federal monument
   at Chickamauga

5. Fort Pulaski yard
   in Sa nah

Left to right, top to bottom:

1. Atop Snodgrass Hill at Chickamauga

2. Cannons pointing to Hornets' Nest at Shiloh

3. Confederate cemetery at Appomattox Court House

4. Cannon at Port Hudson

Left to right, top to bottom:

1. Mississippi monument at Vicksburg

2. Interior of Fort Jackson Museum

3. Lee's surrender table at Appomattox Court House

4. Wilder monument at Chickamauga

5. Kirkland monument at Fredericksburg

Left to right, top to bottom:

1. Fort Pulaski casemates

2. Monument at Spotsylvania

3. Fort Sumter in Charleston

4. Confederate breakthrough at Chickamauga

5. Church at Shiloh

Left to right, top to bottom:

1. Jackson and guns in Lexington

2. Virginia monument at Gettysburg

3. Graves at Brices Crossroads, Mississippi

4. Grant's surrender table at Appomattox Court House

5. Fort Pulaski in Savannah

Left to right, top to bottom:

1. Ohio monument at Vicksburg

2. Sherman's headquarters in Savannah

3. Fort Donelson

4. Cannon at Fort Sumter in Charleston

5. Cemetery in Andersonville

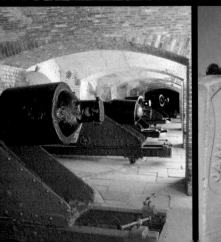

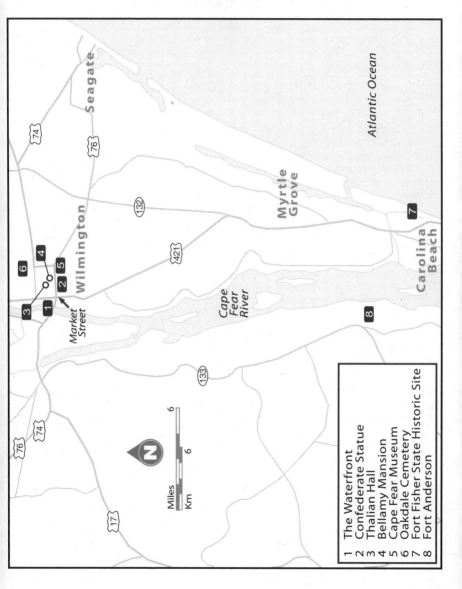

Seagate

Atlantic Ocean

74

76

Myrtle Grove

132

7

421

Carolina Beach

4

6

5

2

Wilmington

3

1

8

Cape Fear River

Market Street

133

76

74

N

17

Miles

Km

6

6

1 The Waterfront
2 Confederate Statue
3 Thalian Hall
4 Bellamy Mansion
5 Cape Fear Museum
6 Oakdale Cemetery
7 Fort Fisher State Historic Site
8 Fort Anderson

WILMINGTON TODAY

There is little evidence today of Wilmington's role as the South's leading blockade-running port. The riverfront where the blockade runners tied up is still there, but these days, the only ships regularly seen along the riverfront are a U.S. Coast Guard cutter assigned to Wilmington and the occasional warship visiting from another country. Across the river is the *U.S.S. North Carolina*, a battleship dating back to World War II. There are no replica blockade runners in the water, and there is no blockade-running museum.

Wilmington, the blockade-running city, has become Wilmington, the movie-making city. For twenty years, movie studios and producers have been trying to make it a small version of Hollywood East, with varying degrees of success. The city woke up to the idea of historical preservation late, so few buildings remain from the Civil War on or near the waterfront. That does not mean that the city is not without some charm, just that the historical buildings that have been preserved have little to do with the Civil War. Still, there is plenty for the visitor to see and do here.

POINTS OF INTEREST

1. The Waterfront ★

The waterfront in downtown Wilmington was once teeming with adventurers; Southern and foreign-born captains, and crews of blockade runners who were either loading or unloading cargos. There is no evidence of this part of Wilmington's history here today. What is here is a pleasant waterfront boardwalk that stretches for over a mile, a few scattered waterfront shops and restaurants, and the occasional visiting warship.

2. Confederate Statue ★

Market Street and Third Street.

This beautiful bronze statue is based on a real soldier, Gabriel Boney, but the interesting thing about the work is what the figure in the statue is doing. He is reaching into his cap box with his left hand. Civil War soldiers had to "cap" their muskets with a small brass container of mercury fulminate. When the musket's hammer struck the cap, it created a spark that caused the ignition of the black powder inside the barrel of the musket. That ignition propelled the musket ball toward its target. Muskets always had their cap locks on the right side of the weapon, so capping meant that the soldier had to hold the weapon in his left hand while putting on the cap with the right. This statue is trying to accomplish an impossible task.

3. Thalian Hall ★

301 Chestnut St.
T: 910-343-3660 (business office)
T: 910-343-3664 (box office)
Call for times of presentations.

Wilmington surrendered to Union General Alfred Terry, who designed the successful attack on Fort Fisher, on the steps of this combination city hall and playhouse on February 22, 1865. Thalian Hall is still an active theater today and hosts a broad range of musical and theatrical productions. During the war, Thalian Hall had been one of the few places where residents could find amusement as war news grew steadily worse. Immediately after the war, a man arrived from Washington to lease the facility because an unfortunate incident had occurred in his own playhouse that forced him to close it. The man was John Ford, owner of Ford's Theater in Washington D.C., where President Lincoln was assassinated. Eye witnesses claim Thalian Hall is home to a well-loved, often-seen ghost, a Victorian-era actor who enjoys watching dress rehearsals.

One of the rare civilian volunteer officers who was offered a regular generalship, General Terry, who had no military training, stayed in the U.S. Army after the war. He headed west to fight Indians and hard-headed subordinates who did not like reporting to a man who had not gone to West Point. One of those subordinates was Colonel George Custer, who would ignore Terry's orders to be careful when approaching the Sioux Indians in 1876.

4. Bellamy Mansion ★★★★

503 Market St.
T: 910-251-3700
Tuesday–Saturday, 10 a.m.–5 p.m.;
Sunday, 1–5 p.m. Last tour at 4 p.m.
Admission: $7

Finished just days before the war started, the Bellamy Mansion has been called North Carolina's most beautiful antebellum home. A team of free black laborers constructed the home for a local doctor and his wife and family of ten children. The house itself demonstrates that black artisans were highly skilled in the architectural and construction trades throughout the South. The house, massive even by today's standards, has twenty-two rooms.

After Wilmington fell, the Federal occupying general, Joseph Hawley, and his wife

took over the house. Neither of them appear to have been social conservatives. According to local accounts, the Bellamy Mansion became the scene of wild parties of Union officers and prostitutes during the six months the Hawleys lived here before the Bellamys could reclaim their home. The only apparent damage left in the house during that time was tobacco-juice stains on the marble. One story claims that on the day the Bellamys finally took possession of the house, Mrs. Bellamy found a drunken prostitute in one of her children's bedrooms. The last time anyone saw the nude woman, a fierce, broom-wielding Mrs. Bellamy was chasing her down Market Street.

5. Cape Fear Museum ★★★★

814 Market St.
T: 910-341-4350
Memorial Day through Labor Day
Monday–Saturday, 9 a.m.–5 p.m., Sunday 1–5 p.m. Winter hours 1–5 p.m. Closed Sunday and Monday.
Admission: $5

The most fascinating Civil War exhibits in the Cape Fear Museum are two dioramas: one showing the bustling waterfront as blockade runners slip in and out of the city, and the other showing the intense fighting for Fort Fisher. Also on display is an interesting newspaper headline describing how President Davis assigned his old friend General Braxton Bragg to command Wilmington. The newspaper headline says "Bragg assigned to Wilmington. Goodbye Wilmington." In the copy of the newspaper is the observation that wherever Bragg has been assigned, "an omen of impending evil like a dark, cold, dreary cloud" has descended. Other artifacts to be found on display include a sword belonging to General W.H.C. Whiting. Whiting had changed the "USA" on the hilt of the sword to read "CSA."

6. Oakdale Cemetery ★★

520 North 15th St.
T: 910-762-5682
Four blocks north of intersection of 15th
Street and Market Street.
Office hours: 8:30 a.m.–noon, 1–4:30 p.m.
Gate hours: 8 a.m.–5 p.m.

This 165-acre cemetery is the final resting
place of several famous people, including
the architect who designed the Lincoln
Memorial in Washington, D.C.; two
Confederate generals; the Confederate
major who mistakenly ordered the volley
that wounded Stonewall Jackson at
Chancellorsville; a famous Confederate sea
raider who captured twenty-two Union
ships before becoming a blockade runner;
and the South's most famous spy, Rose
O'Neal Greenhow.

Greenhow is credited with warning
Confederates about the impending movements of Union forces just before First
Manassas in July 1861. Imprisoned by the
Federals, she was eventually released and
returned to spying. The ship carrying her
from England in 1864 with dispatches
and gold was about to be captured off Fort
Fisher when she climbed into a rowboat to
try to reach shore. The boat capsized and
she drowned. When her body was recovered, she was buried with full honors. The
office has maps showing locations of the
famous Confederate-related graves.

Look on the cemetery map for the statue
dedicated to the unknown Confederate
dead. The same statue honors Union dead
in several Northern cities. For some reason, the soldier is casually resting his left
wrist over the muzzle of the musket. A
glance at the hammer shows it at full
cock—the soldier is about to blow his
hand off. One possible explanation for this
intentional "mistake" in the way the soldier is handling his weapon is that the
stone carver who designed this statue for
the mass market was playing a joke on the
unwary towns who bought it.

OUTSIDE WILMINGTON

7. Fort Fisher State Historic Site
★★★★★

Kure Beach near the ferry landing to the
mainland (20 minutes southeast of
Wilmington)
T: 910-458-5798
8 a.m.–5 p.m. visitor center and museum.
Park hours vary; open as late as 9 p.m.
during summer months.
November–February, office open
Monday–Friday
Free admission.

First-time visitors expecting a brick fort
when they arrive at Fort Fisher may be
surprised to see five tall mounds of sand
standing in a line facing north. That is all
that is left of the fort's land face, barely
ten percent of what was here in 1865.
None of the ocean face, a line of mounds
and sand walls more than a mile long, still
stands. All of the sea face and most of the
land face were washed into the Atlantic
years ago. Ironically, it was the U.S. Army,
which occupied the site during World War
II, that contributed to the destruction of
the scene of one of its greatest victories.
Although most of the fort had already
washed away, the Army built a landing
strip right through a portion of the remaining land face.

Luckily, the remaining mounds of grass-
covered sand are enough for visitors to get
a good idea of how Fort Fisher was constructed—by shoveling sand as high as
possible. Impressed slaves, free blacks, and
soldiers all worked shoulder to shoulder

for more than two years to construct the fort. The remaining walls are impressive; nearly forty feet tall, they demonstrate how intimidating the fort was with its numerous cannons and riflemen aiming down on any approaching enemy. In front of the land face is a reconstructed wood palisade that was designed to deter or at least slow any advance by any enemy.

The visitor center has an electric map display that describes the two battles for Fort Fisher, numerous artifacts from the fort and blockade runners that ran aground nearby, and several dioramas describing various moments during the battles. Also on display is a breech-loading Whitworth cannon that blockade runners imported from England. The cannons were technologically far more advanced than anything else the Confederate or Federal armies had. Their accuracy, in the hands of skilled gunners, frightened Union ship captains. The only problem was that Fort Fisher was always short of rounds for the guns, so they were used sparingly.

Just outside the visitor center is the fort's famous Armstrong cannon, a multibanded cannon designed in England and smuggled through the blockade. The cannon fired an odd-looking 150-pound projectile studded with bumps. Those studs lined up with the grooves inside the cannon barrel so that the shell would spin more efficiently. The range of the Armstrong gun was more than five miles. Once the fort put the cannon in place, the Union ships moved themselves a safe distance from it, which allowed blockade runners more opportunity to run into port. The Armstrong gun was captured after Fort Fisher's fall and transported to the U.S. Military Academy in West Point, New York. It is on loan to Fort Fisher until February 2006. After that it will return to West Point, but a replica gun will be put on display in its place.

A trail leads from the visitor center around the land face and then back to the visitor center. A low fence keeps tourists from walking on the mounds, but visitors' views are not obstructed. At the far end of the fort, near the Cape Fear River, is Shepherd's Battery, named after the cannon battery that anchored this end of the fort. This is the point where the Federals first broke through Confederate defenses during the January battle. From here the Federal soldiers fought as they moved toward the sea face. On the day after the battle, a bombproof blew up, killing scores of Federals. At first the Union commanders believed retreating Confederates had planted a slow-fused bomb in the works. An investigation uncovered that a drunken U.S. Marine carrying a torch while looking for war souvenirs had wandered into one of the fort's undamaged powder magazines.

The battle losses at Fort Fisher were surprisingly light. Fifty-five Union warships hurled nearly 20,000 shells into the fort over the two engagements, but only 500 Confederates were killed or wounded out of a garrison of 1,900. That is a testament to how safe it was inside Fort Fisher's bombproofs. By contrast, nearly 2,000 Federals were killed and wounded in the two fights because they were charging across open ground into the muzzles of both cannons and muskets. While the Confederates were behind sand walls, the Federals were in the open.

In a low building west of the Fort Fisher parking lot is an exhibit on underwater archaeology that many tourists miss. The explanation of how wrecks are found and explored is definitely worthwhile.

8. Fort Anderson ★★★★
Brunswick Town State Historic Site

S.R. 133 on west bank of Cape Fear River
20 miles southwest of Wilmington
This site is best accessed by taking a river

ferry from below Fort Fisher across the Cape Fear River to Southport and then north on S.R. 133. From there drive north to U.S. 17, then return to Wilmington.
T: 910-371-6613
Tuesday–Saturday, 10 a.m.–4 p.m.
Closed Sunday and Monday
Free admission.

This combination pre-Colonial town site and Civil War fort shows visitors two historical eras. Brunswick was first settled in 1726 as a port from which pine pitch was shipped. At one time it was the home of the royal governor.

In 1765 the town's residents protested England's move to issue tax stamps. This defiant act against the Crown was eight years before the famous Boston Tea Party was staged to protest taxes on imported tea. With the growth of Wilmington and the move of the royal capital to New Bern, the town began to decline.

During the Civil War, Fort Anderson was built in order to provide a last line of defense for the city in the event that Fort Fisher fell. Designed by the same man who built Fort Fisher, its sand walls are still formidable-looking since it is on a river and has not been pounded by the Atlantic as Fort Fisher has been over the years. Once the Confederate garrison realized that the Union forces were overwhelming, they evacuated the fort just before the Union combination land-and-water force arrived. While the Federal soldiers were walking around inside the fort, the Union ships, which had not been signaled of the fort's capture, began shelling. The soldiers within quickly ran a white flag up the fort's flagpole, meaning that the Union Army surrendered to the Union Navy in order to stop the firing.

SOURCES & OTHER READING

The Wilmington Campaign: Last Rays of Departing Hope, Chris E. Fonvielle, Jr., Stackpole Books, 2001.

Fort Anderson: Battle for Wilmington, Chris E. Fonvielle, Jr., DeCapo Press, 1999.

Confederate Goliath: The Battle of Fort Fisher, Rod Gragg, Louisiana State University Press, 1994.

Confederate Lifeline: Blockade Running During the Civil War, University of South Carolina Press, 1991.

Gray Phantoms of the Cape Fear: Running the Civil War Blockade, Dawson Carr, John F. Blair Publisher, 1998.

Hurricane of Fire: The Union Assault on Fort Fisher, Charles M. Robinson, Naval Institute Press, 1998.

Lifeline of the Confederacy: Blockade Running during the Civil War, Stephen Wise, University of South Carolina Press, 1991.

Getting to and Around Wilmington

Wilmington International Airport is served by two commercial carriers and several rental car agencies.

Visitors need a vehicle and a good local map to see all of the Civil War sites around Wilmington. Fort Fisher is at least a twenty-minute drive from Wilmington to Kure Beach. Fort Anderson is a half-hour ferry ride from Fort Fisher area, then an additional fifteen-minute drive north from the ferry dock.

Two types of tours can be found along the waterfront. Carriage tours are offered April through October starting at Water and Main on the waterfront. Cost is $9 per person. The *Henrietta III*, a river boat docked at Water Street, offers a variety of river cruises, from daytime sightseeing to sunset and evening dinner cruises.

Accommodations

Rosehill Inn Bed & Breakfast

114 South Third St., Wilmington
T: 800-815-0250
www.rosehill.com
6 rooms
$129–$189

This 1848 Italianate-style home was once owned by Henry Bacon, the designer of the Lincoln Memorial in Washington. It is three blocks to the riverfront from the front door.

Murchison House Bed & Breakfast

305 South Third St., Wilmington
T: 910-762-6626
www.murchisonhouse.com
5 rooms
$185–$200

Originally built in 1878, the house had been changed considerably until the current owners, working from 1910 photos, returned the house to its original look, reflecting the Second Empire style. Several movies have been filmed here.

C.W. Worth House

412 South Third St., Wilmington
T: 800-340-8559
www.worthhouse.com
7 rooms
$130–$150

Built by the grandson of a North Carolina governor in 1893, it was converted into a B&B in 1985. It is located a short distance from the waterfront.

Blue Heaven Bed & Breakfast

517 Orange St., Wilmington
T: 910-772-9929
www.bbonline.com/nc/blueheaven
4 rooms
$90–$100

This 1897 Queen Anne–style house was built with seven fireplaces, which remain as decorative touches. It is a five-minute walk to the downtown and the waterfront, Bellamy Mansion, and Thalian Hall.

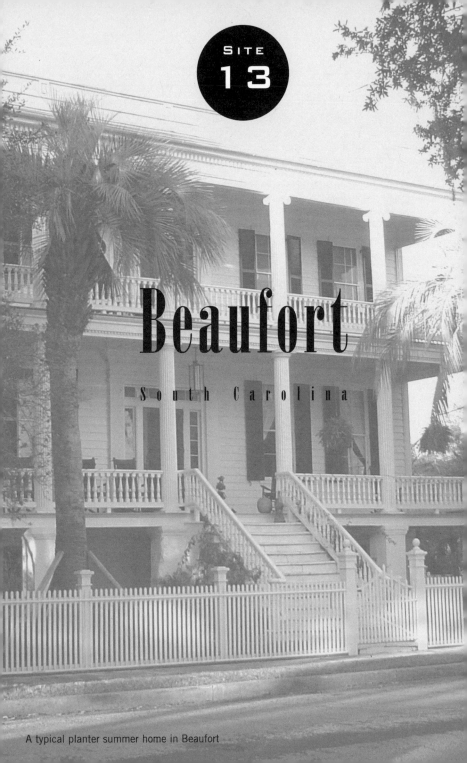

Beaufort

South Carolina

A typical planter summer home in Beaufort

THE WAR YEARS

The capture of Beaufort and nearby Port Royal Sound was one of the first major Union victories of the war. From this base on coastal South Carolina, the Federals were able to begin the slow but sure process of closing Southern ports. If the idea of South Carolina finally going through with secession after decades of threats took root in any one place, it was in Beaufort.

Founded in 1712 as an agricultural city dedicated to the growth and exportation of indigo (from which a bright blue dye was produced), Beaufort was transformed in 1790 when the Elliott family perfected the art of growing sea-island cotton on nearby Hilton Head Island. Prized by the textile factories of London for its long strands, which were used to weave elegant, silky shirts, sea-island cotton quickly overtook all other cash crops such as indigo and rice. Within a decade it was the principal crop on scores of island plantations stretching down into the Georgia sea islands.

As sea island cotton grew in popularity, so did the need for slaves to cultivate it on the muddy tidal flats. Any talk of abolition of slavery drew the ire of the state's planters and politicians, who feared the loss of the large workforce needed to grow, pick, and process the crop. The most vocal among them was Beaufort's own Robert Barnwell Rhett, Sr., who had first talked of secession as early as the 1830s in response to the high tariffs imposed on imported goods by the federal government. By the 1850s, as tensions over states' rights and abolition were boiling over, Rhett was using his newspaper, the *Charleston Mercury,* to actively call for a "confederation" of slave-holding states that would shift the South's loyalty from the Union to its own region.

Rhett's rantings were not fully thought out. Secession could mean trouble with international trade at least and war at worst. Either circumstance would disrupt life in Beaufort, where by 1860 the townspeople were living quite well. The two- and three-story houses owned by the planters as "town homes" away from their muggy and buggy island plantations rivaled anything built in Charleston, or even Boston and New York.

Beaufort history records that in December 1860, its local delegates were the first to agree that leaving the Union was their only choice. After that vote at a meeting in Rhett's house, they moved on to Charleston, where other delegates debated the issue and agreed to leave the Union on December 20, 1860.

War came to the sea islands much sooner than the secessionist planters ever expected. Within days of the war opening on April 12, 1861, the U.S. Secretary of the Navy handed President Lincoln a report suggesting the capture of Port Royal Sound, just south of Beaufort. The plan called for the conversion of the bay into a huge coaling station to supply the ships that would carry out Lincoln's proposed blockade of Southern ports.

When seventy-seven Union warships and transports carrying 12,000 soldiers arrived on November 7, it was the largest naval force the U.S. had ever assembled. Their targets were two hastily built Confederate sand forts on either side of the sound.

Despite the overwhelming show of force, success was not assured. The Union had lost major land battles at Manassas, Virginia, in July; Wilson's Creek, Missouri, in August;

and Ball's Bluff, Virginia, in October. Only on North Carolina's Outer Banks in August had the Union won any ground since the war began. Morale among the Federal soldiers waiting to land after the expected naval battle was low.

The Federals need not have worried. Thanks to a careful battle plan in which the Federal ships stayed in a circling line bearing their guns on the forts, the Battle of Port Royal went perfectly their way. The Confederate forts and their outdated cannons had been poorly placed by inadequately trained engineers, while the Union naval forces were led by old salts who knew how to attack stationary targets. Within hours the Confederate forts' guns were silenced and the way was opened for the Union soldiers to land unopposed.

Early capture by the Union in the war and the planned need for a naval base ultimately worked in Beaufort's favor. When the planters fled inland, Federal garrison troops moved in and made themselves at home. For the rest of the war, Beaufort, Port Royal, and its surrounding islands served as a base for the South Atlantic Blockading Squadron, ships assigned to run down and capture Confederate blockade runners.

Though the Union later took to burning private property in an attempt to bring Southern civilians to their knees, Beaufort was spared such a fate. Six months after the war started, it essentially had been brought back into the Union—at least its property was. The houses that were there in 1860 survived the war and remain today.

Robert Smalls, the first black hero of the Civil War, was from Beaufort. Born a slave, Smalls, relatively speaking, enjoyed a great deal of freedom from the McKee family, who recognized early on that the young man was smart. They apprenticed him to a ship captain in Charleston, who trained him to be a ship's pilot. A pilot's job was to guide ships around sand bars and snags. It was a job that required an intelligent man with a great memory, someone who could read the water's surface and know what dangers lay below.

In May 1862, Smalls was working as pilot for the *C.S.S. Planter,* a supply ship to the Confederate forts around Charleston. Throwing on the coat and hat of the white ship's captain who normally stood in the bow, Smalls and the all-slave crew successfully stole the *Planter* early one morning. He surrendered the ship to the crew of a Union blockading vessel seconds before it fired on the ship that had been rushing at it from the dark.

A crew of slaves successfully stealing the flagship of the Confederate commander of Charleston made national news. It proved to a startled, skeptical North and an embarrassed South that black people were capable of thinking for themselves. Smalls was made into a hero and given command of the *Planter,* which was converted into a raiding vessel. He was the first black man ever handed command of a U.S. ship. Eventually he would return to Beaufort and represent his district in the U.S. Congress.

The Confederates fought a few battles within a day's march of Beaufort, but never tried to recapture Port Royal, which proved to be key to the eventual strangulation of Southern ports. Beaufort remained in Union hands and was a popular posting throughout the war. It was far from the fighting, a town with fresh food and water, and inhabited by a populace who early on got used to the idea that they were back in the Union.

SITE
13

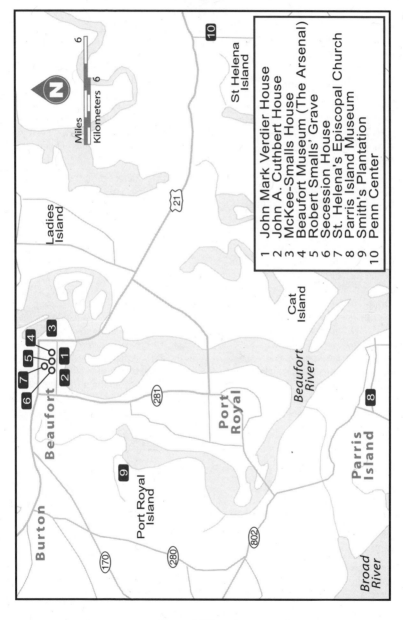

1 John Mark Verdier House
2 John A. Cuthbert House
3 McKee-Smalls House
4 Beaufort Museum (The Arsenal)
5 Robert Smalls' Grave
6 Secession House
7 St. Helena's Episcopal Church
8 Parris Island Museum
9 Smith's Plantation
10 Penn Center

BEAUFORT TODAY

With many fine examples of residential architecture from the 1830s to the 1860s, the historic district of Beaufort today is like a Civil War time capsule. Many of those houses were sold at tax auction during the war when their Confederate owners did not show up to pay the government. Their new owners, often Northern cotton agents who made sure they controlled the local municipal government, kept the houses up. Beaufort's occupation early in the war saved it for posterity.

There are no battlefields to see in and around Beaufort, but there is plenty of history. Edmund Rhett, the man who came up with the term "confederacy" to describe the alliance of secessionist states, lived here. Sea island cotton, a product that needed slave labor to cultivate it, was developed in small, experimental plots in nearby plantations, and that land is still there. The graves of the family who developed the cotton strain—men whose agricultural experimentation led to the continued demand for slave labor in the South—are here. The remnants of the school that was home to the Port Royal Experiment—the first attempt to teach large numbers of newly freed slaves to live independently—is on a nearby island.

Movie fans will recognize Beaufort's compact downtown and riverfront homes, which have appeared in several films, dating back to *The Great Santini* in 1979. Other movies that have used Beaufort as a backdrop include *The Big Chill, The Prince of Tides,* and *Forrest Gump.*

Because they are on the way to several beachfront communities, Beaufort's Bay Street and Business U.S. 21 passing through town can be crowded during the summer afternoons and evenings. Cars move at a crawl. Visitors who arrive early in the day will find it easiest to find a parking spot on the edge of the business district, then spend the rest of their stay exploring on foot. Consider riding in one of the carriage tours of the historic area.

POINTS OF INTEREST

1. John Mark Verdier House ★★

801 Bay St.
T: 843-379-6335
Monday–Saturday, 10:30 a.m.–4 p.m.
Admission: $5

This is the only historic house in Beaufort that is open to the public. Administered by the Historic Beaufort Foundation, it tells the story of Beaufort's fortunes. Its original owner was an indigo merchant who went broke when that market dried up and then became wealthy again when sea-island cotton was developed. Built in 1801, the house, like almost all the large houses in the town, was used by the Union during the war. It served as a military headquarters while most other houses were converted into hospitals. Tour guides use this house to describe Beaufort architecture.

This house's preservation in the 1940s marked the beginning of the town's preservation movement, which has kept the historic area intact for visitors to enjoy today.

2. John A. Cuthbert House ★

1203 Bay St.
View from sidewalk. This is a bed and breakfast, not a touring house.
T: 843-521-1315

During the war, the Union occupying commander, General Rufus Saxton, purchased this house at a tax auction. When General William T. Sherman was passing through on his march through the Carolinas, Saxton invited him for dinner. Sometime during the evening, Saxton made a comment in support of abolition. Sherman gave his host a hard stare, then said that he would just as soon South Carolina and Massachusetts be sawed off from the rest of the United States, towed into the Atlantic, and sunk. Sherman blamed the war on Northern abolitionists as much as he did on the secessionists of South Carolina. He believed radicals on both sides pushed for war when compromise might still have been possible.

3. McKee-Smalls House ★

511 Prince St. (private)

Robert Smalls, the slave who stole the Confederate ship *Planter* in Charleston, was born on the grounds as the property of Henry McKee. Later, he used his share of the prize money from selling the *Planter* to buy this house at public auction (it was available due to nonpayment of taxes). Smalls was living here when he launched his political career, and eventually served three terms as one of the first black U.S. Congressmen. One of his pet political projects was pumping money into the former U.S. Naval coaling station on Parris Island. Thanks to Congressional bills filed by Smalls, that coaling installation grew into the U.S. Marine Corps Training Depot

on Parris Island. Marines recruited from east of the Mississippi River complete their basic training here.

4. Beaufort Museum (The Arsenal) ★

713 Craven St.
T: 843-379-3331
Monday–Saturday, 11 a.m.–4 p.m.
Admission: $3

Located in an arsenal built in 1789, the Beaufort Museum, often called "Beaufort's attic" because of the artifacts stored here, traces the area's history from its founding through modern times. The arsenal was occupied by Union forces after the capture of the city, but it was never defended.

5. Robert Smalls' Grave ★★★★

Tabernacle Baptist Church
907 Craven St.
Daylight hours

A bust of Smalls depicting him as a Congressman is inscribed: "My race needs no special defense for the past history of them and this country. It proves them to be equal of any people anywhere. All they need is an equal chance in the battle of life." Behind the bust is his grave, which has a simple tombstone. There are no markers telling his life story.

6. Secession House ★★

Milton Maxcy House (private)
1113 Craven St.

The Secession House, first built in 1743, is a private residence, so it cannot be toured. But it is a fine example of Beaufort architecture, and it is historically significant. In the 1850s it was the home of Edmund Rhett, the editor of the *Charleston Mercury,* who regularly held meetings of like-minded secessionists. After more than a decade of such meetings, Rhett finally got his wish—a statewide vote for secession. Local history says the Beaufort delegation voted in advance in this house that they would support secession at the general meeting to debate secession in December 1860. Once Port Royal fell, Rhett was unable to return to this home.

7. St. Helena's Episcopal Church ★★★

505 Church St.
Graveyard open in daylight hours.

Union troops used the church as a hospital after they destroyed the organ to show local residents that the building was no longer their church. In the front of the church graveyard to the right is the Elliott family plot under an obelisk. Among the graves is that of General Stephen Elliott, Jr., grandson of the man who developed sea-island cotton. Elliott was severely wounded in July 1864 at Petersburg when a mine that Pennsylvania mining engineers dug under Confederate lines exploded under his South Carolina brigade. He died of complications from those wounds nearly two years later. He was just thirty-six years old.

At the rear of the church is a wrought-iron fence surrounding a large stone marker honoring Richard Herron Anderson. Anderson was a lieutenant general in the Army of Northern Virginia whom General Robert E. Lee trusted as "my noble old soldier." A study of Anderson's engagements found him always in the thick of the fighting. His division gained the high ground of Cemetery Ridge at Gettysburg on July 2 before being pushed back—creating the need for the following day's charge, which became known as the Pettigrew-Pickett-Trimble Assault. It was his division's swift march from the Wilderness to Spotsylvania Court House in May 1864 that saved the rest of Lee's army from being cut off from Richmond.

After the war, Anderson, a professional soldier who knew no other trade, fell on hard times. He was working as a railroad laborer in 1879 when one of his former soldiers recognized him. Given a job as phosphate inspector, he died of a heart attack within days of taking on his new and better job. A Union general who admired Anderson's fighting ability donated the iron fence around his grave. Admirers said Anderson never failed to take or defend any ground under orders from Lee.

OUTSIDE BEAUFORT

8. Parris Island Museum ★★★★

Building 111, Panama St.,
Parris Island Marine Corps Recruit Depot
T: 843-228-2951
Daily, 10 a.m.–4:30 p.m.
Free admission.

Although hosted by and focused on the U.S. Marine Corps, this museum also features exhibits on the development of the sea islands, and includes Civil War–era photographs of Beaufort homes.

Among the artifacts is a uniform from 1st South Carolina Volunteers, one of the first black regiments created during the war. Be prepared to present photo identification for every member of the party wishing to gain access to the base. The museum is found on a street to the right not far from the base's public entrance.

9. Smith's Plantation ★★

Port Royal Island (visible from U.S. 21 bridge)

The major point of historical interest found in Port Royal must be seen at a distance from the bridge leading over to the sea islands from the mainland. Security concerns have closed the U.S. Naval Hospital in Port Royal, where the site is located, to all civilian vehicular traffic, but this should not deter visitors from glimpsing two of the most historically relevant spots in black American history.

On January 1, 1863, the Emancipation Proclamation was publicly read for the first time by Union General David Hunter on a river beach on what had been the Smith Plantation, which is now enclosed by the Naval Hospital grounds. The audience on that day was a group of slaves whose masters had fled the area in November 1861. While the slaves had theoretically been free for over a year (since the Battle of Port Royal), they had actually been under the control of a Federal government unprepared for the question of what to do with slaves who no longer had masters.

The confusion over what to do with freed "property" extended all the way to the Executive Mansion. Within several months of the Battle of Port Royal, Hunter, the Union military commander of the area, acting on his own initiative, had declared the slaves free. Lincoln himself later countermanded that order.

After Hunter finished reading the Proclamation, the slaves looked at each other, unsure of the meaning of the words they had just heard. Then one slave burst into song with a rendition of "America," better known in that day as "My Country 'Tis of Thee," a patriotic song written in 1832. These South Carolinians were the first to be officially freed by the document, though they had been living free for more than a year.

Within weeks of this dramatic reading, the Smith Plantation was the site of another major historic moment in black history. The 1st and 2nd Regiments of South Carolina Volunteers, made up of freed slaves from the area, were raised and trained on this same ground. These men were the first of around 180,000 blacks who would serve in the Union army.

The regiments had first been raised in 1862, but when President Lincoln heard about the military organization of former slaves, he ordered the regiments disbanded out of fear that arming blacks would anger the slave-holding border states. Although Hunter publicly rescinded the order, he secretly kept one regiment under arms in defiance of the President. He believed that Lincoln would eventually give in to abolitionist pressure to arm the blacks so they could fight for their own freedom.

Finally, the Smith Plantation was home to another significant moment in black history. The 54th Massachusetts Regiment, a regiment of free blacks raised in the North and often mistakenly believed to be the first black regiment, trained on this same ground as the South Carolina regiments. The 54th Massachusetts left here in the summer of 1863 to make its famous, disastrous attack on Battery Wagner in Charleston Harbor (as depicted in the movie *Glory*.)

To see the Smith Plantation beach, look to the right (or south) while crossing the bridge on U.S. 21 from the mainland to Lady's Island. The U.S. 21 bypass is just north of the entrance to the Naval Hospital on S.C. 802. The beach is the point of land sticking out into the river.

10. Penn Center ★★

St. Helena Island
T: 843-838-2432
Monday–Saturday, 11 a.m.–4 p.m.

After crossing over the bridge, continue east on U.S. 21 and cross onto St. Helena Island. All of this land was once cultivated in sea-island cotton. After driving five miles from the bridge, watch on the right for Martin Luther King Drive (also called Land's End Road). Drive 0.7 miles and turn right into Penn Center, named in 1862 for Quaker William Penn.

While only the brick church across the road dates back to the Civil War, this area was the center of the Port Royal Experiment. Founded by two white women and one black woman, all abolitionists who came down from Massachusetts and New York right after the military victory at Port Royal, the movement set up schools for the freed slaves. Everyone from children to adults was taught to read, write, and count to achieve the Experiment's ultimate goal—teaching a suddenly independent society how to be free.

The Penn Center today is dedicated to preserving the Gullah culture of black sea islanders. Unique to this area of South Carolina, the Gullah language can still be heard in the sing-song cadence of speech and unusual words that outsiders often confuse with Caribbean dialects. In fact, the culture can be traced back to slaves imported from the West African country of Sierra Leone, who were originally brought over for their skills in growing rice.

The Port Royal Experiment was more successful than the federal government had hoped. Lincoln cabinet officials tried to persuade the new freedmen to continue operating the sea-island–cotton plantations on their own so that the profits from the sale of the cotton could be transferred into U.S. government coffers. Instead, most of the slaves opted to farm small plots of land to grow their own food. They wanted no part of a free life that reminded them of their former lives as slaves.

GETTING TO AND AROUND BEAUFORT

Savannah/Hilton Head International Airport, forty-five miles to the south, is the closest airport. Eight airlines serve the airport. Rental cars are available.

The Beaufort County Airport is a general services airport with no regularly scheduled flights, but it does have a 3,400-foot runway. Private pilots should keep a sharp eye out for faster traffic, as not far away is the Marine Corps Air Station with a complement of jet aircraft.

Like a much smaller version of Charleston, Beaufort, population 14,000, is a walking or biking town. Because of the heavy vehicular traffic heading to the beaches during the warm months, parking along Bay Street can be a problem. Overnight visitors wanting to view the exteriors of the houses or just watch the Beaufort River roll by will want to choose accommodations convenient to downtown so that they can park their car and explore on foot. Bay Street has a wide variety of restaurants and shops, including a bookstore frequented by Fripp Island resident and author Pat Conroy. Visitors could spend several days in town and not even leave the compact historic area.

One good way to get oriented is to take the hour-long carriage ride ($14.50 per person). The carriage passes more than eighty antebellum homes and inns.

For those wishing to see more than history, Hunting Island State Park, several miles east of Beaufort, gets more than a million visitors a year to its sandy beaches. The other islands, such as Fripp, are private, and visitors will be turned back.

Golfers might want to visit Hilton Head Island thirty-five miles south of Beaufort. Now carved up into residential plantations, Hilton Head was home to twenty-eight sea-island–cotton plantations before the war. Most evidence of the sand fort on the northeastern side of Hilton Head that tried to protect Port Royal Sound has been lost to development.

ACCOMMODATIONS

The Cuthbert House Inn

1203 Bay St., Beaufort
T: 800-327-9275
www.cuthberthouseinn.com
7 Rooms
$175–$265

Once the headquarters of the Union occupying general of the area, this house hosted William T. Sherman for a few nights. Today it overlooks Beaufort Bay and is located two blocks from the commercial part of Bay Street. If you are not inclined to walk, loaner bicycles are available.

The Rhett House Inn

1009 Craven St., Beaufort
T: 888-480-9530
www.rhetthouseinn.com
17 rooms
$150–$350

Built as an inn in 1820, Rhett House was renovated several years ago and continues to serve its original function. It is a favorite of visiting Hollywood actors, including Barbra Streisand, who famously called up the Marine Corps Air Station and asked them to stop flying while she was making *The Prince of Tides.*

The Craven Street Inn

1103 Craven St., Beaufort
T: 888-522-0250
www.bbonline.com/sc/craven
10 rooms and suites
$125–$215

Built in 1870 as a private residence, the inn is one block from the bay. There are rooms in the main house, a carriage house, and a separate cottage suggested for longer stays.

The Beaufort Inn

809 Port Republic St., Beaufort
T: 843-521-9000
www.beaufortinn.com
25 rooms and suites
$145–$350

Built in 1897 as a private home, this inn was converted into a boarding house in the 1930s. The inn also serves dinner.

SOURCES & OTHER READING

Gullah Statesman: Robert Smalls from Slavery to Congress, 1839–1915, Edward A. Miller, Jr., University of South Carolina, 1995.

Captain of the Planter: The Story of Robert Smalls, Dorothy Sterling, Doubleday, 1960.

From Slavery to Public Service: Robert Smalls 1839–1915, Oken E. Uya, Oxford University Press, 1997.

"Dupont and the Port Royal Expedition," in Daniel Ammen, *Battles and Leaders of the Civil War,* Vol. I, Thomas Yoseloff, Inc. (reprint 1956).

Official Records of the Union and Confederate Navies in the War of Rebellion, Washington, D.C. 1894–1927, Series 1, Vol. 12.

Charleston

South Carolina

A Fort Sumter cannon aims at downtown Charleston.

THE WAR YEARS

hough the fort where the war started looks nothing like it did before thousands of shells began slamming into it, the core of the city where the war started has not changed much since those times.

Founded in 1670 as a port city at the confluence of the Cooper and Ashley Rivers, Charleston had been a major population and import-export trade center for nearly 200 years, far longer than most interior Northern cities had even existed. In 1860, Charleston was a busy seaport, center of Southern social life, and a major city of 40,000, one of the largest cities in the nation.

One of its long-standing imports would play a role in launching the war. Until the federal government legislated the importation of slaves out of existence in 1808, Charleston was the largest receiving port for Africans (New York City was the second largest). Most of the slaves who had been brought to Charleston had arrived in ships owned by slave dealers living in northern states like Rhode Island, Massachusetts, New York, and Connecticut. As the market for slaves waned in the North in the late eighteenth century, the merchants adjusted their marketing. The slave trade into the South became a more selective business, with Northern slave catchers mapping African populations to find tribes already skilled in such knowledge as growing rice, an emerging Southern export.

As the practice of slavery matured in the South, it crossed economic and racial boundaries. Most owners allowed their slaves to hire themselves out on their own time and to keep that earned money. The most skilled slaves sometimes made enough to buy themselves and their families. By 1860, Charleston had more than 3,000 free blacks and mulattoes. Some not only lived next to wealthy whites, they also owned their own slaves.

In the summer of 1860 the decades-long political battles between North and South were coming to a head. Questions were debated in the halls of Congress and in each town's public square. Was the nation a union of states forever bound together, or a collection of states that cooperated as long as each state's rights were respected? What goods should be taxed and at what rate? How much protection should one region's industries have from overseas competition? Did the nation's future rest with agriculture or industrialization? Which region would have the most power in the nation?

No question loomed larger than the future of slavery. Would it expand into the western territories? Should it exist at all? A vocal Northern-based abolition movement with growing national political influence was calling for unconditional freedom for the South's 4 million slaves. The Southern planters saw immediate abolition as an attack on their existing agricultural workforce, accumulated wealth, and future livelihood. The average Southerner, who did not own any slaves, resented the people in his region being told what to do by faraway Northerners. Many Southerners of all classes shared a common fear of slave rebellions, which had occurred several times around the South, including in Charleston. John Brown's Harpers Ferry Raid in October 1859 was seen throughout the South as a failed but organized attempt by the North to launch a national slave revolt.

When the Democratic National Party met in Charleston that summer of 1860 to choose its presidential candidate for the November election, the party split into Southern and

Northern factions with the future of slavery at the core of their differences. Former Whigs who didn't like either branch of the Democrats formed a third party called the Constitutional Union Party. The fourth party was the four-year-old Republican Party, who nominated a former one-term Congressman named Abraham Lincoln.

Southerners sensed that the splitting of the Democrats, plus the addition of the Constitutional Union Party, would almost certainly throw the election to the Republicans, who had talked about limiting the expansion of slavery. When the vote was held, Lincoln won, as expected, but in protest, most Southern states did not carry his name on the ballot.

Lincoln's election and the uncertainty of what his administration might do about slavery was all it took to spark a second American revolution. Lincoln had hinted that he might limit the growth of and eventually abolish slavery. The South decided not to wait to see what he would do. On December 20, 1860, within weeks of Lincoln's election, but before he was inaugurated, South Carolina politicians voted their state out of the Union, hoping that other Southern states would join them in a "confederation" separate from the U.S. Six days later, Major Robert Anderson moved his ninety-man garrison of U.S. Army soldiers from the vulnerable Fort Moultrie, located on Sullivan's Island across the Cooper River from Charleston, to Fort Sumter, a strategically located, but uncompleted brick fort in Charleston's harbor. Within a month of South Carolina's seceding, six other states also left the Union to form the Confederate States of America.

From January through March 1861, the new leaders of the Confederacy demanded that Fort Sumter be vacated, as it was now a U.S. fort in what was now the sovereign state of South Carolina in the new nation of the Confederate States of America. Both outgoing U.S. President James Buchanan and incoming President Lincoln refused to surrender the fort or even to acknowledge that any states had left the Union.

On April 12, 1861, Confederate siege cannons began firing on Fort Sumter when it was learned that a supply ship was bringing provisions to the soon-to-be-starving garrison. Curiously, not a single soldier died in the thirty-hour bombardment before Sumter surrendered, but two soldiers would die when a cannon they were firing to salute the lowering U.S. flag exploded. The only deaths associated with the historical start of the Civil War resulted not from Confederate aggression, but from poor training of U.S. gunners.

After Fort Sumter's surrender, President Lincoln called for 90,000 volunteers to put down the rebellion of the Southern states. He asked each state governor not then in the Confederacy to supply the Federal government with several regiments. That call for Southerners to invade their neighbors drove four more states into the Confederacy, creating a total of eleven core states in the Confederate States of America. Thousands of volunteers from the border states of Missouri, Kentucky, and Maryland also joined Confederate armies, while their state's official loyalties remained with the Union.

Over four years of warfare, constant Union bombardment from the sea and from nearby captured islands reduced the Confederate-held, three-story Fort Sumter to one story. Charleston itself did not see any fighting between armies, but the U.S. army did shell the city's civilians for 600 days in 1863 and 1864, firing from the same hidden emplacements in the swamps east of the city that they used to fire on Sumter.

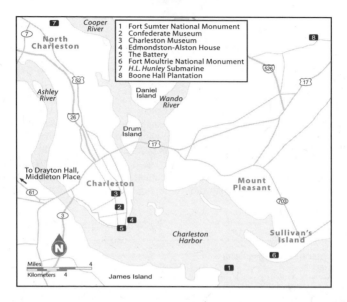

1	Fort Sumter National Monument	
2	Confederate Museum	
3	Charleston Museum	
4	Edmondston-Alston House	
5	The Battery	
6	Fort Moultrie National Monument	
7	H.L. Hunley Submarine	
8	Boone Hall Plantation	

Neither the fort nor the city, the two most powerful symbols of secession, fell. The closest battle came about ten miles to the southeast in June 1862 when a Union force was stopped at the Battle of Secessionville. In April 1863, a large force of Union ironclads tried to reduce Sumter, but sharp-shooting Confederate gunners holed the supposedly invincible ironclads. That summer the 54th Massachusetts, a regiment of black soldiers trying to prove their fighting virtues to skeptical white generals, stormed a sand fort named Fort Wagner at the mouth of Charleston harbor. They were repulsed with heavy losses, and Wagner was never captured.

The most curious military action at Charleston came in February 1864 when a Confederate submarine, the *H.L. Hunley,* was hand-cranked out to a Union blockading ship, the *U.S.S. Housatonic.* A torpedo run under the ship's keel resulted in the first underwater victory in maritime history.

As the war neared its end, Charlestonians feared that their city would be destroyed as had been threatened by Northern politicians wanting to make an example of the place where secession was born. Instead, Union General William T. Sherman turned north from Savannah and targeted Columbia. Columbia would burn instead of Charleston.

Although Charleston was spared total destruction, after two years of shelling, the city, once the center of Southern culture, was little more than a shell of what it had been in 1860. It would take decades of investment and the emergence of historical tourism more than 100 years after the war for Charleston to return to its gentle splendor.

CHARLESTON TODAY

With a population of just over 100,000, Charleston is South Carolina's second-largest city after the capital of Columbia, but it feels much smaller. Most visitors head straight to the historic area bordered by Market Street, Ashley River, and Cooper River. The core of the historic area is bordered by Broad Street on the north and Meeting Street on the west, with the two rivers to the east and south.

Charleston is best explored on foot. While there are parking lots on the fringes of the historic area, there are none in the historic neighborhoods of multimillion-dollar antebellum homes, which are the area's primary attraction. Driving in the neighborhoods is also hampered by horse-drawn carriage tours, which is the only other way to see the houses aside from on foot.

POINTS OF INTEREST

1. Fort Sumter National Monument
★★★★★

Fort Sumter is accessible only by private boats and tour boats that depart from two locations: in Charleston at the Liberty Square Visitor Education Center at the intersection of Calhoun Street and Cooper River, and on Sullivan's Island on the north side of the Cooper River from Charleston at Patriots Point, where the *U.S.S. Lexington* aircraft carrier is docked.
T: 843-883-3123
Daily, 10 a.m.–4 p.m., March 1–30;
10 a.m.–5:30 p.m., April 1–Labor Day:
10 a.m.–4 p.m., day after Labor Day–November 30; 11:30 a.m.–4 p.m.,
December 1–February 28, except week of Christmas; 10 a.m.–4 p.m. December 26–31. Closed major holidays.
Liberty Square Visitor Education Center open 8:30 a.m.–5 p.m.
Call 800-789-3678 to confirm tour boat schedule.
Boat ride: $12 (no charge to enter fort).

Fort Sumter is perhaps one of the most unimpressive forts to look at among the dozens that one can visit along the nation's coastline and waterways, but outside looks belie its importance in American history and what it used to look like before a war started within its walls. Today's one-story fort was three stories high in 1860. From 1863 to 1865, constant bombardment from Union ironclads and shore batteries reduced the upper two stories to rubble. To the delight of defending Confederates, the lowered profile of the fort just made it harder for Union batteries to hit, so they never rebuilt the upper floors. They just shoved the rubble into any exposed parts of the fort and continued their defense until the war was over.

The hour allotted to visitors at Sumter is enough time to visit the northern wall facing Fort Moultrie, where most of the damaging fire was delivered. The cannons in place in Fort Sumter are probably the same ones that were here in 1860, as those guns were discovered buried under sand and silt years into its restoration process. One cannon remains pointed skyward, evidence of an early attempt by Union defenders to create a makeshift mortar. A period photo shows that the gun has not been moved from its original location. The guns at Sumter facing westward toward Charleston were not powerful enough to have reached the city.

Walking along the wall atop Sumter gives visitors a sense of how strategic this fort was for harbor protection. Cargo and cruise ships pass between Sumter and Fort Moultrie, just one mile away. Any ship trying to attack Charleston would have taken heavy fire from both forts, which explains why Charleston was not shelled from the sea. The same walk gives distant views of Morris Island, the location of Fort Wagner, which the 54th Massachusetts fatally attacked. Interpretive signs describe the two attempts to take Sumter, once by ironclad reduction and once by a bold if foolhardy landing by Union sailors.

2. Confederate Museum ★★★★

188 Meeting St.
T: 843-723-1541
Tuesday–Saturday, 11 a.m.–3:30 p.m.
Admission: $5

Housed on the top floor of an 1841 building at the west end of Charleston's famous market, the Confederate Museum is administered by the Charleston Chapter of the United Daughters of the Confederacy. This one-room museum takes at least an hour to tour because it is full of original artifacts, including uniforms, weapons, and flags donated by the very men who used them. The museum is old enough that some of the identifying tags on the artifacts were filled out by Civil War veterans. This is not a museum designed by professional historians to tell a story, but a wonderful collection of artifacts preserved by the loving descendants of the men who experienced the dangers of combat.

3. Charleston Museum ★★

360 Meeting St. (one block north of Calhoun)

T: 843-722-2996
Monday–Saturday, 9 a.m.–5 p.m.;
Sunday, 1–5 p.m.
Admission: $9 for museum only, $14 for two sites, $18 for all three sites.

America's first museum, opened in 1773, is still open to display Charleston's social, natural, and architectural history. Though the museum seemingly covers everything from natural history, complete with skeletons of prehistoric creatures and stuffed birds, to sobering social displays, such as the metal tags slaves were required to wear so their owners could be readily identified, the Charleston Museum gives visitors a sense of the city and its inhabitants before the war. Note that one of the outdoor landmarks of the building is an old, now inaccurate cast-iron model of what the *Hunley* was thought to have looked like before it was actually discovered at the bottom of Charleston's harbor.

Visitors wishing to see how Charlestonians lived in the late 1700s can tour two houses owned by the museum. The Joseph Manigault house, built in 1803, is next door to the museum, and is typical of the houses that rice planters built. The Heyward-Washington House, built in 1772, is located one block off the Battery in the historic area, and was the home of a signer of the Declaration of Independence. It features gardens that the upper classes would have enjoyed in this time period.

4. Edmondston-Alston House ★★★

21 East Battery
T: 843-722-7171

Tuesday–Saturday, 10:30 a.m.–4:30 p.m.,
Sunday–Monday, 1:30 p.m.–4:30 p.m.
Admission: $10

The porches and roof of this house, built in 1825, were crowded with excited or anxious, dread-filled spectators on the early morning of April 12, 1861, as the

Confederates opened fire on Fort Sumter in the predawn hours. In fact, General P.G.T. Beauregard, commander of all Confederate forces and the man who gave the order for the cannons to fire, did observe the bombardment from the roof of this house. Several months later, Robert E. Lee spent the night at this house when a fire (unrelated to the war) threatened to spread to the downtown hotel where he was staying. This is the only house on the Battery that is open to the public. The rest are all private dwellings or bed and breakfasts.

5. The Battery ★★★★

The Battery, the loosely defined neighborhood spreading westward from the intersection of East Battery and South Battery Streets at the southeast end of the historic area, is the epicenter of historic Charleston. Named for the cannon batteries that once occupied the site in Colonial times, the neighborhood now includes White Point Gardens, an oak-shaded public space stretching for several blocks westward from the confluence of the Cooper and Ashley Rivers. The gardens have several cannons in place that point out to sea, including one recovered from a sunken Federal ironclad and used by the Confederates.

Set back from the park are the multimillion-dollar planter-era homes that give Charleston its distinctive flavor. It is definitely worth walking the sidewalks to see these homes, many of which were already 100 years old when they survived the Federal army's shelling. Built with narrow facades so that owners could reduce property taxes, which were based on street frontage, the houses stretch back into deep lots. Almost all have long porches designed to catch the sea breezes during the humid summers. The ceilings of those porches are traditionally painted a light blue to ward off "haints," or evil spirits, who supposedly detest the color.

A seawall running along Cooper River and then curving to run along Ashley River makes a perfect introduction to the neighborhood. During the day tourists can peek through the hand-wrought ironworks to see gardens that Charlestonians have kept for centuries. At night, many of those same Charlestonians graciously keep their curtains open so out-of-towners can see what the interior of a Colonial-era house brought into the twenty-first century looks like by lamplight. Watch your step as some streets are paved with uneven cobblestones and some sidewalks have been broken by tree roots poking up through the earth.

While walking along the streets to view the houses, visitors should pay attention to the ironwork of the fences. Those fences with multidirectional spikes on top were put up during Colonial or pre–Civil War times by owners who feared slave uprisings such as the Stono Revolt, which took place outside the city in 1739. The spikes were supposed to keep slaves from climbing the fences.

RELATED SITES BEYOND CHARLESTON

6. Fort Moultrie National Monument ★★★★

1214 Middle St., Sullivan's Island. From U.S. 17 in Mount Pleasant, turn southeast onto S.C. 703. Follow brown signs to the fort.

T: 843-883-3123
Daily, 9 a.m.–5 p.m.
Closed major holidays.
Admission: $3

Though commonly associated with Fort Sumter, as it was one of the forts that fired on the harbor fort to open the Civil War, the site of Fort Moultrie dates back to the American Revolution. Here, American Patriot gunners firing from a sand fort reinforced with palmetto palm-tree trunks successfully fought off a British invasion of Charleston in 1776. The South Carolina state flag's palmetto palm tree celebrates its role in the defense of Charleston.

Today's one-story, brick Fort Moultrie was finished in 1809, making it one of the oldest of the nation's coastal forts. It was the primary garrison of the Union army in the Charleston area through December 1860, when its commander realized that secessionists could easily scale the fort's low walls on the land side. Under cover of darkness, he moved Moultrie's garrison to Sumter, setting up the stand-off that would result in the bombardment in April 1861.

The fort's bricked, windowless chambers and bombproofs give visitors a good sense of how claustrophobic garrison life must have been. Along the top walls, visitors can see Sumter just one mile away, within easy range of Moultrie's cannons. The cannons on display are of the type that would have been in use during the war and may even be some of the originals. The extensive concrete structures on the grounds of Moultrie date back as recently as World War II, when military planners believed enemy ships and submarines might shell the coastline.

7. H.L. Hunley Submarine ★★★★★

Warren Lasch Conservation Center on North Charleston's now closed naval base. From I-26 in North Charleston, exit 216-B (Cosgrove Avenue North). At the third light, turn left onto Spruill Ave., At the next light, turn right onto McMillian Ave. Proceed through Naval Base gate. At first light turn right onto Hobson Ave. Drive one mile and turn left onto Supply Street.

T: 1-877-448-6539
Saturday, 10 a.m.–5 p.m., Sunday, Noon–5 p.m.
Admission: $10

Now submerged in a bath of fresh water that has stopped further deterioration, the Confederate submarine *Hunley,* the first underwater vessel ever to sink another warship, has yet to reveal all of its 136-year-old secrets. The primary mystery is why it sank in February 1864 after completing its mission. Raised from a spot in the Atlantic beyond Fort Sumter, the *Hunley* was brought here in 2000 with its eight-man crew still buttoned up inside. The crew were removed and buried in 2004 after forensics specialists were able to re-create what they looked like, and even identify that some of them were European-born based on wear patterns on their teeth and other information gleaned from DNA analysis.

The tour begins with a talk describing the *Hunley's* mission before visitors climb the steps to view the submarine in its tank. The vessel itself continues to surprise its researchers as well as tourists. Most surprising was that the boat was much more aerodynamic than historians, who had depended upon drawings for information about it, once believed. Its rivets were counter-sunk into the metal skin of the hull, then capped so as to present no upraised profile that would cause water drag. Other surprises were that it had a sophisticated gearing arrangement attached to the propeller and it was driven by a joy stick rather than a wheel.

As visitors leave the boat they can see the gold coin *Hunley* commander Lieutenant George Dixon carried with him as a good-luck charm. Eventually, the *Hunley* will have its own museum in North Charleston, but for the foreseeable future, it will be undergoing preservation at the Lash Center.

8. Drayton Hall ★★★

3380 Ashley River Rd., Charleston
Follow the signs to the plantation after
crossing the Ashley River west of
Charleston.
T: 843-769-2600
March–October, 10 a.m.–4 p.m.;
November–February, 10 a.m.–3 p.m.
Admission: $12

Finished in 1742, Drayton Hall is
described as the oldest preserved plantation house in America. Displayed without
furniture, the house is preserved down to
the original paint on the walls, just the
way it was left by its Colonial owners.
Remarkably, it was one of the few plantation houses along the Ashley that escaped
the raids and burns of Union General
William T. Sherman's forces.

9. Middleton Place ★★★

4300 Ashley River Rd., Charleston
Follow the signs to the plantation after
crossing the Ashley River west of
Charleston.
T: 843-556-6020
Daily, 9 a.m.–5 p.m.
Admission: $10

It is hard to imagine what Middleton Place
must have been like in Colonial and Civil
War times because Union raiders burned
the main house. What is left is the still-
elegant "gentleman's guest wing"—about

a third of the house that was once on a
rice plantation. This was home to one of
the most prominent families in Charleston,
that of Henry Middleton, who was a president of the First Continental Congress,
and Arthur Middleton, who signed the
Declaration of Independence. It remains a
working rice plantation, so during season,
visitors can watch the rice shooting up
through the lagoons—a sight viewed by
many slaves for over one hundred years.

10. Boone Hall Plantation ★

1235 Long Point Rd., Mount Pleasant
North of Charleston, across Cooper River
Bridges.
T: 843-884-4371
Monday–Saturday, 9 a.m.–5 p.m.;
Sunday, 1–4 p.m. April–Labor Day,
Monday– Saturday, 8:30 a.m.–6:30 p.m.;
Sunday, 1–5 p.m.
Admission: $14.50

The period-looking house was not built
until 1936, but TV fans will recognize the
avenue of oaks ending at the Boone Hall
house from several Civil War–period minis-
eries. Original to the site are the several
brick slave cabins in the front yard, which
date back to 1800. Slave quarters were
usually close to the master's house so that
owners could keep track of their workforce. These brick cabins are among the
best-preserved slave quarters in the South.

GETTING TO AND AROUND CHARLESTON

The city is served by six major airlines at
Charleston International Airport. The airport is eleven miles from downtown, about
$20 in cab fare. Most major rental car
companies are here.

If the destination is downtown historic
Charleston, visitors may not need a car.
Charleston is a walker's city, and strolling
along the sidewalks looking at historic
houses is often the lure of the entire trip.

Finding a parking spot along the Battery
can be impossible during peak tourist season, so a vehicle is only necessary if visitors intend to visit the plantations, all of
which are over ten miles from downtown.

A good way to learn the city's history is to
take a carriage ride from the City Market.
The one-hour tours run about $20 per per-
son. The tours branch out into several
parts of the city so as not to crowd the part

most tourists are interested in—the Battery. Ask the driver whether the tour will visit an area in which you are interested.

Gray Line offers motorized tours leaving the visitor center every half hour. The average tour lasts one and a half hours and covers 300 years of history. Stops include historic Charleston, the sea wall, and the carrier *Yorktown* on Sullivan's Island.

Accommodations

Phoebe Pember House

26 Society St., Charleston
T: 843-722-4186
www.phoebepemberhouse.com
6 rooms
$125–$225

This is the birthplace of famed Confederate nurse and diarist Phoebe Pember, who fought to be accepted as a female nurse at Richmond's Chimborazo Hospital. It offers amenities such as yoga classes, as well as tourist packages.

Governor's House Inn

117 Broad St., Charleston
T: 800-720-9812
www.governorshouse.com
11 rooms
$179–$395

This elegant bed and breakfast was the home of Edward Rutledge, the youngest signer of the Declaration of Independence and a governor of South Carolina.

Zero Water Street Bed & Breakfast

31 East Battery, Charleston
T: 843-723-2841
www.zerowaterstreet.com
Third-floor suite
$275

The view from the veranda overlooking the harbor gives an unobstructed view of Fort Sumter, the same view 1861 residents would have had during the bombardment. No credit cards are accepted.

King George IV Inn

32 George St., Charleston
T: 843-723-9339
www.kinggeorgeiv.com
10 rooms
$89–$185

Located just a five-minute walk from the King Street shopping district and a minute from the historic market, this bed and breakfast is further from the Battery, but more reasonably priced.

Sources & Other Reading

Confederate Charleston: An Illustrated History of the City and the People During the Civil War, Robert Rosen, University of South Carolina Press, 1994.

Allegiance, Fort Sumter, Charleston and the Beginning of the Civil War, David Detzer, Gene Smith, Harvest/HBJ, 2002.

Gate of Hell: Campaign for Charleston Harbor, Stephen Wise, University of South Carolina Press, 1994.

The Siege of Charleston 1861–1865, E. Milby Burton, University of South Carolina Press, 1992.

The Bombardment of Charleston 1863–1865, W. Chris Phelps, Pelican Press, 2002.

Raising the Hunley: The Remarkable History and Recovery of the Lost Confederate Submarine, Brian Hicks, Schulyer Krope, Ballantine Books, 2002.

SITE

15

Savannah

Georgia

Old Fort Jackson's cannons still take aim at Savannah River shipping.

THE WAR YEARS

When General William T. Sherman captured Savannah without firing a shot, he sent President Lincoln a telegram on December 20, 1864, offering the city as a Christmas gift. It was Savannah's lucky day, considering Sherman had burned down Atlanta just months earlier. Thanks to Sherman's gift, the city's colonial squares and the homes on those squares have been preserved and today give visitors a sense of prewar life. Nearby is Fort Pulaski, a Confederate-held brick fort that fell to concentrated fire from rifled cannons—the advent of which marked the end of masonry forts as defensible military structures. The fact that the city was the site of a major change in military technology, combined with two centuries of residences that survived two wars, makes this a rewarding area for the Civil War traveler.

Georgia and Savannah were both founded in 1733. Georgia was the thirteenth and last English colony, and Savannah was the spot where General James Oglethorpe first claimed the land for England. Oglethorpe recognized the opportunity he had to create something from nothing, so he planned the city with twenty-four open squares that he hoped would become public meeting sites. With twenty-one squares still serving the city, Oglethorpe's vision remains today.

While colonists in New England and Virginia famously struggled just to survive from one winter to the next, Savannah seemed to flourish from its early days. The water flowing down the Savannah River was fresh; the soil along the river was rich; the Indians were friendly. Everything about the new colony and the new city worked seamlessly. Even the capture of the city by the British during the American Revolution did not slow the city's progress toward becoming a major American port community.

On the eve of the war, Savannah was a smaller version of Charleston and New Orleans. Though accidental fires had nearly burned the city down twice, and yellow fever had killed 10 percent of its population in 1820, Savannah had always been rebuilt. In 1860 it was the largest city in Georgia, with a population of 23,000. Although port cities in South Carolina and New Orleans dwarfed it in population, Savannah had an atmosphere that signaled a new period of growth. Now that the newest colony was 130 years old, it was living up to its potential. Rail lines stretched from the interior of the state to the Savannah River. Trade goods ranging from cotton to lumber flowed downriver to Savannah, where they were loaded on ships bound for Europe and the North. The merchant class was building homes with materials imported from Europe.

Only the closure of the port could have a detrimental effect on Savannah. That fear did not take long to materialize when in November 1861 the Federal navy captured Port Royal Sound in South Carolina just forty-five miles to the north. By the end of that month an opportunistic Union landing force had occupied Tybee Island at the mouth of the Savannah River. Though the Confederates had been successful in defeating Union forces in Virginia near Washington, Yankees were within twenty miles of Georgia's largest city and were poised to shut down one of the South's busiest ports.

Because Georgia had rushed most of its early recruits north to fight in Virginia, there were no forces left to attack the Federal toehold at Tybee Island. As nervous Savannah residents watched, an increasing number of Union troops landed at Tybee. The Federals were in no hurry to push inland. Instead, they spent their time mounting heavy cannons in the marsh, aimed at Fort Pulaski.

Pulaski was a brick fort started in the 1830s as part of the nation's coastal network to defend its ports. The engineer who designed a system of canals to drain the area of water so the fort would have a solid foundation for its brick walls was a young second lieutenant just out of the U.S. Military Academy, named Robert E. Lee. Strategically situated next to the river and near its mouth leading to the Atlantic Ocean, Pulaski was designed to keep foreign naval vessels from sailing upriver to attack the port city.

Had cannon technology remained static, Pulaski would have been able to fulfill its mission against an eighteenth-century foe, as low-velocity cannon balls usually bounced off masonry walls. But this was the nineteenth century. While fort engineers were still laying bricks throughout the nation's fort system, farther-thinking cannon designers were rifling the smoothbore insides of their siege guns. The rifling put a spin on the newly designed bullet-shaped charges, increasing their range, velocity, and accuracy beyond those of the older, round-shaped explosive and solid cannonballs that had been standard for 200 years.

Cannon design had overtaken fort architecture, but as there had been no war in America since 1814, no one on either side knew it. That changed on April 10, 1862.

On that day, Federal gunners under the command of Union General Quincy Gilmore, a student of the new type of artillery, began firing on Pulaski. To the surprise of Confederates and the delight of Federals, the Yankee shells burrowed deep into Pulaski's walls before exploding. Soon they opened a breach in the wall. Rather than risk a shell roaring through the open space and into the fort's magazine, the Confederate commander chose to surrender.

While the citizens of Savannah were devastated at the loss of what they considered their first line of defense, the Federals decided not to take advantage of it and attack the city. Instead, they turned their attention to strengthening the growing blockading squadron of ships in the Atlantic. Instead of losing men in battle by attacking what they assumed was a fortified city, the Federals simply choked off Savannah's shipping traffic.

It would be two years before Union General William T. Sherman presented a land threat to the city. Sherman fought a few minor engagements around the city late in 1864 and one major fight at Fort McAllister south of the city on the Ogeechee River while preparing for an all-out assault. Rather than be trapped in a city filled with civilians, Confederate General William J. Hardee chose to evacuate his army in the middle of the night. He headed north, where he connected with remaining Confederate forces still in the open and fought one more major battle in North Carolina.

Savannah's nervous city leaders, mindful that Sherman had forced the civilians of Atlanta from their homes before burning down the entire city earlier that summer, expected the worst when forced to open the city to Sherman. The general's March to the Sea with his 60,000-man army had inflicted a sixty-mile swath of destruction on the Georgia countryside between Atlanta and Savannah. But Sherman surprised the residents. Instead of attacking or burning down the city, he just accepted its surrender.

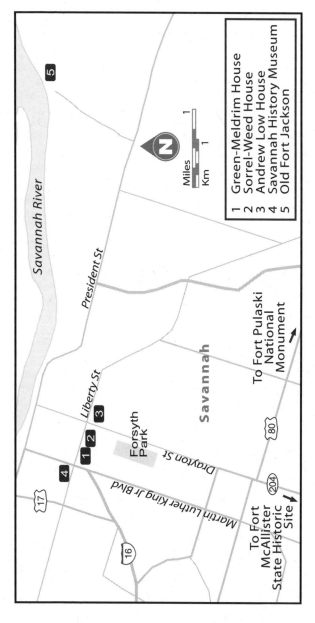

Savannah River

President St

Liberty St

Drayton St

Martin Luther King Jr Blvd

Savannah

Forsyth Park

To Fort Pulaski National Monument

To Fort McAllister State Historic Site

17
16
80
204

N

Miles
Km

1 Green-Meldrim House
2 Sorrel-Weed House
3 Andrew Low House
4 Savannah History Museum
5 Old Fort Jackson

SAVANNAH TODAY

Savannah today is no longer the state's largest city, but with more than 310,000 residents in the metropolitan area, it remains one of Georgia's five largest cities.

During the urban renewal frenzy of the 1950s and '60s, concerned citizens realized that they were about to lose what the original settlers under General Oglethorpe had envisioned. In a story that was repeated throughout the South, a band of preservationists convinced city leaders that tearing down historic buildings to put up office buildings and parking lots might not be wise in the long run. The officials agreed, and the city began to celebrate its eighteenth-century origins and to remake itself into a historical destination.

Of the twenty-four squares Oglethorpe originally drew on a grid, twenty-one still exist. Each is a small, square park with statues, fountains, shrubbery, and benches, with each square a little different from the next. The visitor center offers maps with histories of each square.

There are some intrusions on the historic downtown, notably a large riverfront hotel and a soaring, cable-stayed bridge that carries Business U.S. 17 over the Savannah River. The squares are also separated from the riverfront by a strip of "main street" businesses, but once you're past the modern facade, the eighteenth century reappears.

POINTS OF INTEREST

1. Green-Meldrim House ★★★

14 Macon St. on Macon Square
T: 912-233-3845
Tuesday, Thursday, and Friday, 10 a.m.–3:30 p.m.
Admission: $5

This parish house for St. John's Episcopal Church next door is the most significant Civil War–related house in Savannah because it served as the headquarters for Union General William T. Sherman after he captured the city. Built in 1850, it was Savannah's finest house when Sherman claimed it. It was from here that he sent his famous telegram offering Savannah as a Christmas present.

A line rarely quoted in the same telegram, but probably much more important to

Lincoln, was the offer of 25,000 bales of sea-island cotton that Sherman had captured. Throughout the war, the Union had been selling captured Confederate cotton to keep cash coming into Federal coffers.

It was here at Sherman's headquarters that a cursory investigation of a potential war crime was conducted. Several hundred slaves were drowned on Ebenezer Creek west of Savannah when one of Sherman's generals pulled up a pontoon bridge, forcing the slaves to try to swim the rain-swollen creek to continue following Sherman's army. When word of the deaths reached the newspapers, Secretary of War Edwin Stanton came down to Sherman's headquarters and held a private meeting with black ministers in the area to ask them how Sherman was treating them. The ministers, who may not have been familiar with the number of deaths involved in the incident, assured Stanton they had no problem with him. Stanton left without disciplining anyone.

It was also here that Sherman issued Special Field Order 15, which set aside a thirty-mile-wide tract of land stretching from Savannah to Charleston that would be given to freed slaves to farm. Issued in hopes that the thousands of former slaves would stop trailing his army, Sherman's granting of "40 acres and a mule" would be rescinded six months later when President Andrew Johnson ordered the land returned to the white land owners.

2. Sorrel-Weed House ★

6 West Harris St. on Macon Square
Private home. View only from street.

The 1841 Sorrel-Weed house is located just yards away from the Green-Meldrim house on the northwest corner of the square. This was the childhood home of Moxley Sorrel, a bank clerk who rose through the ranks from Confederate private to general. He is best known to historians as one of the best staff officers in the Army of Northern Virginia in the service of Lieutenant General James Longstreet. Late in the war, he was given his own command and was wounded twice. General Lee visited here in 1870 on his grand Southern tour.

3. Andrew Low House ★★

329 Abercorn St. on Lafayette Square
T: 912-233-6854
Monday–Wednesday, Friday, and Saturday, 10 a.m.–4:30 p.m.;
Sunday, noon–4:30 p.m.
Admission: $7

Andrew Low, the future father-in-law of Girl Scouts of America founder Juliette Gordon Low, was the richest man in Savannah when the war started, thanks to his fleet of ships hauling sea-island cotton to England. When this house was finished in 1849, it was the finest in the city. In 1870 Robert E. Lee stayed here while on his Southern tour. One of the dinner guests during Lee's stay was his old friend General Joseph Johnston, the man whose wounding in May 1862 at the Battle of Seven Pines opened the slot for Lee to take over command of the Army of Northern Virginia. The next day the two men posed for a remarkable set of photographs depicting the two old generals and old friends in their declining years. Lee would die a few months later, but Johnston survived until 1891. He died of pneumonia he contracted while walking with his hat off in the rain during the funeral of his old adversary in the Atlanta Campaign, General William T. Sherman.

4. Savannah History Museum ★★★

303 Martin Luther King Jr. Blvd.
T: 912-238-1779
Monday–Friday, 8:30 a.m.–5 p.m.,
Saturday–Sunday, 9 a.m.–5 p.m.
Admission: $4

Housed in an old railroad passenger shed, this museum tracks the history of Savannah from its founding to the present day, with special emphasis on the American Revolution and the Civil War when the city was occupied by its enemies. The museum gives visitors a good overview of the city's history before they head out to explore it on their own.

5. Fort Pulaski National Monument
★★★★★
US 80 E, about 15 miles east of
Savannah
T: 912-786-5787
Daily, 9 a.m.–5 p.m. Closed major holidays.
Admission: $3

Fort Pulaski is located about fifteen miles
east of Savannah on U.S. 80 on Cockspur
Island, a tidal marsh island apparently
named in Colonial days for the thorny
weed that grows in the sandy soil.

U.S. Park Service rangers tell a tale of
remarkable civil engineering when dis-
cussing the 1830s construction of Fort
Pulaski. Using nothing more than pencil,
paper, slide rules, surveying equipment,
and the principles of mathematics, U.S.
Army engineers designed a series of ditches that would drain the inherent moisture
from Cockspur Island. Once they'd accomplished that, they figured out how to build
a brick fort weighing thousands of tons on
what once was marsh. According to the
rangers, they can find few settling cracks
in its 170-year-old foundation. The only
cracks to be found in the fort came from
the Union bombardment.

A walk along the western side of Fort
Pulaski reveals that the bricks look almost
new. Watch out for the alligators who live
in the moat and in the surrounding marsh
grass. A walk along the top of the fort
reveals a system of drainage ditches that
still keeps the ground around Pulaski's
foundation dry. While the ditches are not
much to look at, Robert E. Lee designed
and placed them, making Pulaski one of
the few places where Lee's engineering
skill can be readily seen.

A walk to the eastern wall reveals that the
fort is not as new as it looks. It went
through through hell in 1862. Deep

gouges and filled-in holes in the wall facing east show the damage caused by the
thirty-six heavy Union siege guns firing
from behind the dunes at Tybee Island,
less than a mile to the east.

The quick fall of the fort embarrassed Lee.
In March 1862 the general was in Georgia
on assignment by Confederate President
Davis to evaluate the Confederacy's
coastal defenses. Just days before the
Federals began firing on Pulaski, Lee filed
a report calling the brick facility impregnable. After all, its walls were more than
seven feet thick and it had been built with
more than 25 million bricks. Lee, who had
graduated from West Point more than thirty years earlier, just had no idea that rifled
cannons had been developed with that
kind of penetrating power.

Visitors should allow an hour to explore
Fort Pulaski. Rangers give occasional
talks, but the tour is self-guided.

6. Old Fort Jackson ★★★★
1 Fort Jackson Rd. (3 miles east of
Savannah)
T: 912-232-3945
Daily, 9 a.m.–5 p.m.
Admission: $4

Though the two forts are similar in looks
(as both are made of brick), Fort Jackson
is much older than Fort Pulaski, having
been commissioned by President Thomas
Jefferson and finished in 1809. The fort
was designed to be a last line of defense
against attack by an enemy most
Americans had assumed would be British.
The United States did go to war with
England again in 1812, but Fort Jackson
never came under fire. The Union army,
having captured Fort Pulaski and the
approaches to the lower part of the
Savannah River, never even bothered to
scout Jackson for an attack.

One reason the Federals never attacked Fort Jackson rests on the bottom of the Savannah River, marked by a buoy visible from the fort's walls. There lies the *C.S.S. Georgia*, an ironclad similar in design to the *C.S.S. Virginia*. Despite their design similarities, the two ships' successes in combat vary greatly. The *Georgia*'s iron plating was so heavy and its engines so weak that the ironclad was never put under her own steam. Instead, she was tied up in front of Fort Jackson in hopes that the threat of a broadside from her would deter any wooden Union ships from venturing up the river to attack Savannah.

In 1865, as Sherman's Federal army advanced on Savannah, the *Georgia* was scuttled by her crew. Dredging over the years has scattered part of her, but preservationists remain hopeful that one day, there will be money to dive on the ironclad to see how much is left that might be salvaged and put on display at Fort Jackson.

What makes Fort Jackson interesting is its vantage point for watching oceangoing vessels. The channel runs very close to the fort, so ships seem to pass by just yards away. Allow an hour to take the self-guided tour and to watch a few freighters pass.

7. Fort McAllister State Historic Site
★★★★★

3894 Fort McAllister Rd.,
Richmond Hill
30 miles south of Savannah off Exit 90 on I-95, follow Ga. 144.
T: 912-727-2339
Monday-Sunday, 8 a.m.–5 p.m.
Admission: $4

The Confederates defending Fort McAllister must have felt like the Texans defending the Alamo in 1836. McAllister's garrison was about the same size as the defenders of the Alamo, two full companies numbering 200 men. Swarming toward them was a division of 6,000 Federals.

Land assault was the only way that Fort McAllister would ever be taken. Started as a four-gun redoubt in 1861, by 1864, the fort, located on a point in the Ogeechee River south of Savannah, had been built into a formidable structure of sand and logs. Several times Union navy ironclads had tried to reduce the fort, but McAllister was built of sand, not the proven-vulnerable bricks of Fort Pulaski some thirty miles to the northeast. Every explosive shell that spiraled into the mounds of the fort exploded harmlessly, hardly moving any sand at all. All that was needed to repair the damage was a few more wheelbarrows of sand, and there was plenty of that to be had.

When Sherman's army finally neared the completion of its march to the sea, he was faced with several choices. He could ignore McAllister and concentrate on developing a siege of Savannah, he could surround McAllister and try to starve out its garrison, or he could attack it directly and rid himself once and for all of its threat. While surrounding the garrison would have been easier and safer, Sherman's army had been marching for weeks in the field since leaving Atlanta. The uniforms of his men were in tatters. Their shoes were worn out. Sufficient food for 60,000 men was scarce.

In the distance, beyond the Ogeechee, lay the Atlantic Ocean. On that ocean were Federal supply ships waiting for Sherman to figure out a way to silence McAllister so that they could run up the river and meet his threadbare army. Sherman's choice was clear—he simply had to capture McAllister.

Sherman did not know the size of McAllister's garrison, so he ordered a full division against its walls. The overwhelming size of the force virtually assured that the fort would be taken, but the first men to rush toward the sand walls were killed by the main Confederate defense. McAllister's commander had prepared all of the approaches to the fort with torpedoes, the Civil War equivalent of land mines.

The Battle of Fort McAllister lasted no more than fifteen minutes. The Federal force was so overwhelming that the Confederates did not have time to fire and then reload their cannons before another charge was upon them. Battle reports indicate that most of the Federal casualties, twenty-four killed and 110 wounded, came from men stepping on torpedoes. The Confederates lost just seventeen killed and thirty-one wounded. Captured were twenty-four cannons and more than sixty tons of ammunition and black powder.

Today, the fort is a state park with camping and recreational facilities located a good distance from the fort. A movie orients visitors before they move on to a nicely appointed museum that includes some smaller artifacts from the *C.S.S. Nashville,* the first ship commissioned by the Confederacy. The *Nashville* operated as a privateer for a short time, meaning that it was a private ship licensed to

attack Northern ships. That created a national controversy—President Lincoln even threatened to hang all captured privateers as pirates. Lincoln backed down when the Confederacy threatened retaliation against captured U.S. Navy sailors. After a relatively short career as an Atlantic raider, the *Nashville* ran aground near Fort McAllister and was sunk in the river by Union ironclads. The state of Georgia is still recovering artifacts from her that are on display here.

Allow at least one and a half hours to tour the dirt fort, which is remarkably preserved for having been shelled repeatedly by Union ironclads and then left to the elements for 140 years. Grass-covered gun emplacements and bombproofs are easily recognized. Pause at the placement of the eight-inch Columbiad cannon to ponder that Confederates reported that an ironclad shell passed between the heads of two men who were working this cannon. The distance between the two unharmed men could not have been more than two feet.

GETTING TO AND AROUND SAVANNAH

Savannah/Hilton Head International Airport, fifteen minutes from downtown on the northwest side of the city, serves as both the commercial and private air access to the city. All the major national airlines and their regional partners fly into this airport.

Taxis and shuttles are available to downtown, but Savannah is a walking city where visitors will find it easier to have their own vehicles. Fort McAllister is more than thirty miles from downtown and Fort Pulaski is eleven miles east on a crowded, two-lane road.

First-timers to Savannah might opt for a ninety-minute motor tour that makes four-

teen stops around the historic part of the city and includes some of the tourist hotels. Cost is $21.

A slower, more historic way to see the city is by carriage tour. There are departures every thirty minutes from 9 a.m. to 3 p.m. After a lull, evening tours begin at 6 p.m. and go until 9 p.m. Cost is $21.

Once you've visited Fort McAllister, Fort Jackson, and Fort Pulaski, it is best to park the car at the hotel or find an off-street parking lot. On-street parking is difficult on most streets and virtually impossible to find—or negotiate—around the historic squares. Traffic runs into the squares from all directions, so Savannah has what amounts to twenty traffic islands scattered around its most visited section.

Bicycle touring is possible, but drivers unsure how to negotiate around the squares are not going to be paying attention to slow cyclists looking at houses.

Accommodations

The Confederate House

808 Drayton St. (Forsyth Park), Savannah
T: 800-975-7457
www.confederatehouse.com
3 rooms
$135–$150

Built in 1854 in Greek-revival style, the inn is decorated with period antiques.

Eliza Thompson House

5 West Jones St., Savannah
www.elizathompsonhouse.com
T: 800-348-9378
25 rooms
$149

Built in 1847, this inn has twelve rooms in the main house and thirteen in the carriage house. It also has a Civil War Reflections tour that includes a book on Civil War Savannah, admission to Old Fort Jackson and Green-Meldrin house, and accommodations for two nights for $378 per couple.

Olde Harbour Inn

508 East Factors Walk, Savannah
T: 800-553-6533
www.oldeharbourinn.com
24 suites
$149

Built as a riverside cotton warehouse in 1892, the inn was created in 1987. Located along the cobblestone streets of Factors Walk, it allows visitors to enjoy both the city's nightlife and river traffic.

Gaston Gallery Bed & Breakfast

211 East Gaston St., Savannah
T: 800-671-0716
www.gastongallery.com
15 rooms
$90–$275

Built in 1876, this Italianate-style house looks similar to Sherman's headquarters house and reflects the architecture and European influence that was favored in the post–Civil War period when the South was finally emerging from reconstruction.

Sources & Other Reading

Civil War Savannah, Derek Smith, Frederick C. Bell, 1997.

Fort Pulaski and the Defense of Savannah, Herbert Shiller, Eastern Acorn Press, 1997.

A Present for Mr. Lincoln: The Story of Savannah from Secession to Sherman, Alexander A. Lawrence, Oglethorpe Press, 1997.

Among the Best Men the South Could Boast, The Fall of Fort McAllister, December 13, 1864, Gary Livingston, Caisson Press, 1997.

"Siege and Capture of Fort Pulaski," Quincy A. Gilmore, pages 1–12, *Battles & Leaders,* Vol. II, reprint, Thomas Yoseloff, Inc. 1956.

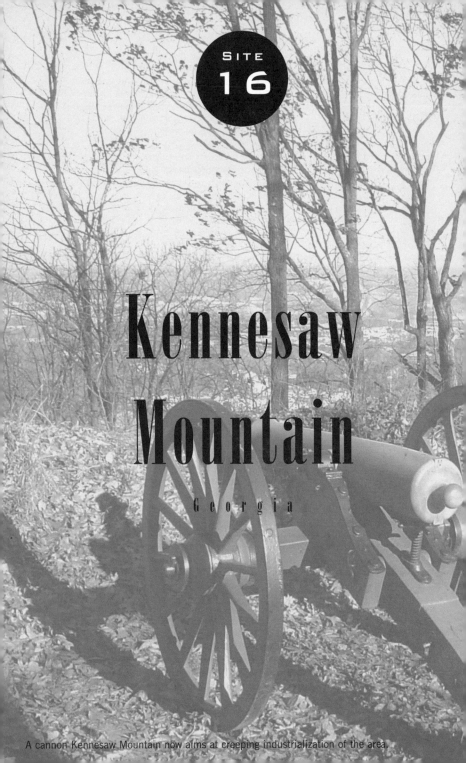

Kennesaw
Mountain

Georgia

A cannon Kennesaw Mountain now aims at creeping industrialization of the area.

THE WAR YEARS

I n the summer of 1864, Union General William T. Sherman decided to finally fight the Confederates standing in his way of capturing Atlanta after weeks of maneuvering around them. Those Confederates would bloody Sherman. As an oasis of historic woods in the heart of Kennesaw, a bedroom community just twenty-five miles north of congested Atlanta, Kennesaw Mountain may be best suited to physically fit travel historians. It is a steep climb to the top of the mountain, and once there hikers can walk or run still more miles of trails over mountainous ridges to see more of the battlefield. This park is for the true adventure traveler.

Kennesaw Mountain and the community at its base, then called Big Shanty, became famous twice during the war. The first time came in April 1862, the second time in June 1864. In both instances the Union did not fare well.

This part of Georgia was still relatively undeveloped in the 1860s, as it had only been thirty years since the U.S. government had pushed the Cherokee Indians off the land, and relocated them to the west. One relatively new development was the construction of the Western & Atlantic Railroad between Atlanta and Chattanooga. This rail line was vital in that any attempt by the Federals to move against Chattanooga to the north could be hampered by the Confederates rushing supplies and men north from the Atlanta area. Union war planners began to plot a way to destroy the line so that a poised Union force could pounce on Chattanooga. The capture of that town was considered a key element in moving westward toward the even larger rail center of Corinth, Mississippi.

Twenty-two men, two civilians and twenty soldiers, volunteered for the raid. The idea was bold: Board a train, steal it, and then stop periodically to burn the ties and the rails. When the crew of the General, the name of the engine pulling a freight and passenger train, stopped at a hotel at Big Shanty for breakfast, the Union raiders jumped into the engine and started heading north. They believed they had left any pursuers in the dust. But they had not counted on the determination of James J. Fuller, the train's conductor, who was not about to let anyone steal his train. Fuller chased the train on foot, then by hand car, then by switch engine, then by appropriating another locomotive called the Texas, which had to run in reverse as it pursued the General.

The raiders, led by a man called Andrews, were stunned at Fuller's tenacity. Every time they would stop to wreck the rails and cut the telegraph lines, they could see Fuller and a small force pursuing them. They could never stop long enough to totally destroy the railroad. Whenever Fuller encountered anyone, he shouted what was happening so that word would spread and others could help in trying to stop the raiders.

Eventually the General ran out of water and wood, and the Andrews Raiders were forced to jump off the train just minutes before the Texas and Confederate cavalry arrived on the scene. The raiders were soon captured. Some, including Andrews, were executed. For their feat in disrupting the train, the U.S. Congress created the Congressional Medal of Honor. Today, the Andrews Raiders would not receive the very medal created in honor of them, as it is reserved for combat heroism. Technically, the Andrews Raiders, dressed in civilian clothes, were not fighting the Confederates, only stealing one of their trains.

The next time Kennesaw Mountain saw action was on June 27, 1864, during a bloody battle started by an overly confident Union General William T. Sherman. In early May, from near Chattanooga, Sherman and his 100,000-man army began moving south toward Atlanta using the Western & Atlantic Railroad as a guide. Confederate General Joseph E. Johnston, with 60,000 men, kept throwing up defenses to slow Sherman. Sherman refused to commit all of his forces to a major battle with Johnston, who kept trying to lure Sherman into attacking his dug-in defenses.

On June 18 Sherman's army had finally arrived in the Kennesaw Mountain area. Union General Joseph Hooker successfully lured part of Johnston's forces under John Bell Hood into attacking him at Kolb's Farm, where the Federals inflicted 1,500 casualties on the Confederates while losing only 250 of their own. Encouraged by this victory, on June 27, Sherman ordered an all-out assault on the eight-mile-long defensive line that stretched around Kennesaw Mountain.

Sherman intended only a feint or false attack on Kennesaw Mountain itself. The main attacks were directed at Pigeon Hill, a mile south of Kennesaw Mountain, and then at Cheatham Hill, two miles south of Pigeon Hill. At both places, Sherman's men ran into a hailstorm of fire through which they could not penetrate. At Cheatham Hill, Union General John Newton created a battering ram of five closely packed columns that he believed would smash through any Confederate resistance. To make sure no one broke ranks to shoot randomly at the Confederates, he ordered the men to charge with uncapped muskets. The weapons were loaded, but could only be fired once the regimental commanders ordered men to put the percussion caps on the nipples of the pieces.

The Union commanders badly underestimated the strength of the Confederates and their ability to fight. No Federal soldier got within fifteen yards of the Confederate trenches at Cheatham Hill, where a salient in the line came to be called the Dead Angle for the piles of Federals in front of it. At the end of the day, Sherman had lost nearly 3,000 dead and wounded compared to only 500 for the Confederates. The Confederates had avenged their losses at nearby Kolb's Farm.

Stung by the loss of so many and embarrassed that he had been drawn into a stand-up fight against an entrenched enemy, a chagrined Sherman decided to return to his successful strategy of maneuvering around entrenched Confederates. Four days after the battle, he simply marched west of Kennesaw, then turned south again toward his real goal of Atlanta. Johnston had to move his men off the ridges of Kennesaw Mountain and head for Atlanta too. The battles around Kennesaw Mountain had slowed Sherman's advance on Atlanta and had whittled down his overwhelming force, but they had not succeeded in stopping him altogether.

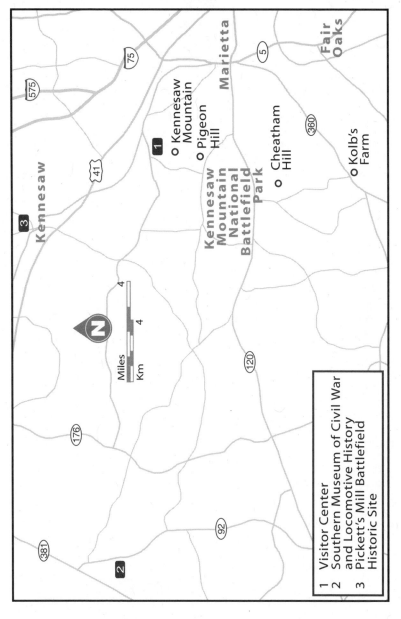

KENNESAW MOUNTAIN TODAY

Visitors to Kennesaw Mountain National Battlefield Park are very likely to find themselves in a traffic jam. Years ago, people working in Atlanta began moving north to Cobb County and the relatively rural confines of Marietta and Kennesaw, about twenty-five miles north of Atlanta. Barrett Parkway, the commercial road leading to Old U.S. 41, which runs in front of the visitor center, is clogged with traffic.

Kennesaw Mountain Battlefield Park is an oasis of wooded calm amid the dense housing and commercial developments around Marietta and Kennesaw. Many of the people who use the national park seem to have little idea that it is a battlefield and are more interested in the sixteen miles of looped running trails through the mountainous woods. On any given morning, the parking lot is filled with joggers ready to challenge the steep inclines up the mountain. People clutching books about the battle are not as plentiful.

POINTS OF INTEREST

1. Kennesaw Mountain National Battlefield Park ★★★★★

Exit 269 from I-75, west on Barrett Parkway to left on Old U.S. 41. From the interstate, the park is four miles.
T: 770-427-4686
Daily, 7:30 a.m.–6 p.m.
Closed major holidays.
Free admission.

The visitor center at the base of Kennesaw Mountain houses one of the better displays of artifacts and explanations of a battle to be found in the park system. It will take at least a half hour to walk through the exhibits, and this should be done before touring the battlefield itself. The modern displays are full of details about the Atlanta campaign.

Note that Kennesaw is like no other Civil War battlefield park. The one-mile dirt trail up Kennesaw Mountain starting behind the visitor center is not a casual walk, but rather a mountain climb. The walking path is quite steep in places. It's a good idea to carry water (which can be purchased at the visitor center). Seeing the entire battlefield by trail will likely take much of the day, so plan accordingly.

If taking the trail, there are several places where you can see downtown Atlanta. It is often shrouded in smog, but sometimes the buildings appear quite clearly. During the spring and summer months, a bus shuttle runs up a paved road to the top of the mountain. When the shuttle is not running, it is possible to walk up the paved road. The road is not as steep as the dirt trail, but it seems about one-third longer.

On top of the mountain are several cannon emplacements. During the battle these guns likely did not fire much, because the Federal attack on Kennesaw Mountain was really a false attack designed to keep the Confederates up here busy while the real attacks came to the south at Pigeon Hill and Cheatham Hill. Unfortunately, these cannons point out onto the roofs of industrial buildings and houses. Once at the top of Kennesaw Mountain, visitors can follow the path to Pigeon Hill and Cheatham Hill, the sites of the two points of heaviest fighting during the battle. Another choice for those who do not have the energy, or the time to hike, is to go back down the mountain, retrieve the vehicle, and drive to Pigeon Hill and Cheatham Hill. It cannot be said enough that taking the trail is for experienced, fit walkers.

It is a sixteen-mile round-trip hike from the visitor center to the top of Kennesaw Mountain and then south to Kolb's Farm. This was the battle that the Confederates lost and that encouraged Sherman to believe he could smash through their defenses. This is also the furthest point of the national park from the visitor center. It is ten miles round trip from the visitor center to Cheatham Hill, site of the Dead Angle. It is five and a half miles round trip to Pigeon Hill. Both Cheatham Hill and Pigeon Hill were the scenes of the heaviest fighting.

If driving to Pigeon Hill and Cheatham Hill, watch for the signs directing you to these sites. There is no direct driving route. Note that parking is limited at both.

There are two monuments at Cheatham Hill, one honoring an Illinois brigade and another honoring Texans. The story goes that when the men of the Illinois brigade raised money for their monument, they were faced with the dilemma of where to put it because they had been in nine major engagements during the war. The veterans chose the Dead Angle because they considered that their toughest fight. The Illinois monument is south of Cheatham Hill's trenches along the trail. At Pigeon Hill are entrenchments dug by the Missouri Brigade, who were attacked by a Union regiment from Missouri. A

reconstruction of a log cabin that was on the property is at Kolb's Farm.

2. Southern Museum of Civil War and Locomotive History ★★★★★

2829 Cherokee St. Leaving the National Park, take Old U.S. 41 northwest and follow the signs to downtown Kennesaw.
T: 770-427-2117
Monday–Saturday, 9:30 a.m.–5 p.m., Sunday, noon–5 p.m.
Closed major holidays.
Admission: $7.50

This excellent museum combines the expected (but well-displayed) artifacts of weapons and uniforms, but its core purpose is to explain the role of railroads during the war. It is doubtful that any other museum in the nation goes into such depth on the importance of railroads in transporting supplies and troops to the front. The museum rightly describes how the South made a fatal, decades-long mistake in failing to build railroads connecting its major population centers. It also failed to standardize a gauge on which trains could run, meaning that the distance between the rails varied from line to line. The different gauges prevented an engine and train cars from one line transferring to another line. In most cases, the cargo on one train had to be off-loaded onto another, a time-consuming process. The many photographs on display here show engines, railroad bridges, troops guarding railroads, and so forth.

The General, the engine stolen by the Andrews Raiders on the Great Locomotive Chase, is the last display in the museum. The museum shows a short movie that explains the chase. Clips from the 1960s Walt Disney movie, *The Great Locomotive Chase,* are deftly blended with updated scenes filmed for the museum. After viewing the movie, visitors walk down a corridor to read about the eventual fates of all of the raiders and the men who chased down the train. One of the original Congressional Medals of Honor, created for the raiders, is on display. At the very end of the tour is the General itself, the same engine the raiders stole. (The Texas, the engine that chased down the General, is on display at the Cyclorama in Atlanta.)

Visitors with an interest in machining will be interested in the Glover Machine Works, which takes up several exhibit halls in the museum. Glover was a Georgia company that helped pull the South out of the depression of Reconstruction by building locomotives. All of the equipment used for heavy manufacturing from iron molds to drill presses is on display.

This museum is affiliated with the Smithsonian Institution in Washington and hosts traveling exhibits on occasion.

3. Pickett's Mill Battlefield Historic Site
★★★

4432 Mount Tabor Church Rd., Dallas
Go 15 miles west of Kennesaw by following Kennesaw-Due West Road from Kennesaw.
T: 770-443-7850

Tuesday–Saturday, 9 a.m.–5 p.m.; Sunday, noon–5 p.m. Closed major holidays. Admission: $1.50–$3

While Sherman's Atlanta Campaign is often regarded as one of his crowning achievements, it was hard on his army because Sherman and his generals continually underestimated their foe. On May 27, 1864, after the Battle of New Hope Church, the Federals tried to outflank the Confederate position and ran into a well-dug-in force here at Pickett's Mill. Believing that they could easily push over the Confederates, the Federals attacked as dusk was falling. They were wrong. The battle went into the night. In the morning, the Confederates were still holding their ground. The Federals lost more than 1,600 men compared to Confederate losses of 500. The trenches here are well preserved. A reenactment is held every year in May.

GETTING TO AND AROUND KENNESAW MOUNTAIN

While Atlanta's Hartsfield International Airport may seem to be the obvious choice for flying in to see Kennesaw, it might be better to fly into Chattanooga Metropolitan Airport. Hartsfield is among the nation's busiest airports, and it is on the southwest side of Atlanta. That means visitors will have to drive north along the city's congested I-285 beltway to I-75 North to reach Kennesaw. Atlanta's traffic is something to avoid if possible.

Chattanooga is not nearly as congested. Visitors could get a rental car there and

drive south along I-75 to reach Kennesaw. The other advantage is that visitors could take in Lookout Mountain and Chickamauga before reaching Kennesaw. There are some historical attractions in Atlanta, but there are no preserved battlefields. The distance from Chattanooga to Kennesaw is about one hundred miles, while Hartsfield Airport is forty miles away. The difference in distance may be worth saving the frustration of being stuck in heavy traffic.

Accommodations

Hill Manor

2676 Summers St., Kennesaw
T: 770-428-5997
www.hillmanor.com
2 rooms
$100

The owners of this bed and breakfast believe Sherman may have stood on this highest spot in town to watch the assault on Kennesaw Mountain. The house was built in 1900 and is two blocks from the Southern Museum of Civil War and Locomotive History.

The Stanley House

236 Church St., Marietta
T: 770-426-1881
www.thestanleyhouse.com
5 rooms
$85–$100

This is an 1895 Victorian house renovated in 1985. Like Hill Manor, it caters to wedding parties.

The Whitlock Inn

57 Whitlock Ave., Marietta
T: 770-428-1495
www.whitlockinn.com
5 rooms
$100–$125

This house was built in 1900 and converted into a bed and breakfast in 1994 after undergoing renovations. It is on the site of a Civil War–era hotel.

Sixty Polk Street Bed & Breakfast

60 Polk St., Marietta
T: 770-419-1688
www.sixtypolkstreet.com
4 rooms
$95–$150

This bed and breakfast is located just off the Marietta Square, where guests will find local restaurants rather than chain fare.

Sources & Other Reading

Kennesaw Mountain June 1864: Bitter Standoff at the Gibraltar of Georgia, Richard Baumgartner, Bleu Acorn Press, 2000.

Kennesaw Mountain and the Atlanta Campaign, Dennis Kelly, Kennesaw Mountain Historical Association, 1999.

Decision in the West: The Atlanta Campaign of 1864, Albert Castel, University Press of Kansas, 1995.

Atlanta 1864: Last Chance for the Confederacy, Richard McMurry, University of Nebraska Press, 2000.

The Atlanta Campaign: May–November 1864, John Cannan, Combined Publishing 1991.

1881 FLORIDA 1865

Chickamauga

Georgia

Florida's is the first monument encountered at Chickamauga National Battlefield.

THE WAR YEARS

he Battle of Chickamauga in September 1863 was the biggest, bloodiest battle in the western theater and the last major victory for the South in the west for the rest of the war. The battle combined simple luck, blind stupidity, and complicated logistics to become one of the most intriguing battles to unfold in all of warfare. Twenty-seven years after the battle, veterans of both sides would reunite to celebrate the dedication of the Chickamauga and Chattanooga National Military Park, the first U.S. national park created in recognition of a battle.

The Battle of Chickamauga on September 19–20, 1863, was fought because both commanding generals, Union General William Rosecrans and Confederate General Braxton Bragg, had been ordered to fight by their respective presidents.

Since early that summer Rosecrans's Army of the Cumberland and Bragg's Army of Tennessee had each been countering the movements of the other in what became known as the Tullahoma (Tennessee) Campaign. It was a bloodless campaign with no battles, only marching around to try to trap the other side into a battle. Rosecrans would maneuver his army to try to cut off Bragg's supply lines, and Bragg would counter by moving his army in whatever direction was necessary to continue to receive supplies. The maneuvers and counter-maneuvers were well executed. Rosecrans forced Bragg to abandon the hills around Tullahoma and fall back into the vital railroad town of Chattanooga. For all the beauty of the maneuvering, both President Lincoln and President Davis were anxious for the two armies to start slugging it out with each other.

To Bragg's surprise, Rosecrans did not initiate battle once the two armies were out of the hills. Instead, Rosecrans divided his army into two pieces and headed one south and the other north—leaving Chattanooga and Bragg behind. Bragg pulled out of the city and followed the two corps heading south into Georgia. Bragg, a terrible field general, soon lost track of the Union corps—a remarkable feat given that it was an army of 30,000 men. Bragg settled down to wait along Rosecrans's line of communications, hoping that the Union commander would worry about a Confederate army separating him from that lone Union corps that had headed north.

Rosecrans took the bait and started his corps back north again toward Bragg, who was waiting for him south of Chattanooga along Chickamauga Creek. Elements of one of Rosecrans's corps stumbled into Confederate cavalry near a mill east of the creek. Scattered fighting broke out that neither general had ordered. Wanting to gather their respective armies into an overwhelming hammer to crush each other's exposed smaller elements, both generals were trying to use the same tactics. Rosecrans and Bragg both spent precious hours trying to move regiments around the battlefield like it was some kind of static chessboard. Those movements confused just about everyone on the field, from subordinate generals to privates. Bragg and Rosecrans would not admit that they were confused themselves. All they would acknowledge was that heavy fighting had taken place without any side gaining an advantage.

As darkness fell on the evening of September 19, Bragg was surprised to meet General James Longstreet and most of his famed First Corps, which had been secretly detached from the mostly idle Army of Northern Virginia. Longstreet and his men had been loaded onto train cars and shipped west to help Bragg establish numerical superiority over Rosecrans. It was a remarkable feat of railroad logistics and secrecy—as Rosecrans had no idea Confederate reinforcements were even on the way. Luckily for the Confederates, Rosecrans had been slow to engage his enemies, so the audacious plan to ship thousands of men hundreds of miles by several different rail lines had worked.

The next day, luck and blind stupidity combined to seal the Union's fate. Earlier in the day, Rosecrans had screamed and cursed at a general named Thomas Wood in front of his staff and men, an unpardonable breach of etiquette among officers. Rosecrans then ordered Wood to "close up on General Reynolds as fast as possible and support him." Wood read the order, shrugged, and then pulled his division out of its defensive line in order to carry out the orders. "Close up" meant for Wood to shift his division until it touched General Reynolds's division on the same line. The problem was that there was another division between the two divisions mentioned in the order. To comply, Wood would have to pull his men out of line and march around the unnamed division. The second part of the order told Wood to march to "support" Reynolds, which meant to line up the division behind Reynolds's division. The order, as written, made no military sense. Wood's division had been ordered to both line up beside and then line up behind Reynolds's division. Wood, peeved about being on the receiving end of Rosecrans's anger, pulled his division out of the defensive line as he was ordered. That created a hole in the Union defense that had not existed before Rosecrans gave the order.

Right after Wood's division left its place in line, Longstreet's First Corps came streaming through the hole in the Union line. Surprised that no one was shooting at them, the men turned first toward the weaker right flank of the Union army and sent the startled Federals flying. The Confederate corps then turned to its right and starting rolling up the Union line one regiment after another. Federals threw down their muskets and ran.

On a low hill called Snodgrass Hill, Union General George Thomas coolly formed his corps. As other Yankees streamed past, some of them found the courage to peel off and join Thomas's men as they waited for the Confederate onslaught. All afternoon the larger Confederate force threw itself against Thomas's corps, which was holding the high ground. No charge was successful. By the end of the day, Rosecrans's fleeing army had made it back to Chattanooga, enabling Thomas to pull his weary, exposed corps out of the fighting. For his resoluteness, Thomas was nicknamed the "Rock of Chickamauga."

Chickamauga was a bloody mess, with the North suffering 16,000 casualties (1,700 dead) and the South 18,000 casualties (2,300 killed)—nearly a third of the numbers engaged. The North probably suffered many more deaths than it officially counted because it had more than 4,000 missing compared to just 1,000 missing for the South. The ironic consequence for the South was that its victory prolonged the war in the west by many months—and brought to prominence a man who would come to symbolize evil in the postwar South. Had the South lost Chickamauga, Rosecrans would have been free to move into Georgia toward Atlanta. With Rosecrans in command and in good favor, Union General William T. Sherman might never have been given command of the armies in the west. He might not have started his destructive "March to the Sea," followed by his sixty-mile-wide burning of South Carolina. A Confederate defeat at Chickamauga might have shortened the war and resulted in less destruction throughout the region.

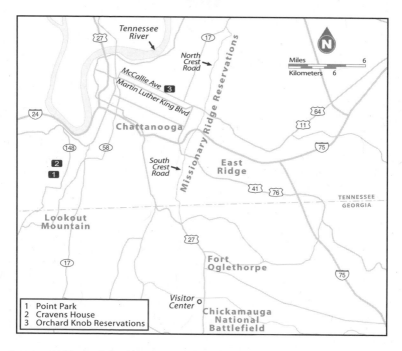

Tennessee
River

27

17

North
Crest
Road

McCallie Ave 3

Martin Luther King Blvd

Missionary Ridge Reservations

Miles 6
Kilometers 6

24

Chattanooga

64

11

148

58

South
Crest
Road

East
Ridge

75

41 76

TENNESSEE
GEORGIA

Lookout
Mountain

2
1

27

17

Fort
Oglethorpe

75

Visitor
Center

Chickamauga
National
Battlefield

1 Point Park
2 Cravens House
3 Orchard Knob Reservations

Bragg could have and should have pursued the Federals right into the streets of
Chattanooga, but as night fell on September 20, he stopped the chase. Instead of moving swiftly against Chattanooga, before the defeated Federal Army of the Cumberland
had a chance to dig in, he decided to lay siege to the city. Bragg's siege was a miserable
failure, as the Federals were able to get supplies from what rescuing Grant and Sherman
called the "Cracker Line," a protected supply trail named after the hardtack biscuits
that made up the staple of the Union soldier's diet. Eventually, the supposedly besieged
Federals would rush forward from a high knoll east of Chattanooga called Orchard Knob
and push the Confederates off the high ground around Missionary Ridge. The siege was
broken. Bragg would be replaced for allowing the Federals to not only keep Chattanooga
but push him around again. Rosecrans was replaced for losing the Battle of Chickamauga.

The battles around Chattanooga in November 1863 were called Lookout Mountain and
Missionary Ridge. The Federals easily captured Lookout Mountain, a very long ridge that
stretches into Alabama, though veterans of this battle made it seem more difficult by
nicknaming it "the Battle above the Clouds." A series of photographs showing U.S.
Grant and other generals and soldiers posing on the cliffs of Lookout Mountain made the
mountain famous in Civil War history.

CHICKAMAUGA TODAY

Lookout Mountain, Tennessee, has a small section of National Park Service land overlooking Chattanooga, but most of the mountain closest to the city is taken up by houses, restaurants, and a few tourist attractions such as Rock City and Ruby Falls. It has the feel of an elevated bedroom community. From the NPS park, visitors can enjoy spectacular views of downtown Chattanooga hugging the Tennessee River. On the east side of the mountain, visitors to Rock City can decide whether the attraction is truly elevated enough to allow views of seven states as has always been claimed. The Federal staging area of Orchard Knob and the battlefield of Missionary Ridge have mostly disappeared under residential development.

The edge of Chickamauga National Battlefield makes a jolting contrast to the heavily commercial town of Fort Oglethorpe, Georgia. The road leading into the park is lined with fast-food restaurants and gas stations. Then, all of a sudden, there are wide, green fields and heavy woods that mark the northern edge of the battlefield.

POINTS OF INTEREST

Chickamauga and Chattanooga National Military Park ★★★★★

Fort Oglethorpe
Reached from Lookout Mountain by following Ga. 193 south to Ga. 2 east and following signs.
T: 706-866-9241
Daily, 8:30 a.m.–5 p.m.
Closed on major holidays.
Free admission.

Of all the national battlefields, Chickamauga has the most modern facilities. A new visitor center has been constructed. At the entrance is a fine display of different types of field cannons that make it easy to compare calibers and the differences between smoothbore cannons and rifled guns. Among the attractions inside is a multimedia show built around the story of two old soldiers, one Union and one Confederate, meeting at the battlefield before the park's dedication. The two men describe the fighting and how the dedication will heal old wounds.

In addition to well-designed displays describing the battle and the life of the average soldier, Chickamauga is also home to the Claude and Zenada Fuller Collection of American Military Shoulder Arms. The collection of 346 long arms includes military muskets, rifles, and carbines. These examples kept in well-lit cabinets likely constitute the best collection of military weapons held in any national park, with the possible exception of the collection held at Gettysburg National Military Park. The Fuller weapons are arranged chronologically by the time period when they were developed starting with matchlocks. The Civil War section has one example of virtually every type of long arm used by both sides. This type of collection is particularly valuable when comparing the various types of carbines used by the cavalry. Carbines were never standardized on any particular caliber or look; regiments carried whatever their commanders were able to find for them—or whatever the Federal government issued once it made a deal with a hopeful contractor. Visitors will also be able to compare the small modifications and differences between "contract" muskets, muskets that the Federal government hired other companies to make based on the Springfield type of musket.

The auto tour does not begin where the battle started, so historians wanting to follow the battle as it progressed will have to read up on the battle, match the landmarks to their maps, grab a compass, and walk some. The park encompasses more than 9,000 acres, has a nine-mile driving tour, and includes more than fifty miles of walking trails. Sites that can be reached by walking trails include Jay's Mill, where the battle first opened on September 19; Braxton Bragg's headquarters; and William Rosecrans's headquarters. Some trails have markers and monuments that you can't view on the driving tour. Numerous markers and memorials—more than 1,900 if you count the metal plaques that mark troop positions—are scattered throughout the park. Visitors whose relatives fought here and who know the names of their ancestors' regiments can ask rangers at the visitor center to pinpoint the location of relevant plaques and monuments.

The following are significant spots on the driving tour:

Stop 2 ★★ is the location of the Federal battle line on the opening of the second day. Unlike some battlefields such as Gettysburg, Chickamauga was covered in dense woods and sparsely settled. The traditional method of advancing in battle lines of regiments of 1,000 men (500 men wide and two men deep) was nearly impossible, as the formations encountered thick stands of trees and brambles, shallow ravines, and streams. Much of Chickamauga has been left wooded. It was here at Stop 2 that probing Confederate units frightened Rosecrans into looking for more Federal units to bring to the aid of Union General George Thomas, whose troops were stationed here. Both sides began shifting units further north from lines to the south as they searched for a weak spot in the line to exploit. As the Federals soon discovered, shifting units in such heavy woods was a risky proposition.

Stop 3 ★★★ is the area where a Union scout, riding to Rosecrans's headquarters a half mile to the west, thought he saw a hole in the Union battle line. During the war, this part of the field was covered with woods, and the scout simply missed the division of Union General John Brannan, who were lying low. Acting on the scout's word, and not having the report checked out by anyone on his staff, Rosecrans impulsively ordered General Thomas Wood's division to pull out of line and move north. Wood did as he was ordered, which created a real hole in the line about a fifth of a mile south of this spot.

Stop 4 ★★★★ is the Brotherton cabin, the site of the hole in the Union line and Confederate breakthrough. It was this hole that was found by elements of General James Longstreet's First Corps of the Army of Northern Virginia, which had been loaned to the Army of Tennessee. Longstreet had arrived the previous night and had not seen the lay of the land in daylight. His attack on the empty Union battle line occurred by pure chance. Longstreet's men swept into the Union rear, turning first to the left to crush the small part of the Union's right flank, then turning right to roll up the Union line.

Stop 5 ★★ is the scene of the heavy fighting that took place on the first day, demonstrating how confusing two-day battles can be to understand when they are interpreted by auto tour.

Stop 6 ★★★★ is the Wilder Lightning Brigade Monument, an eighty-five-foot-tall monument to Colonel John Wilder and his 2,000-man brigade of mounted infantry, which consisted of three regiments from Indiana and one from Illinois. Wilder's concept was new in the war; he equipped infantrymen armed with rifles with horses to enable them to move more quickly around the battlefield. Cavalrymen were normally armed with carbines, a weapon that did not have the range of a rifle. His men's rifles had better range than carbines, and the men were skilled in infantry tactics (compared to cavalrymen who normally dismounted and fought as skirmishers). From this spot, Wilder's men, equipped with Spencer seven-shot repeating rifles, tried to slow Longstreet's men, who were equipped with one-shot muzzle-loading rifles and muskets. Wilder's men did manage to slow Longstreet's men, but were not able to stop them. The tower can be climbed except in winter. Wilder's Lightning Brigade may be thought of as the forerunner of today's military strategy of getting heavily armed ground troops to the scene of fighting in Bradley fighting vehicles or helicopters.

Stop 8 ★★★★★ is Snodgrass Hill, where a good Union general earned a legendary nickname and the Union Army was saved. As Longstreet's corps rushed to the north, his men rolled up the Union line, meaning that the Confederates hit the Union line on a perpendicular plane before the Federals could swing around to face their attackers properly. The sight of the Confederates sent the Union army into a panicked retreat toward Chattanooga.

One Union corps commander, General George Thomas, a Virginian who had stayed loyal to the Union, decided he would not retreat. He brought his corps to the top of steep Snodgrass Hill. As other Union soldiers ran past, some were persuaded to make a stand. Within minutes, Thomas's force was a mixture of dozens of regiments. All afternoon the Confederates attacked Snodgrass Hill and the ridgeline that ran from it to the west. Thomas and his men refused to budge. Some regiments were armed with repeating rifles, which gave them an advantage over the Confederates, who were forced to attack uphill and in the open while the Federals had been able to throw up log barricades.

All afternoon while Thomas's thrown-together force was engaged in combat, the rest of the Union army, including its commander, General Rosecrans, was retreating to the safety of Chattanooga. As the day ended, Bragg ordered his men to stop their fruitless assaults on Snodgrass Hill. Thomas pulled back under cover of darkness. Had Thomas not boldly made his stand on Snodgrass Hill, it is very likely that Longstreet's corps would have overtaken the fleeing Union Army before it had a chance to get back to Chattanooga. The fleeing Rosecrans himself might have been killed or captured.

It is possible that the Union Army of the Cumberland would have been destroyed altogether, leaving the Federal government without a presence in that part of the South. Within weeks, Rosecrans was replaced by U.S. Grant, who would eventually turn over all forces in the area to his friend William T. Sherman when Grant was assigned to head back east to take overall command of the Union forces. Had Thomas, who was given the nickname "Rock of Chickamauga" for his performance at Snodgrass Hill, not made his stand, what eventually became the Atlanta Campaign led by Sherman would have been delayed by months, as there no longer would have been an Army of the Cumberland to launch it.

After Chickamauga, Rosecrans's army was trapped inside Chattanooga with Confederate forces on the high ground all around them on Lookout Mountain and Missionary Ridge. It took nearly two months, but Rosecrans's army was relieved when U.S. Grant's army arrived and broke the Confederate siege. It was then their turn to attack and seek revenge for the disaster at Chickamauga.

LOOKOUT MOUNTAIN

Point Park ★★★★★

East Brow Rd., atop Lookout Mountain; Watch for signs at street corners.
T: 423-821-7786
Daily, 8:30 a.m.–5 p.m.
Admission: $3

Most of the "battlefield" of Lookout Mountain is not accessible since the attack consisted of Union troops climbing and crawling up the sides of the 2,000-foot-tall mountain. Still, there are some gun emplacements one can visit by walking the trails which offer beautiful, expansive views of the Tennessee River, the city of Chattanooga, and miles of landscape. Of particular interest to visitors who have books containing photographs from 1863 Lookout Mountain will be identifying the spots where those photographs were taken. Immediately after the battle, a photographer scaled the mountain and convinced various Union soldiers to pose for him. The photographs are reproduced in many books about this campaign. At some points, one can stand where U.S. Grant stood. There is one famous photo where Grant is looking up at a trapezoid-shaped rock, and the trail passes right by that rock.

Artists will be interested in going inside the Point Park visitor center to see the thirteen-by-thirty-three foot mural "The Battle above the Clouds" painted by James Walker, who witnessed the battle. The painting itself is rather fanciful, but that is because it was commissioned by Union General Joseph Hooker. Hooker was the failed commander at Chancellorsville,

Virginia, in May 1863, who tried to use this painting of a relatively minor battle in Tennessee in November 1863 to secure a more favorable spot in history for himself.

Note that some of these trails are steep and involve climbing stairs. Some spots are also close to the edge of the mountain. Before leaving Point Park, check out the New York Peace Monument, which has a relief of a Union soldier and Confederate soldier shaking hands. All of the property surrounding Point Park and nearby Cravens House was donated to the National Park Service by Adolph Ochs, a turn-of-the-twentieth-century owner of the *Chattanooga Times* who moved from the city when he bought the struggling *New York Times* and saved it from closing.

Cravens House ★★★★

Halfway up Lookout Mountain
T: 423-821-6181
House is open April–October.

The Cravens House, reached by walking the trail from Point Park or by driving there from the main road going up Lookout Mountain, is where the Federals depicted in "The Battle above the Clouds" pushed the Confederates back. A local iron manufacturer owned the house. Because the house was in the direct line of sight of Missionary Ridge, the Confederates used it as a signal station to communicate with their forces across the valley. Later, the Union occupied the same house and used it as a signaling station for their forces. Although the original house was destroyed, Cravens rebuilt it.

Missionary Ridge Reservations ★

Crest Rd., reached from the south from U.S. 27 and from the north by Tenn. 17.

Most of this area has been lost to residential development, and there are few places to pull off the road and get a sense of the slope of Missionary Ridge. Still, the National Park Service has a few "reservations" along Crest Road, such as Bragg's headquarters on the south end of Crest Road and the Sherman Reservation on the north end. On November 25, 1863, the Federals began their assault on Missionary Ridge's steep slopes. Normally, the advantage of having the high ground would have gone to the Confederates, but Bragg had not paid enough attention to the placement of his troops, particularly his cannons. Consequently, many of the Federal soldiers were able to advance up the mountain because the Confederate guns could not be brought to bear on them. In the Federals' final rush up the hill, thousands of Confederates were captured. Bragg's incompetence could no longer be hidden. President Davis relieved him of command after this debacle.

Orchard Knob Reservations ★

Orchard Knob Ave., and East Third St. just east of downtown Chattanooga.

It was from Orchard Knob, a high point of ground facing Missionary Ridge, that U.S. Grant watched the assault. Grant's orders had been only to take the rifle pits at the base of the mountain. He had not yet figured out how to attack such a prominence. To the astonishment of Grant and his subordinates, the Federal soldiers continued crawling up Missionary Ridge in attack mode. It was a true soldiers' fight during which they advanced on their own, having recognized that the Confederates were on the run. When Grant saw what was happening, he turned to his subordinates and asked who had ordered the attack. When no one admitted to issuing any orders, Grant hinted darkly that if the attack failed, there would be hell to pay for his subordinates. The attack was an overwhelming success. The soldiers had found their own way to the top of Missionary Ridge. Though Orchard Knob is no longer the empty plain it was in 1863, one can sense what the Federals faced.

GETTING TO AND AROUND CHICKAMAUGA

Five airlines serve Chattanooga Metropolitan Airport, and several rental car companies are on site.

A vehicle is necessary to reach the Chickamauga battlefield, which is ten miles south of Chattanooga. There is no public transportation to the park. It is possible to get to the top of Lookout Mountain by taking the Incline Railway up the steep slope, which terminates near Point Park ($10 round trip). The Incline Railway has been a Lookout Mountain attraction since 1895, but those with vertigo might want to avoid it. At one point the train car hugs a 70 percent slope. If

staying in one of the bed and breakfasts on top of Lookout Mountain, it may be necessary to drive a car to reach Point Park and the other attractions. While the development atop the mountain is residential, it is still spread out.

Once visitors arrive at Chickamauga, the hardiest among them will be able to walk the battlefield. Except for Snodgrass Hill, most of the battlefield is flat. Trails lace the entire park, and require a map and maybe a compass. As there are fifty miles of trails, walking every one to see every battlefield feature will require more than a single day.

ACCOMMODATIONS

The Garden Walk Bed & Breakfast Inn

1206 Lula Lake Rd., Lookout Mountain
T: 800-617-8502
www.gardenwalkinn.com
6 cottage rooms
$89–$175

The owners say that the inn is located just 100 yards west of where Union General Joseph Hooker's 20th Corps made its attack to capture Lookout Mountain.

Gordon-Lee Mansion

217 Cove Rd., Chickamauga
T: 800-487-4728
www.gordon-leemansion.com
3 rooms, 1 apartment, 1 log cabin
$75–$125

This house was Rosecrans's headquarters before the battle and a hospital after the battle. In 1889, more than 14,000 veterans of the battle ate barbecue on its grounds as they gathered to help make the battlefield into a battlefield park.

Pettit House Bed & Breakfast

109 Ochs Hwy., Chattanooga
T: 423-821-4740
www.bbonline.com/tn/pettithouse
2 rooms
$125–$225

Located at the base of Lookout Mountain, this bed and breakfast is centrally located in relation to Lookout Mountain, Chattanooga, and Chickamauga.

Mayor's Mansion Inn

801 Vine St., Chattanooga
T: 888-446-6569
www.mayorsmansioninn.com
18 rooms
$150–$275

Once owned by a future mayor of Chattanooga, this stone house was built in 1889 and is located in the Fort Wood historic district.

SOURCES & OTHER READING

This Terrible Sound: The Battle of Chickamauga, Peter Cozzens, University of Illinois Press, 1996.

The Shipwreck of Their Hopes: The Battles for Chattanooga, Peter Cozzens, University of Illinois Press, 1998.

Chickamauga 1863: The River of Death, James Arnold, Osprey Publishing, 1992

Guide to the Battle of Chickamauga: The U.S. Army War College Guide to Civil War Battles, Matt Spruill, University Press of Kansas, 1993.

Chickamauga & Chattanooga: The Battles That Doomed the Confederacy, John Bowers, HarperCollins, 1994.

Chickamauga: A Battlefield History in Images, Roger Linton, University of Georgia Press, 2004.

SITE
18

Fort Donelson

Tennessee

Fort Donelson's guns are zeroed in on the Cumberland River.

THE WAR YEARS

When Confederate Fort Donelson on the Cumberland River fell to U.S. Grant in February 1862, it marked the first major victory for the Union in the West, opening the way for the capture of the first Confederate state capital. It also launched the Civil War career of Grant, making this site a benchmark for the coming successes of the Union.

Fort Henry, on the Tennessee River, and Fort Donelson, about ten miles to the east on the Cumberland River, were not like the massive brick and stone forts built along the Atlantic coast by the U.S. in the 1830s to protect the nation's ports from foreign attack. Henry and Donelson had not existed until the war began. They were quickly constructed from dirt on the banks of the rivers to keep U.S. gunboats from entering the two rivers from the Union-controlled Ohio River near Paducah, Kentucky.

The forts' purpose was simple but strategic. The Cumberland ran from west to east all the way across the northern part of Tennessee, passing through Nashville on its way into eastern Tennessee. The Tennessee River stretched from the northern border of Tennessee with Kentucky from north to south deep into Alabama, where it then made a sharp turn to the west and ran across that state. If the forts could sink any Federal gunboats trying to make a run up the rivers, the interior of Tennessee and Alabama—the heart of the Confederacy—could be protected. If the forts fell, then the Confederacy could be split into pieces.

President Lincoln had early on in the war laid out that his favored strategy was to capture the length of the Mississippi River. His generals in the west did not think that was feasible. The river was too long and the cannons mounted on the bluffs of Vicksburg, Mississippi were too formidable.

The generals, principally U.S. Grant, convinced Lincoln that a better tactic was to capture ground in the Confederacy's interior. That plan would push back Confederate forces far enough so that Lincoln's prize of the Mississippi could be captured in due course. Lincoln reluctantly put his ideas aside and adopted the idea of controlling the inland waters. The first targets would be Forts Henry and Donelson.

Whoever designed Fort Henry should have been court martialed. The three-acre, five-sided fort armed with seventeen cannons (twelve facing the river) was solidly built, but it had been built on low ground that sometimes flooded. Higher ground was available, but when the Federals arrived on February 5, 1862, it was too late to build another defensive position.

As expected, the Federals had sent a convoy of four armored gunboats (similar in design to the *U.S.S. Cairo* on display in Vicksburg) to begin attacking the fort. Because it was at river level, some of the fort was flooded; therefore, the ironclads had no trouble shelling the works. That night Fort Henry's commander, General Lloyd Tilghman, knowing that Grant's ground troops could not be far behind the advance of the ironclads, ordered the bulk of his garrison to Fort Donelson, just ten miles away. Tilghman stayed behind with the cannon crews to preserve the honor of the fort. He knew he would surrender, but not without a fight. Fort Henry's gunners hit the ironclads repeatedly, but the ironclads' gunners were also accurate. Finally, satisfied that he and his men had shown a good account of themselves, Tilghman surrendered the 100 men he had.

It was hours later before Grant's infantry finally slogged through the mud and arrived within sight of Fort Henry. They encountered scores of grinning Union sailors, who were only too happy to tease the soldiers that the Navy had already done their work.

Undeterred by the embarrassment of being too late to participate in the battle, Grant turned his attention to Fort Donelson. Donelson was fifteen acres in size, much larger than Henry, but it had only twenty cannons. Its garrison was about 6,000 men, fewer than half the 15,000 men Grant was marching overland.

Confederate General Albert Sidney Johnston, the western theater commander, reinforced Fort Donelson with 12,000 troops, but he made the mistake of putting General John Floyd in command. Floyd was a former governor of Virginia and most recently the former Secretary of War in President James Buchanan's administration. Floyd was a terrible general with no sense of battlefield tactics—and worst of all, he was a coward.

Though Floyd outnumbered Grant by 6,000 men when the Federals first arrived on the scene, Floyd did not attack. It was not until the Federals had surrounded the fort and started to dig trenches that Floyd decided to try to break out. But before the actual attempt, he withdrew the orders on the pretense that it was growing dark. Lower ranking men and officers grumbled that darkness was just what they needed to escape, but Floyd did not relent.

The next day, the same Union fleet that had reduced Fort Henry without the help of Union infantry confidently began shelling Fort Donelson. Donelson, higher on the bluffs than Henry, was much harder to hit. The ironclads moved closer—right into point-blank range of the Confederate cannons. Three of the ironclads were soon disabled. This time it was the Navy that was embarrassed. Grant's infantry would have to capture Fort Donelson by themselves.

On February 15, ten days after the joint Union Army and Navy operation had begun against both forts, the Confederates surprised the encircling Federals when they attempted to escape along the river. They were successful at first, but Federal counterattacks soon pushed them back toward the fort, which other Federal forces had attacked. The fort's outer breastworks were now in the hands of the Federals, with more reinforcements arriving.

That night the Confederate high command met. Floyd turned over command to his second, General Gideon Pillow. Pillow then turned over command to General Simon Bolivar Buckner. Floyd and Pillow and their brigades of Virginians then boarded the last Confederate transports on the Cumberland and motored to the other side of the river and safety. In effect, Floyd and Pillow, the senior commanders, deserted their post and fled, leaving lesser-ranked men to face imprisonment at the hands of the advancing Federals.

Other than the troops of Floyd and Pillow, the only men to escape capture were 500 cavalrymen under Colonel Nathan Bedford Forrest, who would one day be regarded as among the best of the Confederacy's generals. This was the first battle in which Forrest

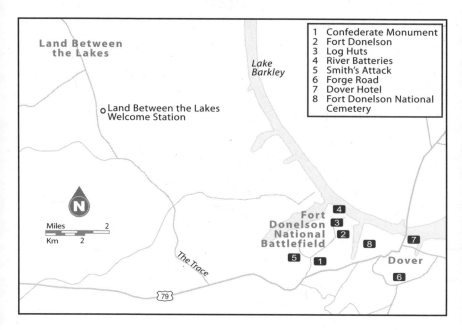

1	Confederate Monument
2	Fort Donelson
3	Log Huts
4	River Batteries
5	Smith's Attack
6	Forge Road
7	Dover Hotel
8	Fort Donelson National Cemetery

Land Between the Lakes

Lake Barkley

Land Between the Lakes Welcome Station

Miles   2
Km   2

The Trace

79

Fort Donelson National Battlefield

Dover

would reveal himself to be an officer who would always refuse to give up. He would have more than twenty horses shot from under him and would kill more than a dozen Yankees in personal combat. On this night, Forrest would lead his men through icy, muddy waters between the encircling Yankee forces.

The next day, Buckner, an old Army friend of Grant, went to the Union headquarters to discuss surrender terms. Buckner may have hoped for some favorable treatment, as he had once loaned Grant money at a time when all of Grant's other friends considered him a drunk disgracing the uniform of the U.S.. Grant told his old comrade that there would be no terms other than "unconditional surrender." Grant was soon known for the term, which matched his initials of U.S.

More than 15,000 Confederates surrendered at Fort Donelson, men who could have been a great help at Shiloh in the coming months. More important, no other forts protected those two rivers. With a loss of life of less than 3,000 men, Grant had split the Confederacy into two separate chunks of territory and opened the way for the capture of the first Confederate capital of Nashville. He had begun to make a name for himself.

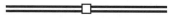

FORT DONELSON TODAY

Though the fort itself with its gun emplacements looking down the Cumberland is part of the Fort Donelson National Battlefield, the park actually controls fewer than 800 acres, less than a quarter of the land on which men died either attacking or defending the fort. Most of the approaches that the Federals took as they tried to surround the fort, as well as the route that Forrest took to escape, remain in private hands. As one of the linchpins in the Union's successful strategy to win the war, the national battlefield is listed as one of the ten most endangered Civil War sites by the Civil War Preservation Trust. It seems unlikely that development pressures will endanger the land bordering the park, but it takes only one landowner to bulldoze a trench line to destroy the area's history.

Dover, just down the road from the park, has a population of 1,400. The nearest city of much size is Clarksville, thirty-five miles to the east, with a population of 50,000. Fort Henry, already disappearing under river water at the time of its battle, has almost totally disappeared under Kentucky Lake, the artificial lake created from an upriver dam of the Tennessee. While that history was lost to demands for hydro-electric power in the 1930s, the trail that Grant used to reach Fort Donelson from Fort Henry is open for hiking from the Fort Henry Recreational area.

Dover and Fort Donelson are at the southern end of a recreation area called the Land between the Lakes that lies mostly in Kentucky.

POINTS OF INTEREST

Fort Donelson National Battlefield
★★★★★

Dover
T: 931-232-5348 (headquarters)
T: 931-232-5706 (visitor center)
Daily, 8 a.m.–4:30 p.m.
Closed major holidays
Free admission

It does not take long to tour Fort Donelson National Battlefield. The park is just one-quarter the size of the actual battlefield. Most of the land east and west of the battlefield, representing Grant's approaches to the fort, remain in private hands.

Still, Fort Donelson is a fascinating place to visit, a must for historians who want to see the battlefield where the future of the

Confederacy was likely sealed. Had the Confederate high command back in Richmond taken a more active interest in building up the forts, had western theater commander General Johnston sent more reinforcements, had the forts had better commanders than Generals Floyd and Pillow, had Fort Henry been built on high ground in the first place, then Grant might have failed in his mission to secure access to the Confederacy via the rivers—and to make a name for himself. Had Grant failed at the forts, he might have faded into obscurity. Well known in the War Department—as well as disliked and distrusted as a potential drunk—Grant attained successes here that made him popular in the public eye. Even if the armchair generals in Washington had wanted to fire him, they could not have done so after he opened the western Confederacy.

Visitors to the battlefield should note that the hours here are a little different from those of the museum: 8 a.m.–4:30 p.m. . There are nearly six miles of hiking trails on the battlefield. Maps are available at the visitor center.

This tour road is more chronologically oriented than some park tours. Stops marking the Federal attack come near the end of the tour, and the last two stops are the site where Confederate General Buckner surrendered and the Fort Donelson National Cemetery.

Stop 1 ★ marks a Confederate statue erected in 1933 to commemorate the Confederate dead. The location of their graves is not known.

Stop 2 ★★ is the outer boundary of Fort Donelson, which was built over the course of seven months into a fifteen-acre fort with dirt and log walls ten feet tall. Historians who have seen other Confederate dirt forts might question the reasons why Donelson's wall height was this low. Fort Donelson's walls were scalable, as proven by the attacking Union forces. Either the work gang used to construct Fort Donelson ran out of time to build the wall to unscalable heights, or the construction supervisor was overconfident that the men could shoot down attackers before they reached the fort's walls. A field of fire 200 yards wide was cleared of trees and brush around all approaches to the fort.

Stop 3 ★★★ shows log huts that are sometimes occupied by weekend reenactors giving programs for the public. During the war, more than 400 log huts were scattered outside the fort. Confederates wrote that they found the duty around the fort "luxurious." These were garrison

troops from Tennessee, Alabama, Kentucky, and Virginia who waited for the enemy to come to them, as opposed to most other Confederate armies, who marched in search of the enemy.

Stop 4 ★★★★ is the most interesting and photogenic stop of the park tour, as it features the river batteries pointing down the Cumberland River. The batteries were divided into upper and lower batteries. The lower had a ten-inch Columbiad (a smoothbore cannon with a ten-inch diameter) and nine smoothbore thirty-two-pounders (meaning the cannon balls weighed thirty-two pounds). The upper battery had a ten-inch Columbiad that had been rifled and two thirty-two-pounder carronades, which were cannons with shorter-than-normal barrels. A carronade had the advantage that it used less powder than a longer-barreled cannon of comparable poundage, but the disadvantage of less striking power.

At least some of the cannons that would have been in place here in 1862 came from the capture of the largest naval ship-yard in the United States, Gosport Naval Yard outside Norfolk, Virginia, in April 1862. The Confederates captured more than 1,000 Federal cannons designed for siege and ship use. Some of them were put aboard trains and shipped at least as far west as Fort Donelson. The fact that the Confederacy had to ship cannons more than 1,000 miles just to protect its inland waters indicates how unprepared the South was to wage war in April 1861.

Admiral Andrew Foote, commanding the Union ironclads, was overconfident when he steamed up the Cumberland to do battle with the Confederate gunners. His ships had easily reduced Fort Henry, and he expected the same results here. He had not counted on better-trained gun crews, who had zeroed in on every spot on the river within their range, and the height advantage Fort Donelson had thanks to its location on the bluffs.

After his ironclads failed to dislodge the Confederates, Foote complained that he had not been ready to attack. He complained that Grant rushed him. Grant, who knew little about gunboats other than that they floated, could not be blamed for what happened, which was that Foote steamed his gunboats too close to the Confederate batteries and they were smashed.

The next noteworthy stop is **Stop 7** ★★★★, southwest of the fort itself, where Union General Charles F. Smith, a former commandant of the U.S. Military Academy at West Point, broke through the outer ring of Confederate earthworks on the morning of February 15. Smith's success in breaching the lines convinced the Confederates that they no longer had time to break out of Fort Donelson. Grant's men were already too thick around the fort.

It was Smith who suggested to Grant that he not agree to any terms with the Confederates other than "unconditional surrender." Until this point in the early days of the Civil War, the losing side had generally been granted some privileges from the winning side. (When Fort Sumter surrendered to the Confederates, its Union commander asked to fire a 100-gun salute in honor of the American flag. That was granted. He also asked that his garrison not be taken prisoner, but be allowed to sail to New York, which was also granted.)

Smith's key roles in the capture of both Fort Henry and Fort Donelson would be rewarded with a commission to major general. Unfortunately, he scraped his shin climbing into a rowboat. The shin became infected, and Smith, Grant's first mentor, died of blood poisoning after Shiloh.

Stops 8 to **10** are found by getting back on the road toward Dover (U.S. 79) and following the signs heading to the southeast.

Stop 9 ★ is the Forge Road. On the morning of February 15, the Confederates briefly cleared this road of Federals, giving themselves one last chance to break out of the fort and try to escape capture. Floyd ordered the men back into the protection of the fort rather than take the chance of escaping. Later that night, he snuck away under cover of darkness. The men who had been on the road to escape were forced to surrender the next day.

Follow the signs to **Stop 10** ★★★★, the Dover Hotel, which has been reconstructed to look like its predecessor, built in the early 1850s as a hotel catering to riverboat traffic. At the end of the battle, General Buckner chose the hotel as the place to negotiate whatever surrender terms he could. The hotel survived the war and operated through the 1930s.

A last stop is the Fort Donelson National Cemetery, started in 1867. Nearly 700 Union soldiers, 500 of them unknown, lie buried here, as do veterans of other wars.

Land between the Lakes ★★★

Non–Civil War buffs will want to know about this recreation area. This region, so named because it is a fifty-by-five-mile peninsula formed by two artificial bodies of water, Kentucky Lake and Lake Barkley, is one large national recreation area administered by the U.S. Forest Service. Within the recreation area is a drive-through elk and bison habitat and a living-history farm where visitors can get a sense of how farmers in the 1860s made their living before war erupted. Visitors to this area enjoy camping, boating, and hiking.

The only Civil War-related site found within the Land between the Lakes is the Fort Henry Trailhead, located off Road 232 at the South Welcome Station of Kentucky Lake. It has ten trails totaling twenty-six miles and includes the approaches Grant's men took to attack Fort Donelson.

Getting To and Around Fort Donelson

Dover is a small town, reached by two-lane highways if you're coming up from the south via I-40. The roads pass through some other small towns, twist and turn, and climb over some small hills. On some stretches, the road borders the Cumberland River. Allow plenty of time to reach Dover and Fort Donelson.

The closest commercial airport is in Paducah, Kentucky, fifty-nine miles northwest, or Nashville, 64 miles to the east. It would make the most sense to combine this visit with a trip to Shiloh. Fly into Nashville, then make a triangular visit to Shiloh, then Fort Donelson, and then back to the Nashville Airport. Both Paducah and Nashville have rental cars available.

A word of caution about Clarksville, Tennessee: It borders on Fort Campbell, Kentucky, home of the 101st Airborne Division, the "Screaming Eagles." There is unexpectedly heavy traffic moving in and out of the base.

Accommodations

The Riverfront Plantation Inn

190 Crow Ln., Dover
T: 877-660-5939
www.riverfrontplantation.com
5 rooms
$95–$110

This house was built in 1859, partially burned down during the war, and then rebuilt in 1869. The guest rooms are all named after Confederate generals.

The Cabin at Stillwaters Farm

Cumberland Furnace
T: 615-219-2408
www.visitthecabin.homestead.com/
Home.html

2 rooms
$105–$115

This is a cabin on the owner's farm. It requires a two-night minimum stay.

The Verandah Bed & Breakfast

108 North College St., Paris
T: 731-642-2371
www.verandabandb.com
2 rooms
$79–$89

Located 31 miles west of Dover, this 100-year-old house promotes its screened porch as a place to relax.

Sources & Other Reading

Where the South Lost the War: An Analysis of the Fort Henry–Fort Donelson Campaign, February 1862, Kendall Gott, Stackpole Books, 2003.

Forts Henry and Donelson: The Key to the Confederate Heartland, Benjamin Cooling, University of Tennessee Press, 1988.

Fort Sumter to Perryville (Vol. 1 of *The Civil War: A Narrative*), Shelby Foote, Random House, 1958.

Unconditional Surrender: The Capture of Forts Henry and Donelson (Civil War Campaigns and Commanders series), Spencer Tucker, McWhiney Foundation Press, 2001.

Shiloh

T e n n e s s e e

These cannons blasted the Hornets' Nest several hundred yards to the north.

THE WAR YEARS

The Shiloh National Military Park preserves the April 6–7, 1862, battlefield that shocked both North and South with its large number of casualties. Until this battle in southwestern Tennessee, losses in the year-old conflict had been relatively small and the battles infrequent. The sprawling combat here was between two armies made up mostly of men who had never fired a shot in anger. This site is important in that it brought home to the civilian population that the war would likely be a prolonged and bloody affair.

The inevitability of fighting at Shiloh (called the Battle of Pittsburg Landing in Northern accounts) was determined two months earlier in February when the Union Navy and General Ulysses S. Grant's army captured Fort Henry on the Tennessee River and nearby Fort Donelson on the Cumberland River. The two forts, 120 miles directly north of Shiloh, had been the Confederacy's main hope of protecting its interior from water invasion. When those forts fell, the way was open for the Union to attack deep into the South, all the way to Alabama if it wanted. Inland ports along the Tennessee and Cumberland and important interior rail lines used for shipping food and supplies all across the South were now at risk.

Grant set his sights on capturing the railhead town of Corinth, Mississippi, which was just four days' march or eighty-five miles from the major port city of Memphis on the Mississippi River. A second Union army under General Don Carlos Buell was ordered to march southwest from Nashville to link with Grant at Pittsburg Landing on the Tennessee River. Once united, the two armies would then move on Corinth, crippling the South's ability to draw supplies from the west and ship them east. Once Corinth was captured, Grant would think about going after the other strongholds along the Mississippi.

There was not much to see at Pittsburg Landing on the Tennessee River where Grant chose to camp his army while waiting for Buell. A small log church named Shiloh Meeting House was a mile away.

Grant was so confident that no Confederate force threatened him that he not only camped his entire army on the west bank of the Tennessee, but took few precautions and didn't even bother to dig defensive trench lines. This proved to be a critical error in judgment, as it meant his army had no room to maneuver if it was attacked from the west—which was where the Confederates were located.

Already on their way from Corinth, twenty miles to the southwest, were 44,000 Confederates under the command of General Albert Sidney Johnston, who knew not only about Grant's 42,000-man camped army, but also about Buell's 25,000-man marching army. Johnston planned to surprise Grant's sleeping men, push them into the Tennessee River, and then lie in wait for Buell's smaller force. It was a plan that depended as much upon surprise and discipline among the Confederates as complacency and confusion among the Federals.

Johnston's army smashed into Grant's sleeping camps at dawn on Sunday, April 6, 1862. The surprise was complete. Union General William T. Sherman had even mocked and berated a nervous colonel who had warned his commanders that his regiment could hear rustling and voices in the woods.

For the first minutes of the attack the Confederates overwhelmed most resistance as the newly minted Union soldiers fled in panic. But the Confederates, including the commanders, were as new at war as the Federals. Attack formations mixed and the regiments became intermingled, creating confusion along the chain of command. Hundreds of hungry Confederates broke formation to eat the breakfasts of the fleeing Federals. The smashing attack waned almost as abruptly as it had begun.

This lull in the fighting gave Union General Benjamin Prentiss time to rally his division on a farm road running past some woods. As the disintegrating army rushed past, some men broke off and joined Prentiss's defenders, whose command would eventually become a mixture of several divisions.

For at least eight hours the Federals in the road held up the Confederate advance. Johnston stubbornly refused to bypass the pocket of resistance. Bullets and cannon shells zinged into and out of the woods so frequently that the Federals named the area the Hornets' Nest.

As this battle within a battle raged, Johnston, who was directing his army's movements from the front lines, was hit in the back of the leg by a musket ball, perhaps fired by one of his own nervous men. He either did not know he had been wounded or intentionally ignored the pain. He did not mention it to his staff, most of whom had gone with Johnston's surgeon to treat Union wounded. After a while Johnston slumped in his saddle. Within minutes, he was dead from loss of blood from a wound that could have been treated with a simple tourniquet.

With night approaching, the Confederates finally took the Hornets' Nest, but by this time Grant had organized a last line of defense of artillery near the river. Confederate General P.G.T. Beauregard, now in command, chose not to attack Grant's thrown-together line in the dark, figuring that he could finish off Grant in the morning.

Fortuitously, Buell's men arrived that night and were ferried across the Tennessee by riverboats, something Beauregard did not know until those fresh 25,000 men, combined with Grant's remaining men, attacked him in the morning. Grant's rejuvenated army swept off the banks of the Tennessee and drove the exhausted and surprised Confederates back toward Corinth. The Confederates had won a dramatic victory on the first day, and the Federals won an even more dramatic victory on the second day. As the Federals were in command of the field, they won the battle.

Shiloh was a battle of historical "what-ifs."

If Grant and Sherman had lost the battle, both emerging generals might have been court-marshaled for failing to deploy their men properly in defense against a Confederate attack. Both might have been dismissed from the army and their future services lost to the Union. The two Union generals most responsible for finally winning the war in both the east and the west might have been forced to resign two years earlier.

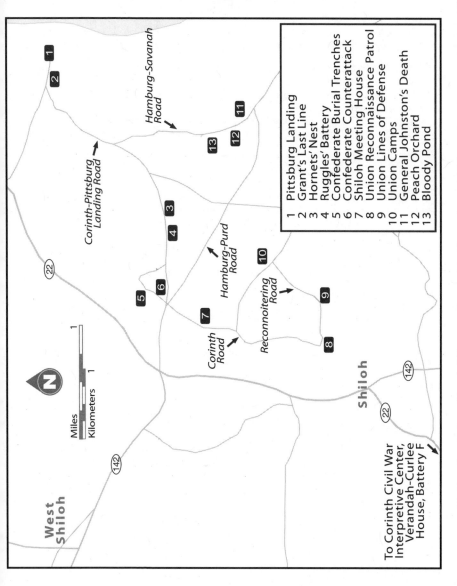

Legend:
1. Pittsburg Landing
2. Grant's Last Line
3. Hornets' Nest
4. Ruggles' Battery
5. Confederate Burial Trenches
6. Confederate Counterattack
7. Shiloh Meeting House
8. Union Reconnaissance Patrol
9. Union Lines of Defense
10. Union Camps
11. General Johnston's Death
12. Peach Orchard
13. Bloody Pond

To Corinth Civil War Interpretive Center, Verandah-Curlee House, Battery F

Hamburg-Savanah Road

Corinth-Pittsburg Landing Road

Hamburg-Purd Road

Reconnoitering Road

Corinth Road

West Shiloh

Shiloh

Miles

Kilometers

22 • 142

Grant almost left the army anyway. After Shiloh, Grant's commander, Henry Halleck, took over personal command of Grant's army for a while as punishment for Grant's allowing himself to be surprised at Shiloh. But Halleck proved so ponderous a commander in moving on Corinth, the original prize, that Lincoln reinstated Grant. Grant eventually erased all doubt about his capabilities by capturing Vicksburg in July 1863.

Had Johnston bypassed the Hornets' Nest, the rumbling Confederate attack might have reached the Tennessee River hours earlier, long before Grant could have set up his defense. Had the Confederates destroyed Grant's army, and then Buell's army the next day, the Union's entire strategy of attacking the western Confederacy would have been in doubt. Johnston might have recaptured New Orleans, captured only one month earlier by the Union Navy.

When Shiloh was over, the tally of the carnage was shocking to both the military and the civilian public. Casualties numbered more than 24,000 on both sides, more than the combined total of all of the major battles in both the eastern and western theaters for the entire war up to that point. Remarkably, both sides' casualty figures were almost identical—about 1,750 killed and more than 8,000 wounded on each side. Even the numbers of captured and missing were close to equal.

At Shiloh, both sides learned that their men had to become more disciplined, that line officers had to learn better field tactics, and that surprise is always the best weapon. Shiloh was a turning-point in the war in that both sides learned how to better kill each other.

SOURCES & OTHER READING

U.S. Army War College Guide to the Battle of Shiloh, Jay Luvaas, Stephan Bowman, Leonard Fullenkamp, University of Kansas Press, 1996.

Shiloh: The Battle That Changed the Civil War, Larry Daniel, Simon & Schuster, 1998.

Shiloh: Bloody April, Wiley Sword, Morningside Books, 2001

Shiloh: In Hell before Night, James McDonough, University of Tennessee Press, 1997.

The Road to Shiloh: Early Battles in the Civil War, David Nevin, Time Life Books, 1983.

Seeing the Elephant: Raw Recruits At the Battle of Shiloh, Joseph Allen Frank, George A. Reeves, University of Illinois Press, 2003.

SHILOH TODAY

Located twenty miles northeast of Corinth, Mississippi, and twelve miles southwest of Savannah, Tennessee, Grant's poorly chosen headquarters for his army at Pittsburg Landing, Shiloh National Military Park is decidedly one of the more remote of the major battlefield sites.

Blessedly, Shiloh is beyond the interest of Civil War battlefields' natural enemies—land developers. There do not appear to be any threats from gas stations or housing developments. The rural location of the battlefield pretty much assures that what tourists see today is just what soldiers saw in 1862.

Although the topography is the same, the battlefield itself is very different. Because Shiloh is one of the oldest military parks, established in 1894, battle monuments and markers abound that show the location of regiments as surviving veterans saw them. While those monuments help descendants find their ancestors' fighting positions, they may be distracting for history travelers trying to imagine full armies emerging from the woods.

POINTS OF INTEREST

Shiloh National Military Park
★★★★★

Pittsburg Landing Road
T: 731-689-5696
Daily, 8 a.m.–dusk. Visitor center open until 5 p.m. Closed major holidays.
Admission: $3

The park is off Tennessee Road 22, reached from Corinth to the southwest and Savannah to the northeast. The major east-west highway in the area is U.S. 64, located north of the park and running through Savannah, and U.S. 45 running north and south, found west of Shiloh and running through Corinth.

The park consists of more than 4,000 acres. The visitor center is near the highway, not near where the battle started, so it would be advisable to arrive with a battlefield guidebook and maybe a compass and global positioning system to follow the flow of action. The U.S. Army War College guide to the battle is available at the visitor center. Each April 6, the woods come alive with historians and historical travelers trying to duplicate what the soldiers saw and heard on the day of the attack. Most of them advance to the northeast toward the river on foot from Stop 8 on the driving tour. It was here, near Fraley Field, that the advancing Confederates first ran into a suspicious Federal patrol commanded by a colonel who chose to ignore General Sherman's pronouncements that the enemy would not be attacking them at Shiloh.

The visitor center has a few displays and a somewhat outdated—and none too authentic—film orienting visitors to the battle. A detached bookstore has a decent collection of books about the battle and the war in the west.

Stop 1 ★★★ on the park driving tour is Pittsburg Landing on the Tennessee River.

Though the site gave its name to the battle (the North generally named its battles after water features such as the landing, while the South named battles after land-based landmarks like churches), there is no evidence today of the riverboat landing that made this location on the river so important. Period-looking paddlewheel steamboats ply these waters today.

Stop 2 ★★★ is out of chronological order. This is where Grant set up his last line of artillery defense, essentially the last thing that happened on the first day of battle, but the second stop on the tour. It was from behind this line of cannons that Grant's and Buell's combined army of 50,000 rushed forward on the second day to push back the Confederates.

Stops 3 ★★★★★ and 4 ★★★★★ are two key stops that deserve at least twenty minutes for a reflective walk. Stop 3 begins at the sunken road that marks the edge of the Hornets' Nest. Stop 4, several hundred yards to the west, marks the line of Confederate cannons that finally dislodged and discouraged the Federals with round after round of explosive shells and canister, tin cans filled with lead balls that turned each cannon into a giant shotgun. Walk into the woods at **Stop 3**, look westward toward that line of artillery, and imagine what it was like for the several thousand Federals holding this position. Visitors who have a compass might take a reading looking toward the Confederate artillery line to get a sense of the direction from which the Confederates were coming when they reaching the Hornets' Nest.

Stop 4 ★★★★★, the line of cannons representing the Confederate line, was organized by General Daniel Ruggles. A former career officer in the U.S. Army, Ruggles was a Massachusetts native but married to a Virginian. Ruggles was slow to deploy his men in the Shiloh attack, but once he saw the resistance at the

Hornets' Nest, he took the initiative to assemble sixty-two cannons from various batteries to blast the Federals into submission. Curiously, though it was Ruggles's initiative that destroyed the battlefield holdup for the Confederates, he was shifted from combat command after the battle, apparently because his gruff, New England manners did not sit well with his more polite Southern-gentlemen general peers.

Stop 5 ★★★★★ is the most sobering and somber stop at Shiloh. Because the Confederates were pushed off the battlefield on the second day, they never had the chance to request a cease-fire to bury their 1,750 dead. Within days of the battle the Federals buried the Confederate dead in five trenches. Two of these trenches are just north and south of this stop. The bodies are said to be buried with as many as seven soldiers lying on top of each other. The largest trench is reputed to hold more than 700 dead and is marked by cannonballs. All five of the Confederate trenches are marked on the park tour road, but you have to walk through the woods to reach three of them.

Because this battle was fought well before the military started issuing identification tags, commonly called "dog tags," the names of those Southerners buried here, from Tennessee, Alabama, Louisiana, Arkansas, Mississippi, Kentucky, Florida, Texas, and Missouri, will forever be unknown. On some other battlefields, particularly those in the North such as Gettysburg, the bodies of the Southern dead were recovered and shipped South after the war. Since these soldiers were already on Southern soil, they remain where they fell in 1862. Visitors who know ancestors were lost at Shiloh often seek out all five trenches to pay their respects.

Stop 6 ★★ marks the last-ditch effort of the Confederates on April 7 to stop the

Union attack. When a counterattack failed to stop the Union advance, Beauregard ordered the men in full retreat to Corinth.

Stop 7 ★★ is the reconstructed Shiloh Meeting House, located next to the modern-day church. Another Confederate burial trench is located behind the log structure. The log structure is open, but the newer building is church property and should not be visited.

Union General William T. Sherman's head-quarters were just northeast of the meet-inghouse. Sherman assured his subordi-nates, nervous about camping with their backs to the Tennessee River, that no Confederates would attack them. He main-tained that opinion until the Confederates swept past his command tent and sent him fleeing with the rest of his men.

Embarrassed by his mistakes, Sherman reacted by fighting vigorously over the two-day battle. It was his performance that helped the Union win the battle, and he was promoted to major general afterward. Supported by Grant in the days leading up to Shiloh, when newspapers were specu-lating that he might be mentally unstable, Sherman returned the favor and became Grant's most trusted subordinate general.

Stops 8 ★★ and **9 ★** mark the opening of the battle, which swept from the south back toward the northeast. Stop 9 marks where General Prentiss first tried to stem the flood of Confederates. His men retreat-ed back two miles to Stop 3, where they dedicated themselves to holding at the Hornets' Nest. There are no trails from this point north to the Hornets' Nest, but the more adventurous can follow the com-pass reading they took at Stop 3 to dupli-cate the Confederate attack. They will have to cross at least one small creek.

Along the way to the Hornets' Nest, hikers will pass **Stop 10** on the auto tour, which is where the Confederates sacked the

Union camps. A Union colonel was killed here trying to rally his panicked troops.

Those following the auto tour will find **Stops 12 ★★★**, **13 ★★★**, and **14 ★★★** worthwhile. At 12, Johnston was wounded behind the left knee by what has been described as a "spent" musket ball, meaning it had either already passed through something or it had been fired so far away that its velocity was very slow. While it seems improbable that Johnston could have been wounded and not known it, it may have occurred that way. Having been wounded in an 1837 duel, Johnston walked with a limp and sometimes com-plained about numbness in his legs. Had Johnston applied a tourniquet to his own leg (and he had one in his pocket), he likely would have survived. He might have lost his leg, but he would probably have fought another day, as amputation of limbs was a common surgical procedure.

Stop 13 ★★★ was the Peach Orchard, replanted now with small peach trees. This was the Federal left flank on the morning of April 6. So many bullets were flying through the air that the peach blossoms were cut from their branches and dropped to the ground as if it were snowing. Eye-witnesses commented on seeing bodies that seemed to be covered with pink snow-flakes. Few who witnessed the scene ever forgot it.

Stop 14 ★★★, the last stop on the park tour, is another eerily named battlefield feature, Bloody Pond. During the fighting on the first day, this small pond became a goal of wounded, thirsty soldiers of both sides. They crawled to it, enemies some-times drinking side by side. Some died and fell face forward into the water. Witnesses said the pond water turned crimson from the blood of men and horses.

OTHER AREA ATTRACTIONS

The Corinth Civil War Interpretive Center
★★★★★

501 Linden St.
Located at the corner of Linden St. and Fulton Dr., just southwest of downtown Corinth.
T: 662-287-9273
Daily, 8:30 a.m.–4:30 p.m.
Free admission.

Opened in 2004, this is the newest unit of the National Park Service. The site of the center is Corinth's most infamous Civil War site. It is built next to Battery Robinett, a Union dirt fort attacked in October 1862 by Confederate forces who were trying to recapture the town.

The aftermath of the attack resulted in a famous series of the most gruesome photographs to come out of the war. While Northern photographers routinely posed Confederate dead, few of those men were ever identified. In the photographs taken just outside the dirt walls of Battery Robinett, the dead commander of the Second Texas Infantry, Colonel William Rogers, lies heaped with several of his men. Close examination of the men visible in the photographs show some missing parts of their heads—a sickening testament to the deadly firepower available in the war. Large blow-ups of the photos are on the wall in the visitor center.

The 5,000 square feet of display space mixes artifact displays with multimedia displays, and includes a multimedia dramatization of the Battle of Shiloh.

Southerners who see the root causes of the war as a myriad of complicated and interconnected reasons might be upset by the fact that the opening displays concentrate on the existence of slavery in the Southern states and expansion of slavery into the western states as the root cause of the war.

Little mention is made of other causes, such as conflicting economic systems, Southern concern for states' rights versus Federal control over states, and the ninety-year power struggle between a South that had controlled much of the national political agenda and a North seeking more attention for its own political agendas.

The seemingly heavy emphasis on slavery comes from Congressional guidelines passed during the Clinton administration that require the National Park Service to emphasize slavery as the cause of the war in its Civil War units. The new law has angered many professional and amateur Civil War historians who maintain that battlefields should be interpreted as battlefields where politics mattered little to the men fighting for their lives.

Regardless of whether visitors of either Southern or Northern proclivities accept, dismiss, or ignore the panels on the causes of the war, the center still offers a good explanation of the war, particularly in this little-studied region of the country. Multimedia exhibits make it easy to absorb information, and those who prefer art over displays will find the courtyard fountain of interest. It has a flowing water feature that symbolizes the growing sectionalism before the war. Blocks of granite symbolizing battles further disrupt the water flow. The stream ends in a calm reflecting pool symbolizing the end of the war.

The Historic Verandah-Curlee House Museum ★★

301 Childs St. at the corner of Jackson St.
Summer hours: Monday–Saturday, 9 a.m.–5 p.m.; Sunday, 1–5 p.m.
In winter open until 4 p.m.
Admission: $5

This house museum served as headquarters for three different Confederate generals and one Federal general. It is now a house museum with furnishings of the Greek Revival period.

Battery F ★ was a Union-built dirt fort west of Battery Robinett that the Confederates captured in October 1862.

Directions: Head west from the Civil War Interpretive Center, pass over U.S. 45, turn right onto Kimberly Street and then left onto Davis Street. The fort, which had four cannons, is on the right. This site is well-preserved for a fort found near a city.

GETTING TO/AROUND SHILOH AND CORINTH

Shiloh and Corinth are not easy to reach by commercial aircraft. The closet airports with airline service are Memphis International Airport, eighty-five miles northwest of Corinth (110 miles west of Shiloh), and Tupelo Regional Airport, fifty-five miles south of Corinth. Private aircraft can fly into Corinth Alcorn County Airport, where there is only one rental car company, Enterprise. Shiloh is about twenty miles northeast of Corinth.

Another option is to fly into Nashville International Airport and drive 150 miles southwest. Nashville is closer than Memphis to another remote Civil War site, Fort Donelson, about 140 miles north of Shiloh. This would allow the visitor to make a triangle of Nashville to Shiloh to Fort Donelson and back to Nashville. Directions to Shiloh from Nashville would be I-40 west to South Tennessee 22.

There is no direct major road heading east toward Shiloh from Memphis. In Colliersville, travelers can head east on

Tennessee Road 57 and link up with Tennessee 22, which leads to the park.

In both Corinth and Shiloh, a car is necessary to see the major sites, as there is no locally operated sight-seeing company.

Once inside Shiloh, visitors should ask rangers for maps detailing both the hiking trails and the historic road traces that can be used for hiking. No vehicles are permitted on these trails. Visitors who feel competent with a compass and walking where there are no trails might want to start at the southwestern end of the park and march north to the Hornets' Nest and then shift northeast to end at Grant's Last Line. This march, including time to view the monuments and interpretive panels, takes several hours, as it is at least four miles from the attacking end of the park to Grant's Last Line.

For walkers and bikers who want to follow the auto tour road, Shiloh is quite flat. The auto tour is nine miles long.

ACCOMMODATIONS

The Generals' Quarters
924 Fillmore St., Corinth
T: 662-286-3325
www.thegeneralsquarters.com
9 rooms
$75–$120

This inn is a little misnamed, as it was not built until 1872, long after the fighting generals had left Corinth.

The Samuel D. Bramlitt House
1125 Cruise St., Corinth
T: 662-396-4979
www.bramlitthouse.com
4 rooms
$85–$110

This house was built in 1892 and featured the first indoor plumbing in Corinth.

Vicksburg

Mississippi

The Union ironclad gunboat *U.S.S. Cairo* on display at Vicksburg National Military Park.

THE WAR YEARS

V icksburg is an important destination for any Civil War buff for several reasons. President Lincoln himself targeted Vicksburg early in the war; it has several sites other than the national park visitor center; the national park has an extensive driving tour filled with artistic monuments; and the park is home to the most amazing Civil War artifact ever recovered—the *U.S.S. Cairo*, an ironclad on which visitors can walk the decks just as if they were crewmen.

Vicksburg was an important city for both sides. Lincoln described it as a key and said that the war could never be won until "that key is in our pocket." He recognized that as long as Vicksburg remained in Southern hands, the North could not control the Mississippi, a major trade route for Midwestern goods, nor could the North split the states of Texas, Arkansas, and Louisiana from the rest of the South.

The South needed the city because the goods unloaded on river wharves could be trans-ported inland on the railroad that ended at the city. Vicksburg was the conduit via which supplies gathered throughout the Trans-Mississippi region reached the warring armies in the eastern theater.

Protecting the city seemed easy enough to the Confederate defenders. Cannons mounted on its 200-foot-high bluffs could blast any Union ship moving on the Mississippi River, while those same bluffs were too high for ship-mounted guns to reach. The city's defenses seemed so high and impregnable that Union Admiral David Farragut called it the Gibraltar of the Mississippi, after the famous citadel island in the Mediterranean.

Still, Union leaders were encouraged after first New Orleans, then Baton Rouge, then Natchez, just south of Vicksburg, fell with little loss of life in the opening months of 1862. Farragut brought his fleet up within shooting range of Vicksburg, but he found, as he had suspected, that he could not elevate his guns high enough to reach the Confederate batteries.

Taking the city became an objective of the army under General U.S. Grant, who had won fame in April for a second-day victory at Shiloh, Tennessee. After Union General William T. Sherman was defeated at Chickasaw Bayou north of the city by a Confederate force less than a third the size of his own, Grant decided on a slow, broad attack that avoided the Confederates rather than confronted them.

Starting in March 1863, instead of moving directly on the city, he marched his men south along the western side of the Mississippi. He marched them as far south as he could to ensure that he met no Confederate resistance. He then crossed the river with 45,000 men on April 30. More important, Federal gunboats had successfully run past the city's defenses earlier in the month. Federal gunboats were at the ready both above and below the city.

The Confederates had a few chances to hit Grant in the open, but confusion over whose orders took precedence bogged down the defense. General Joseph T. Johnston, the over-all commander in the state, ordered General John Pemberton, commander of Vicksburg, to leave his trenches and link up with Johnston's men in Jackson, the state capital seventy miles east of Vicksburg. Johnston's vision was to ambush Grant near the river so there would be no escape for Grant's men. Pemberton was under orders from Confederate President Jefferson Davis to hold Vicksburg at all costs, so he ignored Johnston.

When Pemberton refused to come out of the trenches, the chance of ambushing Grant evaporated. Grant sensed that Pemberton would not leave the trenches, so instead of attacking Vicksburg right away, he shifted his attention to capturing Jackson. Grant wanted to eliminate the potential threat posed by Johnston, who would be in Grant's rear if he concentrated on Vicksburg. In two weeks and two battles, at Port Gibson on May 1 and Raymond on May 12, Grant's powerful army scattered the defenders who were close to the river. He then moved on Jackson.

Pemberton, in a surprise move, then moved out of Vicksburg with the intention of linking up with Johnston, just as Johnston had wanted him to do two weeks earlier. Johnston sent couriers out with orders on how and where to meet, but one of them turned out to be a spy who carried the orders to Grant instead. Knowing now that Pemberton was in the open, Grant smashed into him first at the Battle of Champion Hill on May 16, 1863, then again the next day at the Battle of the Big Black River. Pemberton suffered heavy casualties both days and retreated to the safety of Vicksburg.

Johnston again ordered Pemberton out of Vicksburg to link up for another attack on Grant, but Pemberton had had enough of fighting in the open. He sent Johnston a note saying he would stay in Vicksburg's defenses, as the city "is the most important point in the Confederacy." Pemberton intended to force Grant to come to him and the 170 cannons he had defending the city.

Pemberton was wrong in his belief that Vicksburg was still as important as it once had been. Since running past the guns in April, the Union gunboats virtually owned the river except for the few miles directly under Vicksburg's guns. The railroad line east of the city that had been so important for supplying the rest of the Confederacy had been captured and was now of little use. With Union gunboats on the river, no Confederate supplies could successfully make it across the river from the Trans-Mississippi.

Vicksburg was now a single Confederate city surrounded by Federal forces. Although less important, it was still vital that the Union capture Vicksburg itself because its guns could still sink Union ships moving up and down the river. The city's resistance was also symbolic to Lincoln. He wanted the Mississippi to "flow unvexed to the sea." Grant tried several disastrous frontal assaults on Vicksburg's trenches. All failed. He settled into siege warfare, which involved digging trenches that brought his men ever closer to the Confederate trenches. For the next two months, May and June, the city was constantly shelled by the Federals, who knew their targets included civilians.

Conditions for those civilians and soldiers trapped in Vicksburg were horrible. Civilians hollowed out caves in the hillsides, creating ninety-degree openings so that artillery shrapnel could not penetrate the interior. After they had eaten all the cattle, they ate the horses. When all of the horses were gone, the populace moved on to dogs, cats, and finally rats. Grant was starving the city into submission.

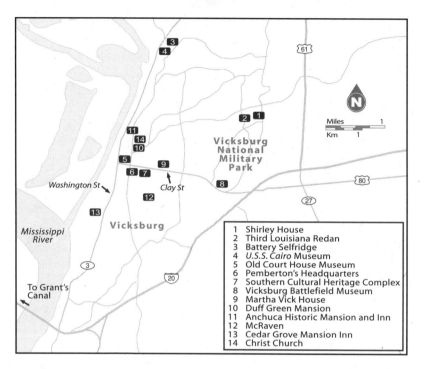

1	Shirley House
2	Third Louisiana Redan
3	Battery Selfridge
4	*U.S.S. Cairo* Museum
5	Old Court House Museum
6	Pemberton's Headquarters
7	Southern Cultural Heritage Complex
8	Vicksburg Battlefield Museum
9	Martha Vick House
10	Duff Green Mansion
11	Anchuca Historic Mansion and Inn
12	McRaven
13	Cedar Grove Mansion Inn
14	Christ Church

After forty-six days of constant bombardment, and with the threat looming of infectious diseases looming that could decimate the city, Pemberton finally sent a note to Grant asking for surrender conditions. On July 4, 1863, just one day after Lee had lost the battle of Gettysburg, Pennsylvania, Pemberton surrendered more than 30,000 men and officers, 172 cannons, and 60,000 rifles. Pemberton had twice as many arms as he had men to fire them.

When the men at Port Hudson, Louisiana, south of Vicksburg, heard that the Gibraltar had fallen, they too surrendered. For the first time in two years, the Mississippi River was once again part of the U.S.

VICKSBURG TODAY

You may be surprised to find four 24-hour-a-day, 365-day-a-year casinos, one of them a fake riverboat boasting more than 1,300 slot machines, here. They do seem out of place for such a historically important town, where most historians believe the North won the Civil War nearly two years before it was officially over.

Vicksburg, population 26,500, still makes a fine destination for the historic traveler who can ignore the lure of the casinos and concentrate on walking the compact downtown. The murals painted on the river floodwall are a noteworthy attraction. A total of thirty-five are planned. Several already exist, including one depicting Davis's reception of the "sad news," when a messenger found him at his nearby plantation and informed him that he had been elected president of the new Confederacy.

Davis had been the U.S. Senator from Mississippi immediately before the war and a highly effective Secretary of War under President Franklin Pierce. When the delegations of the seceding states met, they elected Davis to act as president of the Confederacy in the belief that he was the most prominent man among them who still had ties to the Union. The delegates hoped Davis's old ties might help in negotiating a peaceful leaving of the Union.

Years ago, the Mississippi shifted, and it now bends toward the city five miles south of where it did during wartime, with the result that most of the batteries that protected Vicksburg in 1862 and 1863 no longer point at the Mississippi River. The trickle of water now flowing past Vicksburg is the Yazoo River Diversionary Canal.

POINTS OF INTEREST

1. Vicksburg National Military Park
★★★★★

3201 Clay St., Exit 4B off I-20.
T: 601-636-0583

Daily, 8 a.m.–5 p.m. Closed major holidays.
Admission: $5

The problem with seeing this national park as a Civil War battlefield site is that its 1,800 acres do not represent any single engagement. Most skirmishes were over within a few hours. A few battles lasted a couple of days.

The Battle for Vicksburg lasted forty-six days, much of that time consisting of Union bombardment of the trenches and the city itself. Grant launched a few infantry assaults, once even trying to destroy Confederate lines by tunneling under the trenches and blowing them up with kegs of black powder. But there are not many spots on the sixteen-mile driving loop of the national park where one can look out and visualize a Union infantry attack on a particular Confederate dirt fort (there are nine preserved dirt forts within the park) or trench line (there are twenty miles of trenches within the park). It does not help that the same hilly terrain that confused and exhausted advancing Union troops is still there.

It is difficult to imagine the suffering of the civilians, who lived in caves for much of the bombardment, when not a single cave has been preserved. That said, driving or biking the sixteen-mile loop is important, particularly for those visitors whose ancestors fought here. Because the park opened in 1899, veterans were able to pinpoint their regiment's location on the battlefield. Once the veterans had determined those locations, many states erected monuments to those units. There are more than 1,300 monuments and interpretative tablets here. Most of the individual regimental monuments are for Union regiments, though Southern states erected some spectacular memorials in memory of their troops.

Essential stops on the tour include **Stop 2** ★★★★, the Shirley House, which Federal troops knew only as "the white house." The Shirley House is the only period house within the park boundaries, and it exists only because the retreating Confederate soldier assigned to burn it was killed before he could finish his job. Federals later used the house as a headquarters.

Next to the Shirley House is the Illinois State Memorial, which houses sixty-two tablets listing the name of each of the 36,325 soldiers from Illinois who fought at Vicksburg. Forty-seven steps lead up to the entrance, one step for each day of the siege. Ironically, the memorial was built with granite from Georgia.

Stop 3 ★★★★★ is the Third Louisiana Redan, one of the major earth forts in the park. Grant tried to blow up this fort on two different occasions by tunneling under it and placing black-powder charges. Neither explosion succeeded in breaching the Confederate line.

Stop 7 ★★ is Battery Selfridge, an artillery battery made up of naval guns

and commanded by Lieutenant Commander Thomas O. Selfridge. Selfridge is both the unluckiest and the most-charmed man ever to serve in the Navy. He survived the sinking of three different ships, including two he commanded. Later he was in charge of a disastrous land assault at Fort Fisher, North Carolina, where more than half his men were killed.

Right after Stop 7 is the **U.S.S. Cairo Museum** ★★★★. The *Cairo* alone is worth the entire trip to Vicksburg. This Union ironclad, constructed to operate in the shallow waters of Confederate rivers, is quite possibly the most impressive—certainly the largest—Civil War artifact in existence. Sunk in 1862 by a Confederate torpedo or floating mine in the Yazoo River, it was discovered and recovered 100 years later. The iron plating, cannons, engines, boilers, and so forth are all original. Visitors can walk the deck and follow in the footsteps of the boat's crew. Next to the boat is the museum, filled with artifacts that were on board the *Cairo* when it sank. The boat sank so quickly that every sailor and officer had to leave his personal gear behind. That gear is now displayed and offers the visitor great insights into the life of a Union sailor. Allow at least an hour to tour the *Cairo* and visit the museum.

After leaving the gunboat, take a tour through the **Vicksburg National Cemetery** ★★★. Most of the Union troops buried here are unknown. The U.S. Colored Troops buried here are segregated from their white comrades in arms. At the entrance to the cemetery is a noteworthy tombstone—a cedar tree has grown around it so that a portion of the stone is actually encased inside the living tree.

Continue following the tour road from the cemetery. You'll find many of the Confederate monuments from this point on. The most beautiful and elaborate is Mississippi's, between **Stops 11** and **12.**

2. Old Court House Museum ★★★★★

1008 Cherry St.
Turn off of Clay St. after driving downtown from the park.
T: 601-636-0741
Monday–Saturday, 8:30 a.m.–4:30 p.m.;
Sunday, 1:30–4:30 p.m.
Admission: $5

The Old Court House Museum, opened in 1948, is a great, old-style museum. People whose ancestors owned Civil War artifacts donated them to the museum, so many of the weapons, flags, uniforms, and other articles in the collection can be traced to specific people. One unusual display is of a newspaper printed on wallpaper. When the city was captured, the Union troops reset some of the type and printed the same edition again with a note that they were now in charge of the city. Even the iron staircase leading upstairs tells a story. When a Union soldier noticed that the staircase had been manufactured in Philadelphia, he wondered aloud at the audacity of a region that would start a war when it could not even manufacture its own staircases.

The courtroom looks just as it did when cases were tried in it. One famous case tried here was of the naval officer who was accused of overloading the steamboat *Sultana* with freed Union prisoners. The *Sultana*'s boilers exploded, and the ship sank in the Mississippi with most of its crew and passengers. More passengers were killed in this disaster of 1865 than were lost in the *Titanic* sinking. Visitors should plan to allow at least an hour to properly see and study the display cases.

3. Pemberton's Headquarters ★

1018 Crawford St.
Not yet open to the public.

This house, where Pemberton made all of his command decisions about the defense and surrender of the city, is currently

being restored and added to the National Park Service.

Drive down to the waterfront area and turn left or south on Washington Street (Business U.S. 61). Take this to the Louisiana Circle, an overlook on the **Mississippi River ★★**. This, and nearby South Fort, are the southernmost fortifications that protected the river. This view looking south toward the twin bridges over the Mississippi is especially dramatic at sunset. Leave Louisiana Circle, cross Washington, and follow South Confederate Avenue back into the city. This land used to be in Park Service control but was deeded back to the city. Other Southern state monuments are scattered along here.

4. Grant's Canal ★

Open during daylight hours.

One detached National Park site of interest lies in Louisiana off I-20, exit 186 for U.S. 80. Here is what remains of Grant's Canal, an attempt by engineers to divert the Mississippi River through DeSoto Point and leave Vicksburg high and dry. After losing hundreds of men (mostly slaves confiscated from nearby plantations and forced to work for the army) to malaria and exhaustion, Grant finally abandoned the grandiose idea that the Union army could command the Mississippi River. It took a few decades, but the river eventually did bypass Vicksburg. It is only with human help that water flows past the city today.

5. Southern Cultural Heritage Complex ★

1302 Adams St.
T: 601-631-2997
March–November, Monday–Friday,
8 a.m.–noon, 1-5 p.m.
Admission: $5

The Southern Cultural Heritage Complex is the former St. Francis Xavier Convent and Academy. This was the home of the Sisters of Mercy order, who freely nursed the sick on both sides during the war.

Jefferson Davis himself wrote the order of
Catholic nuns letters of thanks for helping
the wounded. The original academy building, built in 1830, housed troops of both
sides. Staff members offer a tour of the
original academy and the four-story Gothic
Revival–style convent.

6. Vicksburg Battlefield Museum ★★

4139 I-20 Frontage Rd.
Exit 4B near the National Park
T: 601-638-6500
Daily, 9 a.m.–5 p.m. Last show at 4 p.m.
Admission: $5.50

This private museum, located on the
frontage road next to I-20 on the same
exit as the National Park, is built in the
shape of a gunboat. Although it features a
diorama of the siege and a film dramatiz-
ing the siege, the museum's most valuable
exhibit is a collection of scale-model gunboats. Visitors can get a sense of how big
the *U.S.S. Monitor* was compared to the
C.S.S. Virginia, the *Virginia* compared to
the *C.S.S. Arkansas,* and so on.

The following five Civil War–period houses
are open for touring:

7. Martha Vick House ★★

1300 Grove St.
T: 601-638-7036
Monday–Saturday, 9 a.m.–5 p.m.,
Sunday, 1–5 p.m.
Admission: $5

Built circa 1830, this house is the oldest
house open for touring and was built for
the daughter of the town's founder.

8. Duff Green Mansion ★★

1114 First East St.
T: 601-636-6968
Daily, noon–5 p.m.
Admission: $6

Built in 1856 with slave labor, it was used
as a hospital by both sides. It is also a
bed and breakfast.

9. Anchuca Historic Mansion & Inn ★★

1010 First East St.
T: 601-661-0111
Daily, 9:30 a.m.–3 p.m.
Admission: $6

Anchuca's front porch is reputed to be the
spot where Jefferson Davis spoke to the
people of Vicksburg before reluctantly
leaving his nearby plantation to be sworn
in as president of the Confederacy. Built
in 1830, it too was used as a hospital during the war. This house is now a bed and
breakfast.

10. McRaven ★★

1445 Harrison St.
T: 601-636-1663
Monday–Saturday, 9 a.m.–5 p.m.;
Sunday, 10 a.m.–5 p.m.
Admission: $5

McRaven is actually three houses in one; it
was first built in 1797 and renovated in
1836 and then again in 1849.
Confederate troops camped in its front
yard.

11. Cedar Grove Mansion Inn ★★

2200 Oak St.
T: 601-636-1000
Daily, 9 a.m.–4 p.m.
Admission: $6

Cedar Grove Mansion Inn is also a combination bed and breakfast and touring
home. It is situated on a bluff overlooking
the river. It has four acres of gardens in
which to roam.

12. Christ Church ★

1119 Main St.

This Episcopal Church was built in 1839
and held services during the war despite
the daily shelling.

Getting To and Around Vicksburg

Vicksburg is too small to have its own commercial airport, so visitors must fly into Jackson International Airport (JAN) forty-five miles away and rent a car. The airport serves ten cities with eight different carriers. Most of the direct flights are to the Midwest and East.

A private airport, Vicksburg-Tallulah Regional Airport across the river in Louisiana, is owned by the city of Vicksburg.

I-20, heading east and west, crosses the Mississippi just south of Vicksburg. U.S. 61 crosses to the east of the city heading north and south, roughly parallel to the Mississippi.

Visitors need a vehicle to take the sixteen-mile tour of the national battlefield. There are no locally based touring buses. Walking or biking is always possible, of course, but be warned that the same steep landscape that foiled the Federals could slow even the most enthusiastic walker or biker. There are no water stops on the drive. Once visitors leave the park and head downtown to see the Old Court House Museum and historic houses, it is advisable to park the car in a central location and walk.

Accommodations

All four of these bed and breakfasts are also on the historic houses tour.

Cedar Grove Mansion Inn

2200 Oak St., Vicksburg
T: 601-636-1000
www.cedargroveinn.com
34 rooms
$160–$260

This bed and breakfast has an artifact most such establishments don't have: a cannonball lodged in a parlor wall.

Anchuca Historic Mansion & Inn

1010 First East St., Vicksburg
T: 601-661-0111
www.anchucamansion.com
7 rooms
$100–$175

Confederate President Jefferson Davis visited this house on occasion. It is surrounded by oaks in the historic district.

The Duff Green Mansion

1114 First East St., Vicksburg
T: 601-636-6968
www.duffgreenmansion.com
5 rooms
$85–$160

Finished just before the war, this house was hit at least five times by Union cannonballs, and one room's ceiling beam still shows damage. Both sides used the house as a hospital.

Annabelle Bed & Breakfast Inn

501 Speed St., Vicksburg
T: 601-638-2000
www.annabellebnd.com
8 rooms
$98–$125

This house was finished just after the war, but it has the look of the period. The main house has three bedrooms and an accompanying guest house has five, plus a swimming pool.

SOURCES & OTHER READING

Vicksburg Campaign, Edwin Bearss, Morningside Bookshop, 1991,

The Most Glorious Fourth—Vicksburg and Gettysburg, July 4, 1863, Duane Schultz, W.W. Norton & Company, 2001.

Guide to the Vicksburg Campaign (U.S. Army War College Guides to Civil War Battles, Vol 6), Leonard Fullenkamp, Stephen Bowman, Jay Luvass, University Press of Kansas, 1998.

Triumph and Defeat—The Vicksburg Campaign, Terrance Winschel, Savass Publishing, 1998.

Vicksburg and the War, Gordon Cotton and Jeff Gambrone, Pelican Publishing, 2004.

Vicksburg 1863: Grant Clears the Mississippi (Osprey Military Histories), Alan Hankinson, Osprey Publishing, 2000.

Grant Wins the War—Decision at Vicksburg, James R. Arnold, Wiley, 1999.

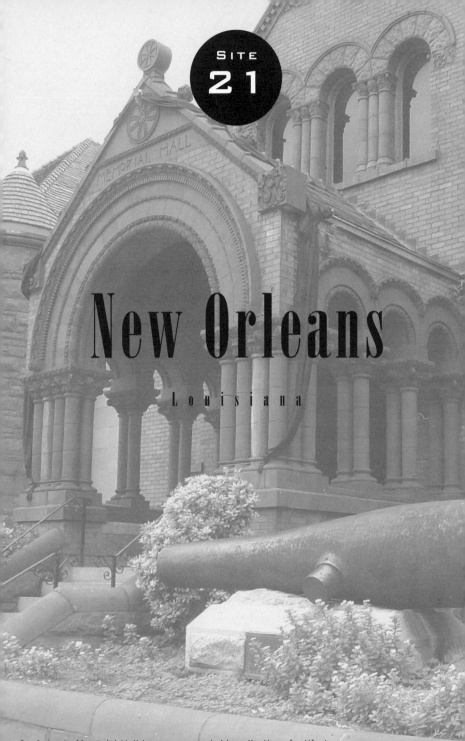

New Orleans

Louisiana

Confederate Memorial Hall houses a remarkable collection of artifacts.

THE WAR YEARS

oday's metropolis on the banks of the Mississippi River is not as important as it once was to the South, but it is home to a fascinating museum with a collection of Confederate artifacts found nowhere else in the South. The presence of those artifacts makes New Orleans one of the nation's great Civil War sites.

If there was one city in 1860 that symbolized the South's great melting-pot of immigration and cultures, it was New Orleans. With a population of more than 168,000, it was the sixth-largest city in the nation and the largest city that had not been a part of the original colonies. Irish, French, and German immigrants made up 39 percent of the population. Fourteen percent of the population was black and they were evenly divided between slave and free. Many of the free blacks owned slaves themselves and were part of the planter society.

New Orleans was not only the pride of the South; it was the economic engine for the nation. A full third of all exported goods leaving the U.S. in 1860 passed through the port of New Orleans. Most of those exports were in the form of cotton bales bound for the mills of England.

When talk in the South turned to secession in the summer and fall of 1860, the merchants of New Orleans, many of whom had been born in the North, were horrified. They recognized that any disruption in the relationship between North and South would be bad for their thriving relationships with the textile companies in New England and "old" England. Still, Lincoln's election and planters' fears that he would disrupt slavery trumped merchants' concerns over trade. The state barely voted in favor of secession in January 1861.

Once the state had committed to leaving the Union, residents of New Orleans gave their wholehearted support. Two companies of free blacks formed the Native Guard and offered their services to the Confederacy. They were turned down by nervous politicians back in Richmond who were unaccustomed to the zeal of blacks defending the South. Several hundred wharf ruffians and mercenaries speaking a dozen languages formed themselves into a regiment nicknamed the Louisiana Tigers that would win fame in the First Battle of Manassas in July 1861. A unit of militiamen from the best families of the city formed the Washington Artillery and became the most famous of Lee's cannoneers.

But while New Orleans residents and Louisianans were volunteering for a region-wide war, Confederate politicians back east were concentrating mostly on defending their new capital of Richmond. They had boldly—maybe foolishly—selected a capital barely 100 miles, or five days' march, from the U.S. capital of Washington. Defense of that capital became the myopic focus of the new government.

Meanwhile, off the mouth of the Mississippi, the first of the Union's blockading ships arrived in late May 1861, barely six weeks after the war had began. Nervous owners kept their ships at the docks, and what had been a thriving port became a depressed used-ship lot.

Despite the pleas of city leaders, the Confederacy was slow to strengthen the city's land defenses or break the still-tiny blockading squadron forming in the Gulf of Mexico about one hundred miles south of the city. The city's military commander was seventy-one-year-old General David Twiggs, a man who may have been slipping into senility while serving as the oldest general in the U.S. Army before he resigned to join the Confederacy. When Twiggs's mind and body finally gave out in October 1861, his replacement was not New Orleans native General P.G.T. Beauregard, the hero of Fort Sumter, but General Mansfield Lovell, a man who had never set foot in New Orleans.

Lovell had proven himself a competent military leader in the Mexican War, but he was not skilled in bureaucratic infighting. Despite his written pleas to Jefferson Davis explaining that New Orleans was a major prize that the Union was targeting, Lovell was sent few troops or supplies. Instead of transferring land troops, Richmond ordered the construction of an ironclad, the *C.S.S. Louisiana*. Typically, however, Richmond did not rush supplies such as iron plating and engines for the ironclad, and it was still unfinished when the Federals began to move on New Orleans.

A Federal naval fleet of seventeen warships and twenty-one mortar boats finally pushed its way past Forts Jackson and St. Phillip on the Mississippi seventy miles below New Orleans on April 23, 1862, after a five-day bombardment. New Orleans was panic-stricken. Lovell's prediction that he had too few troops to defend the city if the Federals made it past the two forts was reexamined. Rather than try to fight, Lovell evacuated his men after destroying some military supplies, so there never was a battle for the South's largest city. It surrendered without firing a single shot in its defense.

From April 1862 through the end of the war, New Orleans was under strict Union military command. The first, most famous, and most hated occupying Union general was General Ben Butler, a career Massachusetts politician who fancied himself a military genius. Butler ruled New Orleans with an iron fist. When a man tore down the U.S. flag outside the New Orleans Mint, Butler had him hanged in front of the Mint. When some New Orleans women persisted in insulting occupying Union officers, Butler issued a proclamation declaring that any woman heard insulting another Union officer would be arrested and tried for prostitution. Butler picked up the nickname "Spoons" when he was caught stealing silverware from a house he had appropriated as his headquarters.

Ironically, Butler also saved New Orleans from being wiped out by disease. When the summer yellow-fever season arrived, Butler, somehow sensing how the disease was spreading, ordered that the city be cleaned of all refuse. That helped eliminate the mosquitoes that carried the disease. He also quarantined ships infected with the disease.

Butler was finally replaced in November 1862 after President Lincoln had heard enough complaints from foreign consuls that he was not treating them with the respect they demanded of the U.S. government.

The Confederates never made any attempt to retake New Orleans from the Federals. It had been given up without a fight, and the Confederates in Richmond did not believe a fight would retake it. Many historians today regard Richmond's disregard of New Orleans' importance to the Confederacy as one of the biggest blunders of the war.

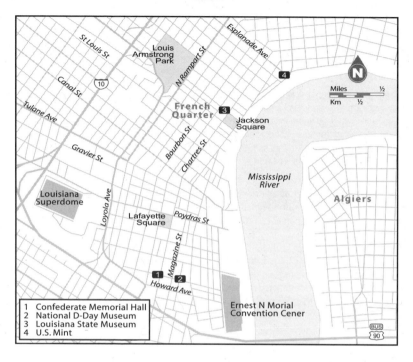

The following legend appears on the map:

1 Confederate Memorial Hall
2 National D-Day Museum
3 Louisiana State Museum
4 U.S. Mint

NEW ORLEANS TODAY

While it is easy to imagine one's self back in the 1860s while strolling through the historic downtowns of some cities, that is not likely to happen in New Orleans. There are too many bars, too much public drinking, too many tarot-card readers, and too many street-theater practitioners angling for the tourist dollar for one to get into the mindset of a resident of the South's largest and most prosperous city on the eve of war.

History tourists have to realize that while Charleston and Savannah have preserved their historical centers, New Orleans has gone a different route by focusing on modern-day entertainment. The "gentility" of the Old South is not in downtown New Orleans, but a few miles away in the Garden District, founded after a Mississippi River flood in 1816 left a heavy deposit of rich soil over the region (thus the name of the neighborhood). There is history to be found in New Orleans, but it takes dedication—and maybe hopping aboard a 1928 streetcar heading to the Garden District—to find it.

POINTS OF INTEREST

1. Confederate Memorial Hall ★★★★★

929 Camp St.
T: 504-523-4522
Monday–Saturday, 10 a.m.–4 p.m.
Admission: $5

When museum aficionados first gaze into Confederate Memorial Hall's one-room gallery, it feels like being inside a church, with its soaring support beams that form a high ceiling. From the first glass display cases to the oil paintings of Confederate heroes, it is clear that it is a special place.

Memorial Hall is packed with artifacts. Indeed, it claims to have the second-largest collection of Confederate artifacts after the Museum of the Confederacy in Richmond. Memorial Hall was built in 1891 as a repository for the wartime artifacts donated by Louisiana's Confederate veterans, and curators estimate that soldiers donated more than 90 percent of the items on display here. That means any of the tears and tatters in a flag or uniform were likely the result of combat.

These items meant a great deal to the men who donated them. On the day the building opened as a museum in 1891, a former member of the Washington Artillery said: "To these sacred and inspiring objects we should extend the fullest measure of our love and protection. We should guard them with the tender care with which a mother watches over her child. We must see that they are transmitted to our descendants as object lessons, which will inspire them with a reverence for the past and excite in them a determination to emulate the courage, patriotism, and devotion to duty of those who have gone before."

The future of Memorial Hall was in doubt for much of the late 1990s and early 2000s due to the maneuvering of the University of New Orleans, which was build-ing an art museum on either side of the hall. The university claimed it had come to own the title to Memorial Hall and would be getting rid of the word "Confederate" and, more important, getting rid of the artifacts. It took eight years of legal perseverance, but Memorial Hall—and history—finally won, and the unabashedly Confederate museum is staying in place.

One of the most popular artifacts is the bloodstained, bullet-riddled battle flag of Hilliard's Legion, a unit formed in Alabama. Museum staff have no written documentation on why an Alabama unit's flag is in the collection of a Louisiana museum, but I am glad it's there. (One of my great-great-grandfathers, Captain Richard Newton Moore, was mortally wounded while following that same flag up Snodgrass Hill at the Battle of Chickamauga, Georgia.) One contemporary account of that battle says bullets pierced the flag more than sixty times.

Nearby is a display describing the actions of the First Louisiana Special Battalion, also called the Louisiana Tigers. The Tigers were under the command of Colonel Roberdeau Wheat, a soldier of fortune who had fought extensively in Central and South America. Wounded and told he was going to die at First Manassas in July 1861, Wheat told the doctors he didn't feel like dying that day. He recovered, only to suffer a fatal wound during the Seven Days Battles in June 1862.

Perhaps the most unusual artifact here is one that some visitors may find startling. It is kept in a display case on a raised deck in the rear of the building where the body of President Jefferson Davis lay in state before his body was put aboard a train bound for his final resting place in Richmond. Among other items of clothing owned by the Davis family is a crown of thorns that Pope Pius IX sent to Davis when the U.S. government imprisoned him. The gift implied that the reigning Pope considered Davis to be persecuted.

The opinion of New Orleans on General Ben "Beast" Butler has not changed much since the war, as indicated by a display on his months as military commander. The display includes a remnant of the flag torn down at the U.S. Mint by William Mumford. Butler later hanged Mumford at the site. The display also demonstrates the cleverness of citizens who wanted to express their displeasure at the Union occupation. Prints of a seemingly mundane floral display titled "Fleurs du Sud" (French for "Flowers of the South") began to appear in Southern homes. If you back away from the print and then look at it again, you will see that that the flowers form the Stars and Bars—the First National Flag of the Confederacy. When Union officers discovered what the print symbolized, they tried to confiscate it.

The Memorial Hall does not back away from displays that depict the mistakes Southerners made in the war, such as refusing to recognize that some black Southerners were willing to fight the Federals. Among the first regiments to volunteer to defend New Orleans from Union invasion were the Native Guards, two regiments of free blacks who felt the same ardor about defending the South as any white man. While Louisianans saw nothing wrong with their volunteering, Confederate officials in Richmond refused to accept their enlistments. Stung by the rejection of their fellow Southerners, the Native Guards reorganized as a Union regiment once New Orleans was captured. The same display offers evidence of individual "black Confederates" who served from the state.

Throughout the museum, visitors will find interesting flags, uniforms, weapons, even hats. One hat worn by a Confederate officer is made of tightly woven grass. A First National flag is emblazoned with the defiant words "Let Us Alone" and "Trust in God." Found in another display case is a flag from the famous Washington Artillery that fought from First Manassas right through Appomattox Court House. Its gunners were renowned for their accuracy.

2. National D-Day Museum ★★★★

945 Magazine St.
T: 504-527-6012
Daily, 9 a.m.–5 p.m.
Admission: $14

Although visitors will not find a single Civil War artifact in this museum, it is just one block from Confederate Memorial Hall, and no historical trip to New Orleans would be complete without a visit. The museum, now somewhat incorrectly named since a recent expansion covers the Pacific Theater of World War II, was built in New Orleans as it was home to the Higgins Boat Company, which manufactured the shallow-water, plywood landing craft that General Eisenhower credited with winning the war. Allow at least three hours for touring this museum and talking to the World War II vets who volunteer their memories of fighting a world war.

3. Louisiana State Museum ★★★★

751 Chartres St. (at Jackson Square)
T: 504-568-6968
Tuesday–Sunday, 8 a.m.–5 p.m.
Admission: $5

This museum has one of the finer displays of the history of a state and a city ever produced. It covers virtually every aspect of the settlement of Louisiana and New Orleans. The comings and goings of so many cultures—from Native Americans, to Spanish, to French, to the Acadians from Nova Scotia—can be difficult to follow, but the displays clarify the area's history.

The second floor has a huge painting and an excellent explanation of the Battle of

New Orleans, which took place out of sight of the city on a swampy plain called Chalmette on January 8, 1815. That battle, which took place after a treaty had been signed ending the War of 1812, would have given Great Britain control over the vast new territories included in the Louisiana Purchase—had the British won. Instead, the British suffered 2,000 casualties compared to only seventy-one Americans lost. The victory cemented the image of Americans as clever fighters on their own soil. All of the principals involved—including pirates, slaves, Indians, and future president Andrew Jackson—are covered in the displays.

On the third floor, a display describes the type of slavery practiced in Louisiana, followed by the museum's section on the Civil War. Slavery artifacts are displayed, and are followed by panels quoting citizens of the state commenting on their emotions on having to leave the Union.

One Civil War artifact currently missing from the museum is the submarine that used to be at the front entrance. It has been moved to Baton Rouge for restoration. Built during the Civil War by unknown Confederates, the hand-cranked submarine was discovered after the war in a canal near Lake Pontchartrain. To date,

no records of who built the submarine or if it ever went on a mission have ever been found. The fat, ungainly-looking machine obviously never benefited from the technology that was used to built the *C.S.S. Hunley*, the submarine that sank a Union warship in Charleston Harbor in February 1864. The submarine will be returned to New Orleans once it is restored.

4. U.S. Mint ★★★

400 Esplanade Ave.
T: 504-568-6968
Tuesday–Sunday, 8 a.m.–5 p.m.
Admission: $5. Discount tickets can be obtained to see both the Mint and the Louisiana State Museum.

The Mint is located about five blocks northeast of the State Museum at the end of the historic district. Inside, exhibits describe the building's use as a U.S. Mint and its short stint as a Confederate mint. It was in the front yard of the Mint that a local man, William Mumford, pulled down the U.S. flag. Union General Ben Butler had Mumford hanged in the same yard to demonstrate his power over the citizens of the city. The effect of the brutal act was to cow the populace into giving up resistance, but it also cemented Butler's reputation as "Beast" Butler.

GETTING TO AND AROUND NEW ORLEANS

Louis Armstrong New Orleans International Airport, served by thirteen airlines, is about eleven miles and a $28 cab fare to the Central Business District.

If the downtown area is the focus of your visit, consider not renting a car and take a shuttle or taxi into the city. However, Fort Jackson, the fall of which sealed the fate of New Orleans, is seventy miles to the south. Visiting it will require a car. As noted in the Bonus Sites chapter, a visit to Fort Jackson is well worth the trip.

New Orleans offers one transportation alternative that few other cities offer—real streetcars. The green streetcars with their wooden seats and polished wood ceilings, still take tourists and residents from Canal Street in the Central Business District out past Tulane University on the St. Charles line. A ride costs only $1.25. Note that the streetcars do not go down Bourbon Street, but a line does run along the Mississippi River.

The most convenient place for visitors to stay is midway between the French Quarter and the Warehouse District, which is the location of the Confederate Memorial Hall and the National D-Day Museum. If the hotel is centrally located, one can walk between the two areas. Because the Mississippi poses a barrier, vehicular traffic becomes more congested further east in the Central Business District. The French Quarter streets are crowded with revelers and carriages during the evening hours, so walking is best.

Numerous walking tours of the French Quarter are offered, but none include the Confederate Memorial Hall. Still, the museum is easy to find.

Accommodations

Ashton's Bed & Breakfast

2023 Esplanade Ave., New Orleans
T: 800-725-4131
www.ashtonbb.com
8 rooms
$105–$140

Finished in 1861 just before the war started, this bed and breakfast is in a 10,000-square-foot Greek-revival mansion.

Creole Gardens Guesthouse

1415 Prytania St., New Orleans
T: 866-569-8700
www.creolegardens.com
20 rooms
$129–$189

This bed and breakfast has decorated part of its facility to resemble what the owners imagine two nearby bordellos looked like.

Dauphine House Bed and Breakfast

1830 Dauphine St., New Orleans
T: 504-940-0943
www.dauphinehouse.com
3 rooms
$65–$125

Built in 1860, this house is one block from the French Quarter. Morning coffee is made with a dash of chicory, which Confederate soldiers substituted for coffee.

Marigny Manor House

2125 North Rampart St., New Orleans
T: 877-247-7599
www.marignymanorhouse.com
4 rooms
$109–$130

This 1840s mansion is in the 150-year-old Creole neighborhood of Faubourg Marigny.

Sources & Other Reading

The Night the War Was Lost, Charles L. Dufour, University of Nebraska Press, 1994.

The Civil War in Louisiana, John Winters, Louisiana State University Press, 1991.

The Capture of New Orleans, Chester Hearn, Louisiana State University Press, 1995.

The Civil War Diary of Clara Solomon: Growing Up in New Orleans 1861–1862, edited by Elliott Ashkenazi, Louisiana State University Press, 1995.

When the Devil Came Down to Dixie: Ben Butler in New Orleans, Chester Hearn, Louisiana State University Press, 2000.

Lee's Tigers: The Louisiana Infantry in the Army of Northern Virginia, Terry Jones, Louisiana State University Press, 2002.

The Louisiana Native Guards: The Black Military Experience During the Civil War, James Hollandsworth, Louisiana State University Press, 1998.

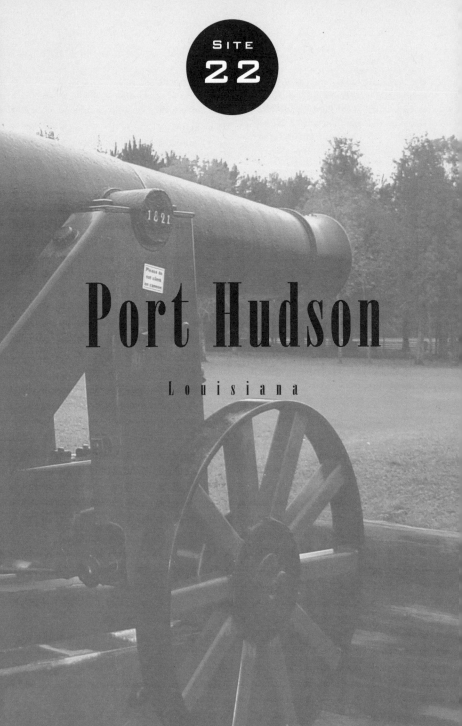

Port Hudson

Louisiana

An old thirty-two-pounder protects the Port Hudson Museum.

THE WAR YEARS

T here are many stories to tell at Port Hudson—it was the longest siege in American military history; Confederates outnumbered ten to one held out for more than two months; and it was the first time black troops got to prove their bravery on the battlefield. All these stories combine to make this a great site.

One of the first wartime objectives President Lincoln voiced was control of the Mississippi River, the lower part of which flowed through Arkansas, Tennessee, Louisiana, and Mississippi. That was a lot of territory to conquer, which meant the Confederacy had a lot of time to build defenses all along the river.

One of the spots the Confederates picked as a defense site was at a bend in the river called Port Hudson, about twenty-five miles north of Baton Rouge and 140 miles south of Vicksburg. Over the course of several months, the Confederate commander at New Orleans, General Mansfield Lovell, wisely constructed a long line of deeply dug earthworks to protect that city and Baton Rouge from a river attack from the north. Unfortunately for New Orleans, the major Federal assault came from the south in April 1862 when Union gunboats ran past two brick forts that had been regarded as impassable. New Orleans surrendered without firing a shot in its defense.

With no defense to the south, Baton Rouge fell soon after New Orleans. That left the way open for the Federals to concentrate on the fortifications at Port Hudson. If they could demolish Port Hudson, that would leave Vicksburg, the most heavily defended city on the river, open to attack. The Confederate garrison at Port Hudson, knowing that it would be attacked once the Federals accumulated enough men and ships, could do little except dig its works deeper, clear its fields of fire in front of its works, and practice its gunnery.

The first Federal attack by the U.S. Navy came on March 14, 1863, a full year after New Orleans had fallen. Accurate Confederate fire destroyed one ship, causing four of the remaining ships to retreat while two ships succeeded in running past Port Hudson. In early May 1863, U.S. Grant crossed the Mississippi River and was north of Port Hudson, though he was concentrating on Vicksburg.

On May 11, 30,000 Federal land troops moved on Port Hudson from the south. The Federals were commanded by General Nathaniel Banks, a former speaker of the U.S. House of Representatives and governor of Massachusetts who had been appointed general as a favor from President Lincoln. The Confederate commander, General Franklin Gardner, a native of New York City who had married a Louisiana woman, had only 3,500 men in his works. That serious shortage of manpower could be traced to the Confederate government in Richmond's underestimation of the importance of controlling the Mississippi. For more than a week, Gardner fought off probing attacks by moving his forces through the trenches to where the Federals were attacking most heavily.

On May 27, Banks finally launched a major assault, but he failed to coordinate the individual attacks along the Confederate line. Gardner was once again able to move his men along his interior lines to where the danger was most intense during the battle.

Hardest hit were the Native Guards, regiments of black men raised from New Orleans. Two of the three regiments were made up of free blacks, including slaveholders who had offered their services to the Confederacy when the war first started. The Confederate government, nervous about arming black men, had turned them down. After the fall of New Orleans, the Native Guards realized that a Union victory in the war could free all black men, so they offered their services to the North.

The First and Second regiments of Native Guards were made up of free men and commanded by black officers. The Third Native Guards, recruited from former slaves around New Orleans, were commanded by white officers after Banks forced their black officers to resign because he did not value their command skills. The three regiments numbered about 1,500 men, half the strength of three normal regiments because Banks believed 3,000 blacks were too many to control. He had left the Second Native Guards behind on this operation for the same reason.

Poor scouting work by white officers caused the First and Third Regiments to attack their portion of the Port Hudson works in a swampy area that bogged down the advance. One captain of the First, a man who proudly called himself "the blackest man in America," was killed while leading the assault. He had been badly wounded earlier in the day but he refused to leave his regiment. The white general leading the black regiments refused to let them withdraw, telling the remaining officers to continue the attack "as long as there is a corporal's guard left."

When the fruitless assault was halted, only one white regiment had suffered as many casualties as the two black regiments. Word spread through Northern newspapers that "the race of serfs had stepped up to the respect of the world." Even Banks, who had not believed the Native Guards would fight, wrote in his official report: "It is no longer possible to doubt the bravery and steadiness of the colored race when rightly led." Curiously, however, Banks never believed the black officers were as intelligent as his white officers. He steadily replaced the Native Guard black officers with white officers, which resulted in morale problems within the ranks of the regiments he had just praised.

When Banks's assault failed, he turned to a siege, hoping to starve the Confederates into surrender. He tried another assault on June 14, but that too failed. Over the next three weeks his force waited as the Confederates resorted to catching and eating dogs, cats, and then rats. Only when word reached Port Hudson that Vicksburg had surrendered to Grant on July 4 did Gardner surrender his garrison.

The number of casualties was surprising. In just over sixty days of fighting and siege warfare, the Confederates, outmanned 3,000 to 30,000, had lost barely 500 men killed and wounded. Thanks to Banks's inexperience as a general, the Federals had lost more than 5,000 killed and wounded. The battles for Port Hudson were among the most lopsided victories in terms of casualties suffered by the winning side.

With the fall of Port Hudson, the Mississippi River came entirely under Union control. No more supplies would come from the Trans-Mississippi Theater of the Confederacy to help supply Robert E. Lee's army in the east. The biggest effect, however, was that the black man had proven that he would not run from fighting.

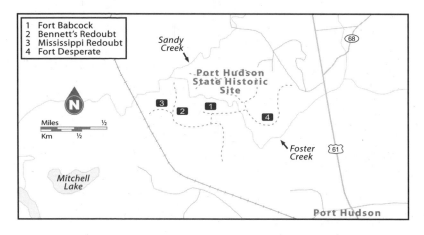

1 Fort Babcock
2 Bennett's Redoubt
3 Mississippi Redoubt
4 Fort Desperate

Sandy
Creek

Port Hudson
State Historic
Site

Miles   ½
Km   ½

Foster
Creek

Mitchell
Lake

Port Hudson

PORT HUDSON TODAY

Port Hudson State Historic Site, thirty minutes north of Baton Rouge and ten minutes south of St. Francisville on US. 61, covers 909 acres of the northern portion of the battlefield. While the land where the heaviest fighting occurred is now protected by the state, significant portions of the battlefield to the southwest are in private hands. The American Civil War Preservation Trust lists Port Hudson as one of its most endangered battlefields.

Since Port Hudson is more than thirty miles north of Baton Rouge, there seems to be little danger of development that would destroy the miles of earthworks hidden in the woods just east of the Mississippi River. Approaching Port Hudson from the south, visitors get a sense of the industrial base of the state of Louisiana. Both sides of the road just out

of Baton Rouge are lined with chemical plants. If visitors approach from the north, they will come upon the small, picturesque village of St. Francisville, population 2,000, and on the east, Zachary, population 11,000. Neither of these communities seems in any hurry to put up tract homes on a battlefield.

This is Louisiana at its most laid-back. You won't find the wild scenes of the French Quarter in New Orleans, or the chemical plants and bureaucrats of the capital of Baton Rouge. This rural setting makes it an easy place to study the war.

Each year, generally around the first weekend of April, close to the anniversaries of the actual battle, there is a public reenactment staged at the state historic site.

Port Hudson State Historic Site ★★★★

236 Highway 61, 10 miles south of St. Francisville.
T: 225-654-3775
Daily, 9 a.m.–5 p.m.
Admission: $2

Visitors to this 909-acre battlefield should come prepared to hike. Other than a small artillery display on the way to the visitor center and a thirty-two-pounder cannon on a carriage displayed outside the visitor center, there is little indication that visitors are on a battlefield. None of the battlefield can be seen by car. All approaches by the Federals and the defensive forts and redoubts manned by the Confederates are reached via six miles of walking trails.

This means that touring Port Hudson requires planning ahead. The park warns on its trail map that there are no bathrooms or water fountains on the trail system. As even fast walkers will need at least two hours to see the entire battlefield along these trails, visitors are advised to bring water bottles. Wear hiking or walking shoes. People with disabilities can likely use the trails, but they are paved with limestone gravel, so rolling a wheelchair might be difficult. The maps distributed by the state park service are not good reproductions, but they do identify the markers so you know where you are on the trail. Many trails, such as the one atop Artillery Ridge, are dead ends. The map is necessary to go from one stop to another.

Among the sites found along the walk:

1. Fort Babcock ★★ was a Union earthwork built 100 yards from the Confederates' Alabama-Arkansas Redoubt.

2. Bennett's Redoubt ★★ was the location of Confederate cannons, which dueled with Union artillery placed upon Artillery Ridge.

3. The Mississippi Redoubt ★★★, on the far western side of the park 1.3 miles from the visitor center, was the point of attack by the Native Guards. This redoubt, a defensive position that is more than an earthwork but less than an enclosed fort, was where two regiments and a cannon battery commanded the high ground looking west toward the Mississippi River.

The ground below them was marshy and in some spots completely covered by water. This was the terrible ground that misinformed officers had ordered the black troops of the Native Guards to attack. Some white officers, realizing the suicidal nature of the mission they were giving their black regiments, ordered the men under their command to take cover more than 600 yards from the Mississippi Redoubt. The officers ordered their men to increase the frequency of the firing of their rifles on the distant Confederate line, so that Union generals behind the lines would hear the firing and assume that the Mississippi Redoubt was being attacked as ordered. The subterfuge was later discovered and the officers punished, but their wise actions in not sending their men over the swampy land likely saved the Native Guards from being entirely wiped out.

4. Fort Desperate ★★★★, nicknamed this by a grim comedian on the Confederate side, is a U-shaped fort best viewed from an observation tower located between the two prongs. An officer apparently designed the fort so that he could move his men quickly from one prong to the other depending upon the severity of the attack on either prong. This redoubt is well preserved, and its U-shape is unusual for defensive works during the Civil War.

Some of the battle's most intense fighting took place here. Among the weapons used were hand grenades. In those days grenades were small hollow balls filled with powder that made them explode into shrapnel. One end of the grenade had a deep hole drilled in it for insertion of a wooden stick fitted with wooden fins. The idea was that the grenade could be thrown further, but the crudity of fuses and contact primers meant that the grenades were often thrown back and forth between opposing sides before finally exploding. Few actually worked as they were designed to, but their appearance at Port Hudson reflected an advance in military technology.

The park also distributes a driving tour of sites around Port Hudson, but like the walking tour, this map is dimly photocopied, and all of the sites are in private hands. Visitors should not leave their vehicles to get a closer look, or they will be in violation of trespassing laws. The driving tour includes the site of a Confederate hospital; Port Hudson National Cemetery, which has some Civil War soldiers' graves; a Confederate cemetery, "Slaughter Field," which was the scene of heavy fighting; and the site of the Confederate surrender.

GETTING TO AND AROUND PORT HUDSON

Baton Rouge Metropolitan Airport, served by four airlines, is the nearest airport. It is a forty-minute drive north to Port Hudson.

At the visitor center, visitors can park the car. All the significant sites can be reached only by walking the park's trails.

ACCOMMODATIONS

Barrow House Inn Bed & Breakfast
9779 Royal St., St. Francisville
T: 225-635-4791
www.topteninn.com
6 rooms
$95–$160

Built in 1780, this bed and breakfast is in St. Francisville's oldest house.

Butler Greenwood Plantation
8345 U.S. Highway 61, St. Francisville
T: 225-635-6312
www.butlergreenwood.com
8 cottages
$135–$185

On this 1790s plantation still owned by the same family, there are eight cottages.

SOURCES & OTHER READING

The Port Hudson Campaign, Edward Cunningham, Louisiana State University Press, 1994.

Port Hudson, Confederate Bastion on the Mississippi, Lawrence Lee Hewitt, Louisiana State University Press, 1994.

Like Men of War: Black Troops in the Civil War, 1862–1865, Noah Andre Trudeau, Little Brown & Company, 1998.

The Civil War in Louisiana, John D. Winters, Louisiana State University Press, 1991.

Pretense of Glory: The Life of Nathaniel Banks, James Hollandsworth, Louisiana State University Press, 1998.

Black Soldiers in Blue: African-American Troops in the Civil War Era, John David Smith, University of North Carolina Press, 2004.

The Sable Arm: Black Troops in the Union Army, 1861–1865, Dudley Taylor Cornish, University Press of Kansas, 1987.

Perryville

Kentucky

Perryville is still as rural today as it was in 1862.

THE WAR YEARS

The Battle of Perryville, Kentucky, was not particularly large in terms of the number of soldiers engaged, nor did it have a major effect on the war's outcome, but the Confederacy's loss here ended any slim chance of getting Kentucky to side with the South. The loss of a border—and slave—state demonstrated the Confederacy's difficulty in winning over the minds of citizens who truly wanted to remain in the Union.

Kentucky, birthplace to both Jefferson Davis and Abraham Lincoln, had always been a slave state, but it also had prominent politicians who believed in a strong Union. Kentucky's two most famous politicians, Henry Clay and John J. Crittenden, had spent many years before the war trying to make peace between the slaveholding states of the Deep South and the free states of the Northeast and Midwest. Clay had even lobbied for outlawing slavery in the U.S. Constitution, but the power of the other Southern politicians always outweighed his sentiments. Crittenden had spent the winter of 1860–1861 proposing compromises to guarantee that the federal government would not interfere with slavery in states where it already existed. Now that war was about to break out and Kentucky needed its great compromisers more than ever, it did not have them to turn to for help. Clay had been dead eight years, and Crittenden was too old to persuade the soon-to-be-warring factions to seek common ground.

The stakes were high in the spring of 1861. No one could predict which way the state would go, but President Lincoln said of the value of having his birth home in the Union: "I think to lose Kentucky is nearly the same as losing the whole game." Though most of Kentucky's national politicians clearly leaned toward the Union, its governor leaned to the South. If war ever erupted, Kentucky would almost certainly be invaded from both directions as North and South fought to get at each other's throats.

As predicted, war did come quickly to the state, and both Confederate and Union generals seized towns along the major rivers and the mountain gaps in the fall of 1861. In January of 1862, the Federals won the Battle of Mill Springs in eastern Kentucky and then in February the Battles of Forts Henry and Donelson, just over the state line in north central Tennessee. Those losses forced the pro-Confederate government officials from the state. For the first nine months of the war, it seemed clear that Kentucky would stay in the Union, though the population itself was split. Estimates are that 80,000 white men and 20,000 black men from Kentucky would fight for the Union, with 40,000 fighting for the Confederacy. Among the most famous leaders fighting for the South was President James Buchanan's Vice President John C. Breckinridge.

The Confederacy wouldn't accept the Union's hold over Kentucky. In the fall of 1862, Confederate General Edmund Kirby Smith's 19,000 men captured Lexington and the state capital of Frankfort and threatened to invade the North at Cincinnati. A second Confederate army under General Braxton Bragg with 32,000 men advanced up the center of the state. Kirby Smith was reluctant to cooperate with Bragg. (Few men in the Confederate army wanted to cooperate with Bragg, as the sour-faced man was vain, mean, and had proved to be incompetent in the field. He had only become a general because he was friends with Confederate President Jefferson Davis.)

As Bragg moved deeper into Kentucky, he became more vocal in his complaints that Kentuckians were not joining in the "liberation" of their state. But the state's men were fighting—just not for Bragg. Kentuckians did not want to have anything to do with Bragg. His reputation for wasting men, resources, and opportunities had preceded him.

Following along behind both Bragg and Kirby Smith was Union General Don Carlos Buell, one of the heroes of Shiloh. Despite his regal name, Buell was born on a farm in Ohio and was a key figure in the opening of the war. A West Point graduate, Buell, acting on behalf of the U.S. Secretary of War, had relayed the secret orders to the commander of Fort Moultrie, South Carolina, to move his troops to the safety of Fort Sumter, the action that initiated the war in April 1861.

Buell's current assignment was to stop Bragg in Kentucky. He had been slowly following the Confederates, and Washington was growing impatient for him to bring Bragg to battle. After sending 20,000 men after Kirby Smith, Buell left Bowling Green and split his 58,000-man army into three columns to advance on Bragg more quickly.

Bragg advanced his army toward Perryville, where he had heard there was enough water to relieve his parched men, who had been marching over land that was suffering a severe drought. Confederate scouts reported back that there was a strong Federal force on its way to Perryville.

Bragg determined it was time for battle. Bragg's reasoning today seems murky, but he apparently never realized—or accepted—the fact that the advancing Federal force was nearly twice the size of his own. Throughout the entire battle, Bragg believed he was facing a single corps, rather than the three that were bearing down on him. Military intelligence—or even acting on the intelligence he did have—was never Bragg's strong suit as a general.

Early in the morning of October 8, 1862, Bragg's subordinate generals formed a defensive line west of Perryville, a prudent decision since they had no idea of the size of the advancing Federal force. When Bragg arrived at 10 a.m., he flew into a rage that the attack he had ordered against the first elements of the Federals was not under way. Bragg's generals reluctantly went into attack mode.

Bragg's rash attack in the open against an unknown superior force was militarily unsound, but his men fought so valiantly that the brash attack worked. The Federals who were engaged fell back in hard fighting.

But not all of the Federals were engaged. One Union corps (at least 15,000 men) was waiting for orders from Buell. Buell was in the rear of his lines and never heard the savage fighting taking place just a few miles away due to an atmospheric condition called an acoustical shadow. This condition, caused by a combination of layers of air and the lay of the land, kept the sound of roaring cannons and muskets from traveling more than a few hundred yards on a horizontal plane. It was as though the Battle of Perryville were taking place in a large soundproof room.

When Buell finally learned of the fighting, he ordered elements of that inactive corps forward. Darkness fell before they became fully engaged. Bragg finally believed the reports

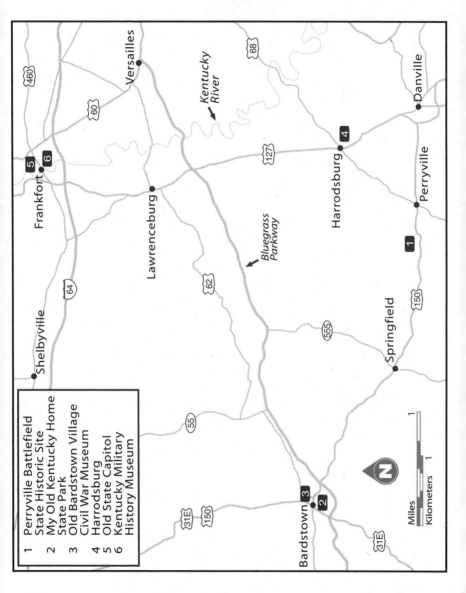

Perryville Battlefield
State Historic Site

1 Perryville Battlefield
    State Historic Site
2 My Old Kentucky Home
    State Park
3 Old Bardstown Village
    Civil War Museum
4 Harrodsburg
5 Old State Capitol
6 Kentucky Military
    History Museum

that the Union army had many more reserves ready to fight the next day. Under cover of darkness, he began a rapid pullback into Tennessee, ordering Kirby Smith to follow him. The invasion of Kentucky, designed to rally Confederate sympathizers, had done nothing more than insult them—Bragg's comments about the level of courage found in most Kentuckians had spread far and wide. Even more important to the Confederates was the more than 500 dead and 2,600 wounded, who would never be replaced with fresh Kentucky recruits. The Federals lost a total of about 845 men dead and 2,800 wounded.

In terms of pure numbers, the battle was not large, but further analysis of the number of casualties compared to the number of troops engaged reveals that Perryville was one of the bloodiest battles of the war. The Confederates alone lost nearly twenty percent of their men thanks to Bragg's insistence on attacking.

Though the Federals lost more men on the battlefield, the Confederates left the field in the middle of the night, so Perryville was recorded as a Union victory. In reality, since neither side actually forced the other from the field, the tactical battle was more of a draw. Strategically, though, it convinced Bragg to retreat back into Tennessee, an important concession.

Bragg would continue to enjoy the good graces of President Davis for the rest of the war, though almost every one of his subordinate generals hated him. Bragg continued to perform poorly in nearly every campaign and battle in which he had a hand.

Buell, on the other hand, was treated poorly by President Lincoln after the battle. Convinced by some armchair generals in Washington that Buell could have decimated the retreating Confederates, Lincoln replaced the general who had won the battle. On top of that indignity, Buell was charged with being a Confederate sympathizer because he had made public comments that he did not like the idea of the Emancipation Proclamation, which had just been announced in late September. Buell had never lost a battle for the Union; his strategy had opened up the Confederate west; and he was the first general to capture a Confederate capital. None of that mattered. If Buell was unwilling to announce his unwavering, blind support of Lincoln's plans to free the Confederacy's slaves while leaving Union state slaves in bondage, the administration considered him a liability. Though U.S. Grant insisted that Buell was one of the best battlefield generals he had ever seen, Lincoln refused to budge. Buell was forced from the army and into civilian life. Lincoln continued to appoint incompetent, sycophantic civilian generals for his entire administration.

Kentucky would continue to see Confederate raids over its borders for the rest of the war, but there would no more major battles. While Kentucky's politicians would reward President Lincoln by staying in the Union, the losers in the state would be its 226,000 slaves. The Emancipation Proclamation, issued just three months after Perryville, applied only to slaves held by Confederate states. Kentucky, a Union state, would be able to keep its slaves until a change in the Constitution had passed.

PERRYVILLE TODAY

The state park commemorating the battlefield is located on Battlefield Road, just north of the town of Perryville, which has a population of fewer than 1,000 people. The rolling hills that both confused and hid each side from the other are still here, untouched by commercial development that has overtaken nearby Danville and Harrodsburg, landmark towns along the march of both armies. (It was to Harrodsburg that Bragg retreated in order to link up with Kirby Smith and begin the march back into Tennessee.)

Just under 300 acres of the battlefield are part of the park, meaning that the approaches and retreats of both armies are still in private hands. The only towns of any size are Harrodsburg, population 8,000 and ten miles to the north, and Danville, eight miles to the east with a population of around 15,000. The large city of Lexington is just forty-two miles away, but at present that seems a sufficient distance to keep development pressures away from Perryville.

Perryville's museum closes in November and does not reopen until April. One aspect of the park that may disturb some visitors is the presence of playground equipment and meeting shelters on a battlefield that includes the unmarked graves of soldiers who died for their country.

Visitors may want to take a few minutes to walk the sidewalks of the small town of Perryville. Many of its storefronts date from the late 1800s, and the town makes a conscientious effort to keep that look.

POINTS OF INTEREST

Perryville Battlefield State Historic Site
★★★★★

1825 Battlefield Rd. (2 miles north of U.S. 150)
T: 859-332-8631
Museum is open daily April 1–October 31, 9 a.m.–5 p.m. Open by appointment the rest of the year. The park is open most days for self-guided tours of the battlefield.
Admission: $2

Heed this word of caution if looking for Perryville on a Kentucky map or trying to use Mapquest to come up with directions from a home address. There are three different Perryvilles in three different counties in Kentucky. That is confusing enough, but all of the Perryvilles are also in the same general area of the state. The site of the battle was in Boyle County, just southwest of Lexington.

One unique thing about visiting the Perryville Battlefield, compared to most national park sites, is that its battlefield tour is entirely a walking tour. So keep this in mind, as the trail does include a few hills. The park actually has three different walking tours; a condensed version that circles the museum, an extended tour, and a further extension of that extended tour. If park visitors choose to do only the short tour of twelve sites, the tour of Perryville

will take one and a half hours (not count-
ing a visit to the museum). If visitors take
the extended tour of all twenty-one stops,
park officials estimate it can take at least
two and a half hours to walk the tour.

Once visitors enter the park, they park
their car across from the museum. If the
museum is closed, there is a box nearby
containing copies of the trail guide. The
interpretative trail starts in front of the
museum at the statue over the unknown
Confederate dead.

During the busier spring, summer, and fall
tourist seasons, visitors follow mown paths
from one site to another. Problems might
arise in late fall and winter when park
employees are no longer mowing the
paths. On the research trip for this book
conducted in late fall, the paths had not
been mown and there were no signs indi-
cating which direction to go. Visitors could
see what they could assume to be the next
battlefield display sign in the distance,
but there was no mown path to those
interpretive signs as promised in published information on the park.

The total distance of the extended tour is
five miles, so should be undertaken by only
the most dedicated of travel historians.
Note that there are no water fountains on
the tour and no bathrooms. (Also note the
irony of cautioning visitors to take water
on a five-mile, two-to-three-hour hike. Part
of the reason the Battle of Perryville was
fought at this particular location was over
the rumor of the availability of water north
of town. Moving through a parched,
drought-stricken countryside, the
Confederate commanders had heard from
civilians living in the area that there were
pools of water in Doctor's Creek, so they
moved there to investigate. Buell's troops
moved in search of the Confederates.)

Informative signs on the trail describe the
pertinent action that took place at each

site. The signs are definitely needed.
Perryville was a confusing battle, with first
one side, then the other side attacking
and retreating.

The Confederates were first in defensive
positions and ordered out of them by
Bragg, who did not study the terrain or the
situation before demanding his generals to
attack. Mistakes happened on the field.
Once during the battle, Confederate
General Leonidas Polk rode up to what he
thought was one of his Confederate
brigades. Polk angrily ordered the officers
to stop firing into a neighboring brigade.
Apparently dry road dust had hidden the
true color of the brigade's uniforms. A
Confederate general suddenly realized he
was giving orders to a Federal brigade. The
confused soldiers and officers were trying
to determine who this unfamiliar general
was when Polk quickly turned his horse
and rode to the safety of his own lines.

On the Federal side, Buell did not even
know a battle was under way at first
because of the acoustical shadow that
masked the sounds of cannons and muskets. Already under pressure and hearing
complaints from Washington for not
engaging Bragg when he first crossed into
Kentucky from Tennessee, Buell spent
much of the afternoon preparing to bring
Thomas L. Crittenden's Second Corps into
the fight.

At the end of the first day, Bragg learned
that he had not even faced all of the
Federals who could have been on the
field. For once, he heeded the intelligence.
Rather than do battle against an army
nearly twice the size of his own, Bragg
decided to withdraw.

Some reluctant history travelers may com-
plain that Perryville is just one big field,
and the truth of their opinion cannot be
denied. It has no massive displays of cannons, no markers erected by veterans

pinpointing where they fought (the park was not officially established until 1958), and no historic houses to visit and break up the walking tour.

But the exercise of walking those paths does put visitors into the shoes of the soldiers who fought over that same ground. Visitors should imagine (or try) running up a grassy hill between markers and then imagine doing it with thirty pounds of weapons, ammunition, and blankets draped on their bodies. Touring the big field that is Perryville is an example of

how history travelers need an active imagination to really appreciate what happened on that unusually hot October day.

One noteworthy feature of the battlefield is the **Confederate soldier statue ★★★★** erected over the mass grave of some 340 unknown Southern soldiers. The statue was erected in 1902 and is of a type that was mass-produced and sold around the turn of the century to small towns to honor their hometown soldiers while they were still alive.

Other Area Attractions

My Old Kentucky Home State Park ★★

U.S. 150, Bardstown
T: 502-348-3502
Daily, 9 a.m.–5 p.m.
Closed major holidays.
Free admission.

Bardstown, thirty-four miles to the west of Perryville on U.S. 150 (known during the war as the Springfield Pike) was where Bragg's army waited just before the Battle of Perryville.

My Old Kentucky Home, officially called Federal Hill, was finished in 1818. The owners of the house were songwriter Stephen Foster's cousins. After leaving from an 1852 visit, Foster wrote the song as a thank-you for the hospitality he received. The song later became the state's official song, and the image of the house appears on Kentucky's quarter. The home escaped destruction by both Federal and Confederate troops and is interpreted as a prewar home. The song is performed regularly through the summer in an outdoor play staged in Bardstown called *Stephen Foster—The Musical.*

Old Bardstown Village Civil War Museum ★★★

310 East Broadway, Bardstown
T: 502-349-0291
Daily, 10 a.m.–5 p.m.
Winter hours may be shorter.
Admission: $6 for main museum and $2.50 for Women in the Civil War Museum.

This museum also administers the adjacent Women in the Civil War Museum. Billing itself as the fourth-largest Civil War museum in the nation, the museum features 8,500 square feet of exhibit space. Like General Sweeny's Museum at Wilson's Creek, Missouri, the Bardstown museum concentrates on the war in the west. (The war's western theater is loosely defined as all of the battles west of Georgia up to the Mississippi River. Across the river was the Trans-Mississippi Theater. The battles in the Carolinas, Virginia, Maryland, and Pennsylvania are considered the eastern theater.)

Harrodsburg ★★

It was to Harrodsburg, ten miles north of Perryville, that Bragg retreated after the battle. Bragg combined his army with that of Kirby Smith here, and they began a retreating march to the southeast and

Cumberland Gap, the famous mountain road where Kentucky's first settlers such as Daniel Boone entered the region.

Established in 1774, Harrodsburg bills itself as the first permanent English-founded settlement west of the Allegheny Mountains. Among the attractions here are houses that date to the Civil War era, and Old Fort Harrod State Park, a reconstruction of a log fort built to protect settlers from the Indians. An outdoor play about Daniel Boone is produced each summer in an amphitheater behind the fort.

Old State Capitol ★
Intersection of Broadway Street and Lewis Street, Frankfort
T: 502-564-1792
Tuesday–Saturday, 10 a.m.–5 p.m.;
Sunday, 1–5 p.m.

Guided tours run every hour. Last tour begins at 4 p.m.
Free admission.

Confederates were about to install their own governor here in October 1862 when the approach of Buell and his forces killed the idea.

Kentucky Military History Museum ★★
East Main at Capitol Ave., Frankfort
T: 502-564-3265
Tuesday–Saturday, 10 a.m.–5 p.m.;
Sunday, 1–5 p.m.
Free admission.

This museum traces Kentucky's military heritage from pioneer times through today. Some displays cover the Civil War.

GETTING TO AND AROUND PERRYVILLE

Blue Grass Airport in Lexington, about forty miles from Perryville, is the closet commercial airport, with five airlines making nonstop flights to twelve hub cities. Most of the major car-rental companies are represented. Lexington is also the nearest airport to land private aircraft.

Getting to Perryville by car is relatively easy. Perryville is about forty-five miles northwest of the I-75 exit (Exit 59) at Mount Vernon and thirty-four miles southeast of the intersection of U.S. 150 and the Bluegrass Parkway at Bardstown. Anyone coming from the Blue Grass Airport should get on U.S. 68 and head south to reach Perryville.

As noted elsewhere, there is only one way to see Perryville Battlefield, and that is to walk it. There is no official driving tour of the approaches both sides took to the battlefield, but there are plenty of crisscrossing paved country roads surrounding the park and the town. Most of the Federals arrived on what was then the Springfield Pike (today's U.S. 150) west of the town. The Confederates mostly congregated north of the town in the vicinity of the state park. The country roads surrounding Perryville give travelers some idea of what the approach terrain looked like in the fall of 1862.

ACCOMMODATIONS

Old Crow Inn Bed & Breakfast

471 Stanford Rd., Danville
T: 859-236-1808
www.oldcrowinn.com
3 rooms
$80–$100

Built in 1780, this is supposedly the oldest stone home west of the Allegheny Mountains.

Jailer's Inn Bed & Breakfast

111 West Stephen Foster Ave., Bardstown
T: 504-328-5551
www.jailersinn.com
6 rooms
$105–$125

This was a real jail, built in 1819. The guest rooms have bars on the windows, and the walls are made of stone. One room is even a real jail cell, though the rest of the building was converted into a house in 1874.

Beaumont Inn

638 Beaumont Inn Dr., Harrodsburg
T: 800-352-3992
www.beaumontinn.com
4 rooms
$93–$185

This bed and breakfast was built in 1845 as a finishing school for young ladies. It was converted into an inn in 1917, and the same family runs it today.

The Golden Lion Bed & Breakfast

243 North Third St., Danville
T: 859-583-1895
www.thegoldenlionbb.com
3 rooms
$89–$95

This 1840 house has its own military museum and three rooms all named after ancestors of the owners.

SOURCES & OTHER READING

Perryville: This Grand Havoc of Battle, Kenneth Noe, University Press of Kentucky, 2001.

War in Kentucky: From Shiloh to Perryville, James Lee McDonough, University of Tennessee Press, 1996.

The Civil War: A Narrative—Fort Sumter to Perryville, Vol. 1 of 3, Shelby Foote, Random House, 1958.

Perryville: Battle for Kentucky, Dr. Kenneth Hafendorfer, self-published, 1989.

The Civil War in Kentucky, Kent Masterson Brown, DeCapo Press, 2000.

Civil War in Kentucky, Lowell Harrison, University Press of Kentucky, 1987.

Pea Ridge

Arkansas

Two Confederate generals were killed on this field at Pea Ridge.

THE WAR YEARS

T his battlefield is definitely one of the best battle sites in the nation. Its battle-ground is almost perfectly preserved, so it looks much the same as it would have looked during wartime; it was the only true battle where American Indians comprised a large number of the combatants; and the Union victory here protected U.S. Grant's distant flank as he moved down the Tennessee River toward Shiloh, Tennessee, where he would win a decisive victory the following month.

Concern for control of the state of Missouri, the border of which lies just a few miles to the north of here, helped make this remote region of northwest Arkansas a battlefield in March 1862.

Though the Confederates had won the Battle of Wilson's Creek, Missouri, seventy-eight miles northeast of Pea Ridge on August 10, 1861, the state's final allegiances had not yet been settled. Wilson's Creek had been fought barely three weeks after the Battle of Manassas in Virginia, and no other large-scale battles had yet taken place in the eastern theater to either defeat the Confederacy or convince the Union to let the Southern states secede. Other than the Union capture of much of coastal North and South Carolina in the summer and fall of 1861, and a disastrous Union defeat at Balls Bluff, Virginia, near Washington in October, neither side had gained an advantage.

In effect, both sides were standing and watching for the other to make a move, hoping the other side would make a mistake.

The Confederates in Missouri were at a logistical disadvantage. Thanks to Union Colonel (later General) Nathaniel Lyon, who acted without specific orders to capture the St. Louis arsenal in May 1861, would-be secessionists in the state were still poorly armed when the spring of 1862 rolled around. Some reports say that as many as a third of the Confederate Missouri State Guard did not have a military-style weapon. They were using their own hunting rifles and shotguns.

More important to the future of the state, the Federal military bureaucracy in Washington had become better organized after an initial concentration on the war in the east. The quiet time after Bull Run had allowed the armchair generals in the nation's capital to realize that holding Missouri in the Union by forcing the Confederates out would likely secure the far flanks of the Union for the foreseeable future.

After Lyon's death at Wilson's Creek, Union General Samuel Curtis was appointed commander in the southwestern district of Missouri. Curtis, a West Point–trained soldier who had fought in the Mexican War, settled on one agenda—driving the Confederates out of Missouri once and for all.

Curtis's main opponent was Confederate General Sterling Price, who had been just about everything in Missouri *but* a military leader. Price was a wealthy planter, former U.S. Congressman, and former governor who had hoped at first that a compromise could be worked out between the slaveholding states and the Union. When the Federals under Lyon seized the Missouri armory in May 1861, Price offered to organize the Missouri State Guard for the South.

The thrill of Confederate victory at Wilson's Creek lasted only a few months before Curtis and 11,000 Union troops started pushing their way toward another engagement with Price's 8,000-member Missouri Guard. Price bought time by retreating into northwestern Arkansas so he could link up with other Confederates under his old companion and adversary General Ben McCullough. Both generals relinquished overall command to West Point–trained General Earl Van Dorn.

Van Dorn was as brash and rough-edged as Price was careful and courtly. The two had little in common, but then few men who served with Van Dorn liked him at all. The Mississippi-born Mexican War veteran seemed in a hurry to duplicate his fifteen-year-old reputation as a hero. He found that playing the hero helped him impress ladies—both single and married.

But Van Dorn's flaws began to show early as he consolidated command of his little army. He had been a dragoon (cavalry) commander while fighting Indians, where it was important to rush the enemy. Army commanders should use their cavalry to scout out the enemy and then carefully plan how to engage their infantry while finding good ground for their artillery. This sort of planning was beyond his capability.

Van Dorn turned the combined army—called the Army of the West and numbering some 16,000—around and headed it back to Missouri. He wanted to capture the Federal-held city of St. Louis, a feat that he hoped would turn the state around for the Confederacy.

Van Dorn's plan was to surprise Curtis's pursuing army before the Federals realized that a battle was about to take place. To accomplish that, Van Dorn ordered his infantry regiments forward in a rush, leaving his ammunition wagons behind. He figured they would secure the victory quickly and there would be no need for ammunition replenishment. Van Dorn was still thinking that he was leading a hit-and-run cavalry raid rather than planning for a major battle.

Efficient Federal scouts discovered the approaching Confederates, crippling Van Dorn's plan from the start. Curtis pulled his men back into a defensive position on Pea Ridge and awaited the Confederates. He would stop them before they even crossed Missouri's southern border.

Skirmishing began near dawn on March 7, 1862, but Price, in keeping with his reputation for caution, did not fully engage the Federals until three hours later. Van Dorn himself had taken ill, or was possibly drunk. Whatever the cause, he was not on the field.

Price's Missouri State Guard finally broke the Union line near Elkhorn Tavern, a wayside village that appears in Confederate records as the name of the battle. At the opposite end of the line, more than 1,000 Cherokees also briefly broke through the Union line. They celebrated by scalping some dead and still-living Union soldiers. However, their joy was short-lived as Union cannons pushed them back into the woods.

When Confederate General Ben McCullough foolishly went forward to survey the situation, a Union sharpshooter killed him. Another Confederate general, James McIntosh, was killed shortly afterward. That end of the Confederate line hesitated, confused now that its two line commanders were dead.

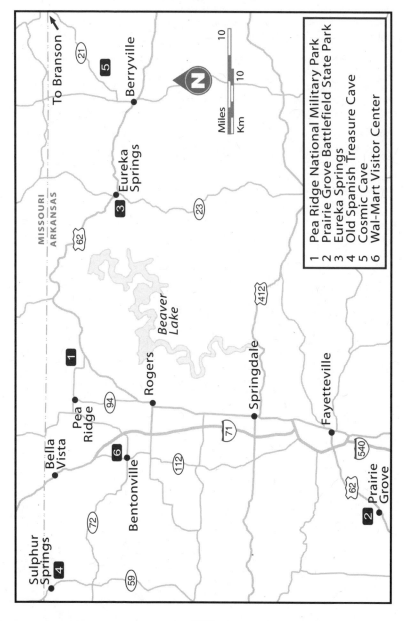

To Branson

21

5 Berryville

10

10

Miles
Km

1 Pea Ridge National Military Park
2 Prairie Grove Battlefield State Park
3 Eureka Springs
4 Old Spanish Treasure Cave
5 Cosmic Cave
6 Wal-Mart Visitor Center

Eureka
Springs

3

23

MISSOURI
ARKANSAS

62

Beaver
Lake

412

1

Rogers

94

Springdale

Pea
Ridge

71

Fayetteville

Bella
Vista

6

112

540

Bentonville

72

62

Prairie
Grove

2

Sulphur
Springs

4

59

As night fell, both sides held their ground, but Curtis consolidated his lines. That night Curtis assessed the situation and speculated that Van Dorn had left his supply wagons behind. If he had, then the Confederate ammunition supply had to be dwindling. Curtis's defensive plan switched from holding onto the ground he had to attacking the superior numbers of Confederates.

On the second morning, two divisions of Federals, under German-born General Franz Siegel, attacked the Confederates around Elkhorn Tavern with the help of some fine shooting by Union artillery men who took out Confederate batteries. As their cartridge boxes emptied, the Missouri State Guard broke. The same thing happened on the other end of the line to the men who had not recovered from the loss of their two generals.

With both ends of his line collapsing in confusion, Van Dorn ordered a general retreat. He was humiliated; his supposedly overwhelming force of 17,000 men had lost to 11,000 Federals. Van Dorn had gone into the battle thinking he would have the advantage of surprise. Instead, thanks to his decision to leave behind his ammo wagons, his men had no choice but to fall back in the face of an inferior force.

The battle losses at Pea Ridge seemed huge to the armies engaged. A thousand Confederates were killed and wounded and 300 captured. The Federals lost around 1,300. Those numbers were minuscule compared to the losses they would experience at Shiloh, Tennessee, the following month, but to the men fighting at Pea Ridge, it had been grueling indeed.

Strategically, Pea Ridge was much larger in significance than the numbers engaged would seem to indicate. This was a small battle. But Curtis had crushed the Missouri State Guard, the main Confederate resistance in the state—the last realistic chance that the Confederacy had of forcing Missouri out of the Union. Though the Confederacy would launch one more battle nearby at Prairie Grove to try to recapture this area for the Confederacy, it was to no avail. The result of the Confederate loss at Pea Ridge was that a large slaveholding state would remain in the Union. The Confederate dream of stretching the Union's resources by forcing them to fight in the Trans-Mississippi Theater was dashed. The war would remain concentrated in the southeast, in the heart of the Confederacy.

SOURCES & OTHER READING

Pea Ridge: Civil War Campaign in the West, William Shea and Earl Hess, University of North Carolina Press, 1997.

Pea Ridge and Prairie Grove, or Incidents of the War in Arkansas, William Baxter and William Shea, University of Arkansas Press, 2000.

The South's Finest: The First Missouri Confederate Brigade from Pea Ridge to Vicksburg, Phillip Thomas Tucker, White Mane Publishing, 1993.

The Blue, the Gray and the Red: Indian Campaigns of the Civil War, Thom Hatch, Stackpole Books, 2003.

Pea Ridge Today

Northwest Arkansas today is not as rural as it was in the 1860s, or even as it was just twenty or thirty years ago, since Wal-Mart, headquartered in Bentonville, has grown into the retailing behemoth that it is. Though the region sees a large number of corporate visitors, the residential and corporate building growth seems to have been controlled. Despite the growth of Wal-Mart, Bentonville retains a population of just 21,000. Fayetteville, its larger neighbor and the home of the regional airport, has a population of 60,000. What this means for the Pea Ridge National Military Park, located about eight miles outside of Rogers, Arkansas (population 40,000), is that it will always be a well-preserved battlefield. Pea Ridge is simply a great place to bring books about the war, throw down a blanket, and start reading. Even if the battle being studied is not this one, it is easy to lose one's self in the peace that is now the national battlefield.

Points of Interest

Pea Ridge National Military Park
★★★★★

15930 Highway 62, Garfield
U.S. 62 east of Rogers.
T: 479-451-8122
Daily, 8 a.m.–5 p.m.
Admission: $3

The Pea Ridge National Military Park, eight miles northeast of Rogers on U.S. 62, is one of two Civil War battlefields in this part of Arkansas (the other is Prairie Grove). Both of the battlefields can be seen in one day as they are no more than an hour's drive apart. Allow at least two hours to properly see the battlefield itself and the visitor center and museum, and to watch the fine movie filmed on the actual battleground. The film, made using reenactors on location, gives an excellent overview of the battle and provides viewers with a good understanding of the uniforms and weapons that were used.

The park museum is light on artifacts compared to many other Civil War sites, but it has two items of particular interest. One is the uniform coat worn at the battle by Union Brigadier General Samuel R. Curtis. The coat, found unused and unappreciated in another museum but confirmed as the authentic article, is displayed in a glass case. A more gruesome but interesting display is the musket ball that is reputed to have killed Confederate Brigadier General Ben McCullough. Park rangers cannot confirm that the flattened piece of lead is definitively the musket ball that killed the foolhardy general who rode into the open on a scouting mission, but all of the written and oral evidence points to its being the one.

Pea Ridge is a battlefield whose 4,300 acres have been bypassed by commercial development. U.S. 62 skirts the battlefield on its southeast side, but once you're on the tour road, road noise subsides, allowing visitors to imagine how the battle progressed without modern-day interference. Rangers are available to answer visitors' questions.

Because the battlefield was not designated a national battlefield until 1956, long after all veterans of the battle had died, it does not have regimental monuments scattered around like other sites such as Gettysburg, Vicksburg, and Shiloh. But stone monuments and iron tablets can be detractions for visitors who are trying to put themselves into the mindset of the combatants. It looks much as it did in March 1862, except that the landscape is more heavily wooded than it was during wartime. Remarkably, the already-pristine battlefield will soon more closely resemble the original, as park rangers report that they are in the process of restoring the fields by cutting timber on the battlefield. They will be using the felled trees to build split rail fences in the same locations as the 1862 fences.

This means that Pea Ridge is almost perfect for historians who have the time and inclination to walk the battlefield to get a feel for what it must have been like for the troops. Those visitors who do not have much time can still absorb the history by taking the ten-stop, seven-mile driving tour. All of the key battle features are within the park boundaries.

Stop 3, Leetown Battlefield ★★★★, is significant in that it was here that the Confederate chain of command fell apart after two generals, Ben McCullough and then James McIntosh, were killed on the northern edge of this field.

McCullough was a fiery leader of the Texas Rangers without military training when he was appointed general. Disdainful of both West Point–educated professional soldiers like Van Dorn, and courtly politicians like Price, McCullough had managed to cooperate with Price to win Wilson's Creek.

Early in this battle, McCullough, ignoring protocol and common sense, rode forward of his lines to see if he could spot the enemy. That was a foolish task for a general, one that lowly scouts are generally assigned to. The general stood out against the grassy fields wearing the shiny black velvet suit he favored over a military uniform. Several Union sharpshooters, incredulous that what was obviously a Confederate officer would present himself as such a target, brought him down.

General McIntosh, angry at the loss of his friend, then did something equally unwise. He rode to the front of a cavalry regiment and led them toward the Union line. Within minutes, two Confederate generals had been shot dead out of their saddles.

After McCullough and McIntosh fell, no colonels of the regiments they were commanding stepped forward to take over battlefield command. Instead, they waited for word from the army's overall commander, Van Dorn. In effect, the battle went into a lull due to a lack of leadership on the Confederate side. The Federals shifted their attention to the heavy fighting that was taking place around Elkhorn Tavern while the leaderless Confederates waited for someone in command to make a decision.

Stop 4 ★★ is the part of the battlefield where two regiments of Confederate Cherokees, about 1,000 men, helped defeat a Union cavalry force. The Cherokees were dressed in uniforms, but many wore traditional turbans dressed with feathers and war paint on their faces.

Stops 6 ★★★, 7 ★★★★, 8 ★★★, and **10 ★★★** are also worthwhile. By walking 150 yards down a short path at Stop 6, visitors get an elevated view of the entire battlefield. Maps here help orient the visitor to the movements of both sides. At Stop 7 is a reconstructed Elkhorn

Tavern, named for the elk horns placed on top of the roof. At one time, this was a thriving little community that catered to travelers. The Confederates named the battle after this tavern. Stop 8 describes the fighting just north of the tavern, which marked the end of the battle. A painting

in the visitor center shows a Confederate assault on a Union cannon battery here on the first day of fighting. At Stop 10 is a display of Federal cannons marking the location of the batteries that helped force the Confederates from Elkhorn Tavern.

OTHER AREA ATTRACTIONS

Prairie Grove Battlefield State Park
★★★★

Prairie Grove, U.S. 62, eight miles west of I-540.
T: 479-846-2990
Museum hours: Daily, 8 a.m.–5 p.m.
Park hours: Daily, 8 a.m.–dark.
Admission: $2.75

Prairie Grove Battlefield State Park contains more than a battlefield and features a one-mile walking tour as well as a six-mile driving tour. Several period structures have been relocated to the park, including a house Confederate General Thomas Hindman used as a headquarters the night before the battle. Other houses and buildings date to the war period, so visitors can see period architecture. The museum has a good display of artillery and a short film that explains the significance of the battle, the last attempt by Confederate forces to try to hold on to power in northwestern Arkansas. Hindman failed to attack an approaching and exhausted Union column. Instead he went into a defensive position. Over the course of a day, another Union column was able to reinforce the first, and Hindman was forced to withdraw all the way to Little Rock in the center of the state. Northwest Arkansas now belonged to the Union.

The park does not have a lot of information on General Hindman, who was minor and ineffectual as a general, but an intriguing war personality nonetheless. A native of

Tennessee, he was Arkansas's most visible secessionist as a U.S. Congressman. He almost single-handedly transformed the disorganized state into an efficient member of the Confederacy, but he raised some hackles as he accomplished that when he enforced the conscription act. His only major battle was Prairie Grove, a stalemate at best.

When the war ended, Hindman refused to surrender. He moved to Mexico for two years before coming back to work with the Republican Party, then ruling the state. He was shot while sitting in his home in 1868. A politician to the end, he gave a speech from his front porch telling his friends good-bye. He then died from blood loss. No one ever claimed credit for his assassination.

Eureka Springs ★★

Just thirty-two miles east of Pea Ridge is the town of Eureka Springs, which did not exist during the war. Founded in 1879, two years later it had grown to become the fourth-largest city in the state. The attraction was the Basin, a spring the Indians and later white settlers believed to have healing powers. One local doctor even bathed the wounded of Pea Ridge in waters drawn from here, but there is no evidence of how well they recovered.

What attracts tourists today is a preserved Victorian downtown that is home to gift shops, dining, and several spa and massage therapy establishments that are carrying on the tradition that built the town in the first place. The spa treatments range from the traditional baths and facials to more mystical evaluations that say Eureka Springs itself is a "'vortex' where body, mind and spirit are aligned."

Branson, Missouri ★★

It is eighty-two miles from Pea Ridge and fifty miles from Eureka Springs, but it's worth considering a side trip to this town where live country-music shows are a staple form of entertainment.

The town's visitor center is open each day from 8 a.m. until 9 p.m. Note that that there are more than 100 shows from which to choose. The closest thing to the Civil War in this town is Dolly Parton's Dixie Stampede, where North and South chase each other around on horseback while carrying flags.

Northwest Arkansas Area Caves ★★

Like most mountains, the Ozark Mountains are honeycombed with caves, some of which are open to the public. The Old Spanish Treasure Cave, twenty-five miles west of Pea Ridge at Sulfur Springs, comes with its own legend of long-lost buried treasure. Cosmic Cave, forty-three miles northeast of Pea Ridge, claims to be the warmest cave in the Ozarks and was discovered before the Civil War.

Wal-Mart Visitor Center ★

105 North Main St. on the Town Square, downtown Bentonville.

Walton's, the preserved five-and-dime store, is open from 9 a.m. to 5 p.m. Tuesday through Saturday. This is Sam Walton's first store in the chain that would become the largest retailer in the world. Wal-Mart opened the visitor center in 1990, fifty years to the day after Walton's originally opened. Many of the museum displays revolve around Sam Walton, a man who believed that employees could be motivated to do more than just take orders. Among the artifacts is the pickup the modest billionaire drove himself; a hula skirt he wore on Wall Street as a dare; and his office, which was moved from corporate headquarters when he died.

GETTING TO AND AROUND N.W. ARKANSAS

Northwest Arkansas Regional Airport, west of Fayetteville, has to be one of the nation's most rural regional airports. Dedicated in 1998, XNA is also one of the nation's newest airports. The airport is several miles from restaurants and gas stations, so it is advisable to take the fuel option if renting a car. Several rental car companies are available.

The highways are well maintained and marked. One word of warning for motorists looking for the regional airport from I-540: Coming from the south, the first airport sign encountered is actually Fayetteville

Municipal Airport-Drake Field, which may be an option for visitors using private aircraft, but don't get confused if you're rushing to catch a plane.

Wilson's Creek is 140 miles northeast of Pea Ridge. Prairie Grove is about forty-three miles southwest. One good strategy is to fly into Northwest Arkansas, see Pea Ridge, drive to Wilson's Creek, and then return to Prairie Grove if there is time. It is best to make this a two-day trip, or longer if Branson or the caves appeal.

Accommodations

Hillside Oaks Inn

285 Green St., Pea Ridge
www.bbonline.com/ar/hillsideoaks
T: 479-451-1810
2 rooms
$150–$200

This inn, a restored 1891 farmhouse, has a Jacuzzi that is ideal for resting after tracking battle lines.

Most of the bed and breakfasts with Civil War–period architecture can be found in Eureka Springs. Billing itself as "a Victorian village nestled in the Ozarks," and bearing the description of "the largest historic district in the United States," the town is located thirty-two miles east of Pea Ridge and boasts more than a dozen bed and breakfasts with architecture that evokes the time and place of the 1860s.

The Piedmont House Bed & Breakfast

165 Spring St., Eureka Springs
www.eureka-usa.com/piedmont
T: 800-253-9258
9 rooms
$79–$155

Built in 1880, the Piedmont House is claimed by its owners to be the oldest continuously operated inn in Arkansas.

1884 Bridgeford House

263 Spring St., Eureka Springs
www.bridgefordhouse.com
T: 888-567-2422
5 rooms
$99–$265

This inn, built in 1884, provides views of the surrounding mountains and of the springs that first drew visitors to the area.

The Crescent Hotel

75 Prospect Ave., Eureka Springs
www.crescent-hotel.com
T: 800-342-9766
79 rooms
$180

This hotel was built in 1886. It features a spa, which is one of the main reasons for visiting Eureka Springs.

The New Orleans Hotel

63 Spring St., Eureka Springs
www.eureka-springs-usa.com/orleans
T: 800-243-8630
20 rooms
$129–$350

Built in 1892, this hotel is reminiscent of the French Quarter in New Orleans. Of its twenty units, seventeen are suites.

SITE
25

Wilson's Creek

Missouri

Wilson's Creek is still a quiet, flowing stream.

THE WAR YEARS

T his well-preserved, little-visited Civil War site marked the third significant
Confederate victory within two months in 1861, following victories at Big Bethel,
Virginia, in June and First Manassas, Virginia, in July. The Wilson's Creek victory
on August 10, 1861, convinced Southerners that the war would soon be over, as
the Northern people realized that the Confederacy was willing to fight both in the
east and in the west for their right to secede. Finally, Wilson's Creek is also an
important site because of the nearby General Sweeny's Museum, one of the best private
Civil War museums in the nation.

When the war broke out in 1861, Missouri was caught in the middle.

Missouri had been a slave state for more than forty years thanks to the 1820 Missouri
Compromise, which let it into the Union as a slave state in exchange for Maine's entering as a free state. The Compromise had tried to limit slavery in the western territories,
but that plan only lasted until the Compromise of 1850 declared that each state should
be allowed to decide if it would be slave or free.

For most of the 1850s, "border ruffians" from both proslavery Missouri and antislavery
Kansas crossed state lines to murder each other in an effort to influence the Kansas
statehood issue. Several hundred civilian lives had been lost to the principle of slavery
long before any soldiers stepped onto a battlefield.

When war loomed, state government officials rejected the idea of leaving the Union in
February 1861. But Missouri's newly elected governor, Claiborne Jackson, was pro-
South. Jackson not only refused newly elected President Abraham Lincoln's April
demands for troops to put down the Southern "rebellion," he mobilized the Missouri
State Guard and seized one arsenal. The Guard was moving on a second, larger arsenal
in St. Louis when a U.S. Army captain, Nathaniel Lyon, acting without any orders from
his superiors, seized it first. Lyon later captured some members of the pro-Southern
Missouri militia.

A cocky Lyon paraded his Federal troops and his captured militiamen through St. Louis
on May 10, 1861. Enraged pro-Southern citizens began protesting, and Lyon reacted by
shooting them. As many as forty civilians in St. Louis were gunned down by Federal soldiers more than two months before the Battle of First Manassas, Virginia, the first major
battle of the war.

Even Unionists were outraged at Lyon's actions. They worried that Lyon's rash attacks on
civilians would tip the state to the Confederacy. But while the governor was pro-South,
the legislature was pro-Union. Lyon believed that it was not enough to win over the
hearts of the legislature. To be on the safe side, he captured Missouri's state capital of
Jefferson City, an act that stunned Unionists once again. Chaos reigned. An officer of the
U.S. army had just occupied the capital of a state that was still in the Union!

Lyon paid little attention to conventional thinking. He intended to crush whatever military forces the Confederates had in Missouri to ensure no resistance in the future. His
first target after taking the capital was capturing Governor Jackson and his pro-Southern

militia forces. Using his newly formed force of regular soldiers and volunteers from Missouri, Kansas, and Iowa, Lyon attacked Jackson's forces at Boonville, Missouri, on June 17. The Federals easily routed the poorly trained militiamen, but that did not eliminate them as a threat.

Lyon, promoted to general, chased the Missouri State Guard due south more than 175 miles. By mid-July, Lyon was in nearby Springfield with 6,000 men. The Confederate Missouri State Guard, under former Missouri Congressman, now General, Sterling Price, was seventy-five miles away. Within days, more Confederates poured into Missouri from Arkansas and soon the Confederate army numbered around 11,000.

The brash Lyon now found himself in trouble. He was outnumbered nearly two to one, and had a Confederate army in front of him. Along with General Franz Siegel, who was a German immigrant, and his German-speaking regiments recruited from St. Louis, Lyon moved out of Springfield, hoping to catch the Confederates asleep.

On August 10, 1861, Lyon attacked the Confederates under the command of the self-taught General Ben McCullough, former head of the Texas Rangers, along Wilson's Creek. It was just one day after McCullough had abandoned his own surprise attack because of the onset of rain.

At first, Lyon and Siegel's two-pronged attack routed the Confederates, most of whom were just waking up and crawling out of their tents. The Federals took command of a gentle, unnamed slope that would gain a name after the battle—Bloody Hill.

The tough, grizzled McCullough and the white-haired, aristocratic Price soon calmed their men and convinced them that the Federals actually had a smaller force than they did. They rallied and started pushing back, forcing Lyon's men into defensive positions on Bloody Hill.

Siegel and Lyon were separated. Lyon was now on the defensive, but Siegel assumed Lyon was still on the offensive. Lyon assumed Siegel would soon be attacking the rear of the Confederates who were now pressing him. Both men's assumptions would lose the Battle of Wilson's Creek for the Federals.

For nearly five hours, the battle raged back and forth over Bloody Hill as the Confederates sought to silence the Federal artillery that gave the Union an advantage.

Lyon kept looking for Siegel's help. Siegel kept waiting for Lyon to arrive.

McCullough's Confederates attacked Siegel, aided by the fact that the Confederates were dressed in blue militia uniforms that Siegel mistook for the blue militia uniforms worn by Lyon's Union men. (The Federals at First Manassas had made the same mistake in correctly identifying the opposing side by the color of their uniforms.)

Siegel now lost his nerve and started a retreat that turned into a rout. The fleeing Federals did not head toward Lyon on Bloody Hill, but toward Springfield. Lyon's men were now alone, facing a Confederate force more than three times the size of theirs.

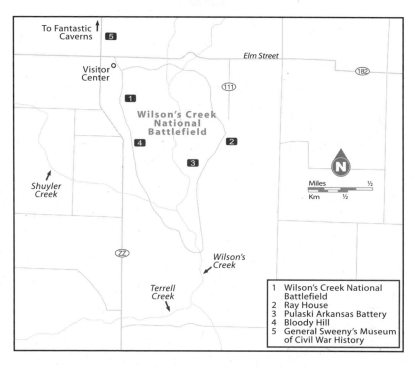

To Fantastic
Caverns
5

Elm Street

Visitor
Center

182

1

111

Wilson's Creek
National
Battlefield

4

2

3

N

Miles   ½
Km   ½

Shuyler
Creek

ZZ

Wilson's
Creek

Terrell
Creek

1 Wilson's Creek National
   Battlefield
2 Ray House
3 Pulaski Arkansas Battery
4 Bloody Hill
5 General Sweeny's Museum
   of Civil War History

Over the next hour, the trapped, virtually surrounded Federals fought as best they could.
Lyon was wounded first in the leg, and then a ball grazed his head. Lyon, who wore his
hair long and allowed his beard to grow into his hair to reinforce the fierce look that
matched his name, ignored his wounds. He rushed from one side of Bloody Hill to the
other, moving his forces to meet first one Confederate charge and then another. Finally,
a third Confederate ball nicked the general's heart and he dismounted from his horse,
lay down on the ground, and died.

Shortly after Lyon's death, the Confederates unexpectedly stopped fighting. On the verge
of overwhelming and either annihilating or capturing an entire Union army, the
Confederates withdrew because they were short on ammunition and rumors were flying
that more Federals were on their way from Springfield. That retreat allowed the surviving
Federals to follow Siegel toward Springfield. Within a few days, the Federals abandoned
Springfield.

Missouri's allegiances to the Union would remain undecided.

WILSON'S CREEK TODAY

The town of Republic (population 8,500) should consider itself lucky that the crossroads community was not directly in the path of the two armies when they met in August 1861.

Republic was not a military objective despite the fact that it was a crossroads, normally a desirable piece of property for one army to own and another to try to take. Instead of fighting for a geographical feature such as a crossroads, both armies were trying to surprise each other in the pre-dawn darkness. They just happened to be in the open fields along Wilson's Creek, three miles east of Republic, when they found each other.

Springfield, thirteen miles to the northeast, is a large city of 152,000. It too saw a small battle early in 1863 as Confederates attacked the Union supply depot, but urban development downtown has wiped out most evidence of the meager fighting, which claimed a total of 400 casualties on both sides.

Today, southwestern Missouri retains a rural feel, with opportunities for outdoor recreation, particularly on the water.

POINTS OF INTEREST

1. Wilson's Creek National Battlefield
★★★★★

6424 West Farm Rd., Republic
T: 417-732-2662
Visitor center: Daily, 8 a.m.–5 p.m.
Park: Memorial Day–Labor Day, 8 a.m.–9 p.m.; April 1–October 31, 8 a.m.–7 p.m.; November–March, 8 a.m.–5 p.m.
Closed major holidays.
Admission: $3

The battlefield is located three miles east of Republic; take Elm Street or Country Road 182 off U.S. 62 running along the edge of town. Travelers arriving by I-44 should take Exit 70 (Missouri MM), then head south. Follow MM past the point where the road name changes to M, and then follow it half a mile until it intersects with State Highway ZZ. Turn right on ZZ and drive one and a half miles to the entrance to the national park on the left.

The Wilson's Creek National Battlefield encompasses 1,750 acres and includes all of the historically significant parts of the battlefield. A five-mile driving tour, a seven-mile horseback trail, and five different walking trails ranging from a quarter-mile to three-quarters of a mile in length are all open to public exploration. Only one significant site, the marker where General Lyon was shot down, requires visitors to leave the auto tour, but the walks are easy. One caution is that the trails are not paved so they're not necessarily suitable for people using wheelchairs.

One word of warning for drivers: The deer in the area have learned that they are safe from hunters if they stay inside the battlefield area. They are not afraid of automobiles. Be careful not to drive over the speed limit within the park because the deer are apt to cross the road at any time.

2. Ray House, Stop 2 ★★★, and the spring house in front of the home, are among the only surviving structures from the battle. A Confederate colonel died in the Ray House, and General Lyon's body was brought here after the battle. This was actually a quiet part of the battlefield with little fighting. On certain days, the house is open and interpreters wearing period clothing explain life in the 1860s.

At **Stop 3** ★★★, visitors can get out and walk to the location of the Pulaski Arkansas Battery, which slowed the Federal attack long enough for the Confederate infantry to form itself. The Confederate battery fired to the northwest toward Bloody Hill. Walking to this spot and looking at Bloody Hill about half a mile to the northwest gives visitors a sense of the distances that artillerymen had to calculate in order to hit their targets.

Stop 7 ★★★★★ is another worthwhile stop with an easy three-quarter-mile walk down the gentle slope of Bloody Hill to the granite marker erected at the spot where General Nathaniel Lyon was shot through the heart. Military tacticians will scratch their heads once they see the location of the marker. West Point men are trained to protect "the high ground," which Lyon did when he took and defended Bloody Hill. But the marker is at the base of the hill. Instead of being near the military crest (just below the high point of the hill), where Lyon should have been, it seems the general was near the base of the hill when he was shot. Visitors take a slight sloping walk down to the marker, not up to it. Lyon was not where he should have been to best see advancing Confederates.

Visitors reading the granite marker should note its wording carefully. The marker is dedicated to "the hundreds of brave men, North and South, who, on this field, died for the right as God gave them to see the right." The marker is not making judg-

ments about either the North's or South's intentions in fighting the war or the battle. It honors both sides as well as Lyon.

Watch for a sinkhole along the trail. According to battlefield reports, thirty Union soldiers were given a quick battlefield "burial" by being dropped into it.

Finally, **Stop 8** ★★★★ is an overlook that gives an elevated view of the battlefield. In the fall and winter, one can look to the southeast and see the Ray cabin at the eastern end of the battlefield. This allows visitors to appreciate the small scale of this compact battlefield (especially when compared to much larger places like Shiloh, Tennessee, Sharpsburg, and Gettysburg, all battles that sprawled over such a broad landscape that no single general could keep track of how his units were faring). At this battlefield, Lyon kept in full contact with the troops under his command, even though he did lose contact with Franz Siegel and his regiments.

Dedicated walkers could spend all day tramping the park, but plan to spend at least one and a half hours touring the museum and battlefield.

One rare feature of Wilson's Creek Battlefield is its large research library. The **John K. and Ruth Hulston Civil War Research Library** ★★★★ features more than 5,500 volumes on the war, with a large number of those volumes concentrating on the Trans-Mississippi Theater (meaning the area west of the Mississippi River). The Trans-Mississippi was a vast region, but its history during the war is not as well researched as that of the fighting east of the river. The library is open 9 a.m.–noon, 1–4 p.m., Tuesdays–Saturdays. It is closed on Sundays and Mondays. Although books cannot be checked out, they are available for researchers.

3. General Sweeny's Museum of Civil War History ★★★★★

5228 South State Highway ZZ, Republic
Just outside the National Park on Mo. ZZ.
T: 417-732-1224
Wednesday–Sunday, 10 a.m.–5 p.m.
Closed November–February.
Admission: $4.50

This privately owned museum on Mo. ZZ, just north of the entrance to the national park, is one of the two best privately owned Civil War museums in the nation (the other is Pamplin Park in Petersburg, Virginia). As of early 2005, the National Park Service was in talks to purchase the museum. Founded by Dr. Tom Sweeny and his wife Karen, General Sweeny's Museum contains more than 5,000 artifacts displayed and described in fifty cases as professionally as in any museum in the nation. There are the items you'd expect to find, such as pistols, swords, and buttons, as well as the unexpected, such as the sword and sash worn by famed Confederate General Patrick Cleburne, who was killed at the Battle of Franklin, Tennessee, in November 1864. Another unusual item is one of the flags carried by the troops under Cherokee Indian General Stand Watie, who fought at Pea Ridge.

Tom Sweeny started the collection when he was twelve years old and bought his first artifact, a pistol. As an adult, Dr. Sweeny learned that he was probably related to the eccentric General Thomas Sweeny, a one-armed Union general who tried to invade Canada after the Civil War. Tom became hooked for life on learning about the war. When Tom retired, he built the museum so he could share his still-expanding collection with the public.

The best displays show the artifact along with images of it in the hands of its owner or user. This personalization makes the exhibit come alive. Many photographs show soldiers from the western theaters and have not been widely reproduced.

The exhibits start chronologically with the Kansas border wars in the 1850s and progress through all of the battles, ending with items from Fort Blakely, Alabama, a battle fought by western-based troops that ended about the same time that General Robert E. Lee was surrendering his eastern theater troops at Appomattox Court House.

Some of the items are rarely seen in museums, such as two of the five Congressional Medals of Honor won by Union soldiers at Wilson's Creek. Some are chilling, such as the displays of photographs of William Quantrill, the James Brothers, and Bloody Bill Anderson, a young man who was more a pathological murderer than he was a Confederate guerrilla. One display shows Anderson immediately after his death, which came when he singlehandedly charged a Union patrol that had been chasing his command. Anderson is wearing the frilly, puffy shirt that identified guerrillas of the day.

Allow at least an hour and a half here. The descriptions are nonpartisan and informative, and the displays are well lit. Anyone interested in the Trans-Mississippi will not be disappointed. Allow at least three hours if combining this with Wilson's Creek. For those familiar with Petersburg, Virginia, the combination of General Sweeny's Museum and Wilson's Creek National Battlefield is on par with Pamplin Park and the National Museum of the Civil War Soldier.

4. Fantastic Caverns ★★

4872 North Farm Rd. 125, Springfield
U.S. 14 north of Springfield
T: 417-833-2010
Daily, 8 a.m.–4 p.m.
Admission: $17

Fantastic Caverns offers a fifty-minute tram ride through the caverns.

GETTING TO AND AROUND WILSON'S CREEK

There are two airports visitors could use to reach Wilson's Creek.

Springfield-Branson Regional Airport is served by five major airlines seven rental car companies.

A second choice would be to fly into Northwest Arkansas Regional Airport in Fayetteville and rent a car to take in both Pea Ridge and Wilson's Creek, battlefields separated by two hours of car travel.

Alternately, visitors can fly into Springfield-Branson and then drive down to Pea Ridge.

Once at the battlefield, those touring on foot will find the trails well marked. The only hill at the vehicle stops will be Bloody Hill, but it is a gentle slope. It is about a mile round-trip walk down to the monument marking the spot where General Lyon was killed.

ACCOMMODATIONS

Walnut Street Inn

900 East Walnut St., Springfield
T: 417-864-6346
www.walnutstreetinn.com
12 rooms
$89–$169

Built in 1894, this inn is located in the historic district of Springfield.

The Amish Country Inn Bed & Breakfast

745 East Clinton, Seymour
T: 417-935-9345
www.amishinn.com
7 rooms
$39–$84

This inn is a restored barn. Located in Seymour, a small Amish-populated town thirty minutes from Springfield, it is ten minutes from where Laura Ingalls Wilder wrote her *Little House on the Prairie* books.

Virginia Rose Bed & Breakfast

317 East Glenwood, Springfield
T: 417-883-0693
www.bbonline.com/mo/virginiarose/
4 rooms
$65–$75

This bed and breakfast is a Victorian-era house that has been preserved, along with a barn, in a modern subdivision.

SOURCES & OTHER READING

The Battle of Wilson's Creek, Edwin C. Bearss, George Washington Carver Birthplace, 1992.

Bloody Hill: The Civil War Battle of Wilson's Creek, William Brooksher, Brassey's, 2000.

Wilson's Creek: The Second Battle of the Civil War and the Men Who Fought It, William Garrett Piston and Richard W. Hatcher, University of North Carolina Press, 2000.

General Sterling Price and the Civil War in the West, Albert Castel, Louisiana State University Press, 1993.

Damned Yankee: The Life of General Nathaniel Lyon, Christopher Phillips, Louisiana State University Press, 1996.

Rebellion in Missouri: 1861, Nathaniel Lyon and his Army of the West, Hans Christian Adamson, Chilton Company, 1961.

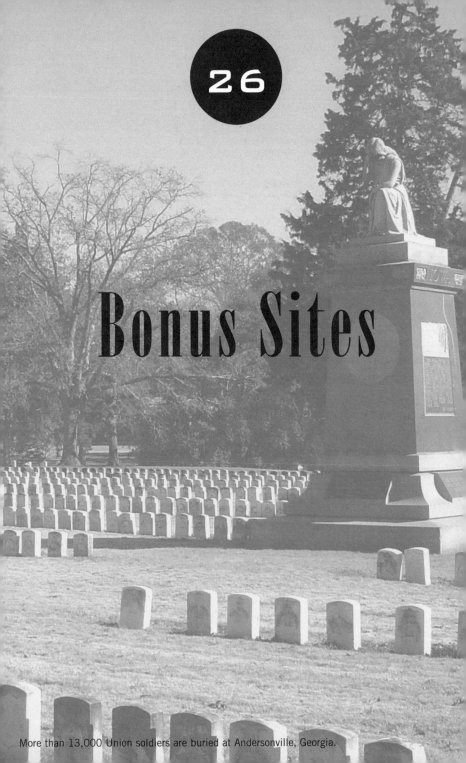

26

Bonus Sites

More than 13,000 Union soldiers are buried at Andersonville, Georgia.

BONUS SITES

I t is hard to select just twenty-five sites since the Civil War took place on such a vast theater. These abbreviated descriptions of ten additional sites are worthwhile for the dedicated history travelers because they are fascinating, a little out of the way, or offer something unexpected.

Andersonville National Historic Site, Andersonville, Georgia

T: 229-924-0343
www.nps.gov/ande/
Andersonville was the informal name for Camp Sumter, the largest prisoner-of-war camp for Union prisoners during the war. Today it is also the site of the National POW Museum and holds artifacts and stories collected from American POWs of all wars. Andersonville has a good, modern museum, the outlined layout of the prison camp, and the marked graves of virtually all of the 13,000 Federal prisoners who died here of disease and exposure. While used as propaganda against the South, Andersonville's death rate was actually less than that of some Northern prison camps for Confederate prisoners.

Atlanta Cyclorama and Oakland Cemetery, Atlanta, Georgia

T: 404-624-1071, Cyclorama
T: 404-688-2107, Oakland Cemetery
www.oaklandcemetery.com
The Cyclorama is a 360-degree painting dating from the 1890s that depicts one of the battles for Atlanta that took place in this part of the city close to downtown. Nearby Oakland Cemetery contains the graves of several thousand Confederate soldiers, including several generals. Here too is "The Lion of Atlanta," an evocative statue of a wounded, grieving lion clutching and protecting a Confederate battle flag as it spends its last, dying minutes standing guard over the graves of the unknown Confederate dead.

National Civil War Naval Museum, Columbus, Georgia

T: 706-327-9798
www.portcolumbus.org
Visitors are surprised when they turn left into this museum and see the huge hulk of the *C.S.S. Jackson*, a Confederate ironclad that never saw combat. The rest of the museum concentrates on the Confederate Navy, offering dual timelines of what was happening during the war both on land and at sea. Among the artifacts preserved here is the uniform that the commander of the *C.S.S. Virginia* was wearing when he fought the *Monitor*. The museum's goal is to have a complete "fleet" of full-scale Civil War–era ships of different types constructed on its lawn so that visitors can get a feel for the wildly varying ship designs that were used during the war. The Museum periodically fires a full-size Brooke cannon recovered from the *Jackson*, perhaps the only place in the nation where visitors can hear—and feel—what naval gun crews experienced.

Fort Delaware State Park, Delaware City, Delaware

T: 302-834-7941
www.destateparks.com/fdsp/index.asp
While Andersonville gets more attention, Fort Delaware on Pea Patch Island in the middle of the Delaware River was just as cruel to Confederate prisoners, and they died the
same deaths from disease, malnourishment, and exposure. Most of the prisoners were
kept in long wooden barracks, one of which has been re-created. During the summer,
reenactors portray prisoners captured at Gettysburg. This park is accessible only by a
ferry. Its drab, foreboding walls almost seem to exude despair, an emotion the
Confederates who arrived here must have felt as well.

Fort Jackson in Port Sulphur, Louisiana

70 miles south of New Orleans, Louisiana
When the Union fleet pushed past this fort and Fort St. Phillip, across the Mississippi,
the capture of New Orleans was assured. This fort, now maintained by the local parish
(county), is in remarkably good condition, though it is occasionally flooded by the whims
of the river. The manager of the fort and her husband themselves dug most of the relics
on display from Civil War camps in and around the fort. The fall of this fine brick fort
may have sealed the fate of the Confederacy as early as March 1862. Fort St. Phillip
still exists, but it is on private land and cannot be visited.

Fort Jefferson in the Florida Keys, Florida

70 miles west of Key West, Florida
T: 305-242-7700
www.nps.gov/drto
It is bizarre to encounter a huge Civil War fort in the middle of the Gulf of Mexico, but
that is also the appeal of Fort Jefferson, one of the defensive forts built along the coasts
by the U.S. government in the 1830s. The Confederates never attacked the fort.
Instead, it was used as a Federal prison—its most famous guests were three of the
Lincoln assassination conspirators in 1865. The fort can reached by sea plane or boat
from Key West. Another fort in this area is Fort Zachary Taylor in Key West, a low-walled
brick fort that is now a state park.

Fort Pickens, Fort Morgan, and Fort Gaines off Pensacola, Florida, and Mobile, Alabama

T: 850-934-2600
www.nps.gov/guis
Visiting these forts may be difficult through 2005 as all three are in areas heavily dam-
aged by hurricanes in the fall of 2004. As of January 2005, only Fort Gaines was open.
Pickens, off Pensacola, never fell to the Confederates, but resupplying the fort almost
meant the war would start there rather than at Fort Sumter in South Carolina. Both forts
were defying local Confederate authorities' demands that they surrender. President
Lincoln chose to force the issue of resupplying the forts by sending the first supply ship
to Sumter. Morgan and Gaines guarded the entrance to the bay of Mobile, Alabama, and
they came under attack in the summer of 1864. Near Fort Morgan, Union Admiral

David Farragut made his famous statement: "Damn the torpedoes! Full speed ahead!" Not long afterward, the *U.S.S. Tecumseh* struck one of those damn torpedoes (water mines) and sank with ninety-nine hands aboard. She still rests on the bottom of Mobile Bay off Fort Morgan.

The *C.S.S. Neuse*, Kinston, North Carolina

T: 252-522-2091
www.ah.dcr.state.nc.us/sections/hs/neuse/Main.htm
The *Neuse* was a Confederate ironclad modeled after the very successful *C.S.S. Albemarle,* a small ship armed with two rifled Brooke cannons. With those cannons and a moderately shallow draft, this ironclad was deadly against the Union's wooden ships. But the *Neuse* never got a chance to go into combat. She was constructed on the shallow Neuse River, and a summer drought made the river too shallow for her to run down the river to fight the Union ships at New Bern, North Carolina. Her own crew scuttled her. Her hulk is on display at the state park, along with artifacts recovered from the wreck. Citizens are building a full-scale model of the *Neuse* in the middle of downtown Kinston.

National Museum of Civil War Medicine, Frederick, Maryland

T: 301-695-1864
www.civilwarmed.org
This museum uses 7,000 square feet to tell the grisly story of what happened when a soldier was wounded or grew sick. He went to "the surgeon," which was not always a good thing since the medical profession didn't universally accept basic ideas such as sanitation. This museum does not deal with the bravery of the men on the battlefield, but with what they faced when they were brought to the field hospital.

National Civil War Museum, Harrisburg, Pennsylvania

T: 866-258-4729
www.nationalcivilwarmuseum.org
More than 850 objects are on display at any one time in this museum thirty-five miles north of Gettysburg, with more objects available when rotating exhibits are staged. Many of the objects can be tied directly to individual soldiers. Subjects such as "Why Men Fought," "Civil War Music," and "Women at War" are covered in galleries. The nearby Battle of Gettysburg gets special attention in one gallery.

BIBLIOGRAPHY

In addition to the books cited in each chapter, the following books were consulted for details on certain sites and personalities.

Current, Richard, Editor, *Encyclopedia of the Confederacy*, New York, Simon & Schuster, 1993.

Hennessy, John J., *Return to Bull Run: The Campaign and Battle of Second Manassas*, New York, Simon & Schuster, 1993.

Rhea, Gordon C., *The Battle of the Wilderness: May 5–6, 1864,* Baton Rouge, Louisiana State University Press, 1994.

Sears, Stephen W., *To the Gates of Richmond: The Peninsula Campaign*, New York, Ticknor & Fields, 1992.

Sifakis, Stewart, *Who Was Who in the Civil War*, New York, Facts on File Publications, 1988.

Sommers, Richard J., *Richmond Redeemed: The Siege of Petersburg*, New York, Doubleday & Company, 1981.

Trudeau, Noah Andre, *Like Men of War: Black Troops in the Civil War 1862–1865*, Boston, Little Brown & Company, 1998.

Warner, Ezra J., *Generals in Blue: Lives of the Union Commanders,* Baton Rouge, Louisiana State University Press, 1959.

Warner, Ezra J., *Generals in Gray: Lives of the Confederate Commanders,* Baton Rouge, Louisiana State University Press, 1959.

Welch, Jack D., M.D., *Medical Histories of Confederate Generals*, Kent, Kent State University Press, 1995.

INDEX

INDEX

INDEX

INDEX

L

Lee, Robert E. 22, 23, 32, 33, 34, 35, 36, 37, 39-40, 43-44, 46, 49-50, 52, 53, 54-55, 59-60, 62, 64-66, 70-72, 73, 79-80, 81, 82-84, 88, 90-91, 98, 100, 105-108, 109, 110, 111, 112, 115-118, 122, 123, 128, 142, 152, 158, 161, 162, 205, 213, 222, 252

Lincoln, Abraham 19, 23, 30, 33, 40, 42, 49, 53, 69, 70, 72, 87, 101-102, 108, 115, 123, 127, 131, 137, 143, 148, 157, 160, 164, 175, 185, 196, 203, 204, 213, 214, 221, 227, 230, 247

Longstreet, James 35, 50, 65, 72, 76, 122, 161, 175-177, 179-180

Louisiana 212-225, 256

Lovell, Mansfield 214, 221

Lyon, Nathaniel 237, 247-249, 250, 251

M

McClellan, George 25, 26, 29, 36, 37, 49, 53, 60, 98, 105-108

Magruder, John 25, 26

Manassas 68-77, 79, 88, 213, 216, 217, 247, 248

Mansfield, Joseph 110

"March to the Sea" 158, 176

Maryland 104-113, 257

Maury, Matthew 35

McCullough, Ben 238, 241, 242, 248

McDowell, Irwin 53, 69-70

McIntosh, James 238, 242

McLaws, Lafayette 55

McLean, Wilmer 79-80

Meade, George 39, 60, 84, 115, 118

Miles, Dixon 102

Mississippi 202-211

Missouri 246-253

Mumford, William 214, 217, 218

N

National Civil War Museum, Harrisburg, Pennsylvania 257

National Civil War Naval Museum, Columbus, Georgia 255

National Museum of Civil War Medicine, Frederick, Maryland 257

Native Guards 213, 217, 222, 224

New Orleans 212-219

Newton, John 168

North Carolina 126-135, 257

O

Oakland Cemetery, Atlanta 255

P

Pea Ridge 236-245

Pelham, John 55

Pemberton, John 203-205, 208

Pennsylvania 114-125, 257

Perryville 226-235

Petersburg 30, 34, 38-47

Pettigrew, James J. 121

Pettigrew-Pickett-Trimble Assault 116-118, 119, 121, 142

Pickett, George 35, 46, 116-118

Pickett's Mill Battlefield Historic Site 172

Pillow, Gideon 186, 188

Polk, Leonidas 232

Pope, John 60, 70-72, 74, 76-77, 105

Port Hudson 220-225

Port Hudson State Historic Site 224-225

Porter, David 128

Porter, Fitz-John 76

Prairie Grove Battlefield State Park 243

Prentiss, Benjamin 194, 199

Price, Sterling 237-238, 242, 248

R

Ramsuer, Stephen Dodson 93

reenactments 15-17

Reno, Jesse 111

Reynolds, John 120

Rhett, Edmund 140, 141-142

Rhett, Robert Barnwell Sr. 137

Richmond 20, 25, 26, 29-37, 43, 62

Rodes, Robert 121

Rosecrans, William 175-177, 179, 180-181

Ruggles, Daniel 198

INDEX